1. The Acropolis

THE
HOMERIC GODS

The Spiritual Significance of Greek Religion

WALTER F. OTTO

Translated by MOSES HADAS

SEVEN ILLUSTRATIONS

PANTHEON

Library of Congress Catalog Card Number: 54-7070

Original title:
Die Götter Griechenlands:
Das Bild des Göttlichen im Spiegel
des griechischen Geistes
Verlag G. Schulte-Bulmke, Frankfurt A.M.

PRINTED IN THE UNITED STATES OF AMERICA
AMERICAN BOOK—STRATFORD PRESS, INC., NEW YORK

CONTENTS

may not be necessary

ILLUSTRATIONS

FOREWORD

A SERVICEABLE IMAGE of the physical environment and daily life of a society remote in time and place may be conjured up by an agile and well-furnished mind, but it is very much harder to apprehend its religious beliefs. Whatever the degree of our attachment to our own traditions, it is almost impossible for us to step out of their framework and strip familiar connotations from words like god, soul, sin, piety. That is why people who have recognized the extraordinary intelligence and perspicacity of the Greeks in other respects have found their religion childish or barbaric or merely decorative. But their literature makes it plain that adult Greeks with refined sensibilities were seriously preoccupied with religious faith; it must therefore follow that our own approach has been at fault.

Professor Otto's book is illuminating because his approach is right. He reaches the essential meaning of the Homeric gods not by working backward from modern notions (as we all unconsciously tend to do) but by working forward from Homeric antecedents, and he emerges with an appreciation of Homer as one of the greatest religious reformers our world has seen. This appreciation generates a degree of fervor, and this combined with the absence of the formidably erudite documentation to which students of ancient religion have grown accustomed may arouse suspicions of Otto's book; let it therefore be said that his work is perfectly sound and has not been shaken by later workers in the field. The latter have scrutinized every shred of evidence, especially archaeological and epigraphical, with meticulous care and even a measure of imagination, and their works, especially such a monumental collection as Martin Nilsson's *Geschichte der griechischen Religion* (2 vols., Munich, 1941 and 1952) are indispensable to the professional student of the subject. But Otto's book remains the most luminous treatment for the non-professional reader who seeks understanding as well as knowledge. For

vii

many years it has been part of my own work to teach the Homeric poems, whether in the original or in translation, and I have found Otto's book, for those who could read the German, the single most useful help towards understanding Homer. Part of my purpose in offering the present translation is to make the same help available to readers of Homer to whom German is an obstacle.

Columbia University   MOSES HADAS
January 12, 1954

ACKNOWLEDGMENTS

Grateful acknowledgments are hereby made to Oxford University Press, Inc., for permission to quote several passages from Goethe's *Faust,* translated by Louis MacNeice; and to The University of Chicago Press for permission to quote passages from *Odes of Pindar,* translated by Richmond Lattimore, copyright 1947 by the University of Chicago; the First, Fourth and Eighth Pythians were first published under the title *Some Odes of Pindar* (The Poet of the Month, New Directions, 1942). The quotations from Hölderlin on pp. 77 and 160 are taken from *Hölderlin Poems,* translated by Michael Hamburger, Pantheon Books, 1952.

I
INTRODUCTION

1

For MODERN MAN it is no easy task to attain a true understanding of ancient Greek religion. Before the images of the gods from the great period he is filled with awe and admiration, and he feels that the majesty of these figures is incomparable and can never be equalled. Their presence may indeed thrill him with a sense of the eternal, but what he hears of these gods and of their relations with mankind evokes no response in his soul. The somber religious reverberation, that melody of ineffable exaltation and consecration familiar and revered from childhood, seems to be wanting. If we examine this impression further we perceive what it is we miss. This religion is so natural that holiness seems to have no place in it. Such stirring of the soul, of the world itself, as is proclaimed by the words "Holy, holy, holy, Lord God of Hosts" or "*Sanctus Dominus Deus Sabaoth*" the presence of no Greek god can provoke. In these gods too, as in the temper of their votaries, we miss the moral earnestness which we regard as the inseparable concomitant of true religion: we cannot call them amoral, but they are much too natural and joyous to reckon morality as the supreme value. And finally, we can only be estranged by the realization that no cordial intimacy can subsist between man and these gods. That he loves and honors them there can be no doubt: but where can we find soulful devotion, sacrifice of what is most precious, even of self, communion of heart with heart, the bliss of oneness? Always the interval between man and deity remains, even when deity loves man and favors him. Indeed the delimitations are purposefully accentuated. The gods retain their own existence, from which man is by his nature forever kept apart. The effect is almost cruel when at a feast of the gods the poet represents the Muses as delighting the immortals by singing of their majesty and of the sorrows and afflictions of mankind.[1] We must not infer that the gods delighted in mischief or were consciously indifferent, but of this there can be no doubt: that such gods could have no thought of redeeming man from the world and raising him to themselves. And if religion does not hold out this promise, what meaning can it have for us?

To be sure, this remoteness does not apply equally to all periods of Greek civilization. The mysteries and Orphism are in many respects a closer approach to our own sensibilities. And if we descend to the post-classical centuries, traits which strike us as familiar multiply. It is for this reason that religious scholarship bestows particular attention on these movements and eras. Yet in essentials it must be acknowledged that the impression of strangeness persists. It is most striking for the observer who looks not at the centuries of waning creativity but rather at the early age of genius whose first and greatest monument is the body of Homeric poems. This is the period where belief in the gods was maintained with the liveliest conviction; and it is precisely here that conceptions of the divine have so little capacity to touch the heart of modern man directly that many critics have denied them any religious content whatever.

This is understandable, and yet most extraordinary. Consider Homer, who is the prime object of the charge. We admire not only the art of his poems but also the richness and depth and grandeur of his thought. Who could think of attributing superficial views on cosmic issues to a work which can still thrill us after nearly three thousand years? And yet upon his belief in gods we bestow an indulgent smile at best, or we explain him as a primitive—as if in a world so spiritually mature a primitive belief would not be the greatest paradox of all. Is not the fault to be found in the prejudices of the critics themselves? One may truly wonder at the assurance with which judgment is passed upon a nation's most inspired ideas on matters of supreme import without testing whether the position assumed produces valid insights into an alien realm of thought.

2

The properties which we miss in ancient Greek religion are the specific attributes of Christianity and kindred religions which derive from Asia. It is by the gauge of these religions that the Greek has regularly been assayed, usually, to be sure, unconsciously, but therefore with all the greater assurance. Wherever religion has been defined in a higher sense, it is these religions, and they alone, that have furnished the paradigm. Hence in the Greek realm of belief men unconsciously searched for oriental religiosity under the illusion that they were seeking religiosity in general. But since astonishingly little could be discovered, especially in the centuries of Greek culture freshest in vitality and spirit, the conclusion that no truly religious content was present seemed inescapable. The early Christian explanation that heathen beliefs were a work of the devil could no longer apply. And yet the early Christians were more competent judges. They did not take paganism lightly, as if it were puerile or superficial, but recognized it with horror as the opposite pole to the Christian viewpoint. A man's soul was not to grow and mature when he accepted the Christian faith, but must be renewed from its very roots. Such was the impression evoked by paganism in its decline; how much stronger would it have been in the presence of the ancient Greek religion, still genuine and unadulterated! But if Greek religion stands diametrically opposed to that which has to this day constituted the gauge for religion in general, we can realize that a true understanding was impossible. Where shall we find a new and better viewpoint?

Where else than in Hellenism itself? Religion is not a possession added on to a people's other belongings which might just as well be different or lacking altogether. In religion what is most venerable to man finds expression. Love and existence are rooted in the same ground and are in spirit one. Everything truly essential is being confronted with the vital ideas of its contents, its power, and its goal, and these ideas are regarded as divine entities. It is therefore inevitable that the eternal should have been revealed to the ancient Greek in a form quite different from that of the Hebrew, the Persian, or the Hindu. And in his religion the eternal could only be reflected in the measure that this creative and discerning race was capable of seeking, beholding, and revering it.

3

The worldliness and naturalness with which the religion of the Greeks is reproached is encountered in their plastic art also. Here

too the difference from the oriental is immeasurable. Organic
structure takes the place of monstrosity; instead of symbolism and
denotation we have what we have learned—through the Greeks—
to understand as forms of nature. And yet all of these works
breathe a loftiness and nobility which lifts us above the transitory
and earthbound world of facts. Before our eyes a miracle takes
place: the natural has become one with the spiritual and eternal,
without surrendering a whit of its abundance, warmth, and immediacy in the amalgam. Should not the spirit for which exact
observance of the natural led to the vision of the eternal and
infinite have made the religion of the Greeks the very thing it
was?

There has never been a religion in which the miraculous, in
the literal sense of transcending the natural order, has played so
slight a rôle as in the ancient Greek. The reader of Homer must
find it remarkable that despite frequent reference to the gods and
their power the narrative contains virtually no miracles. To appreciate how remarkable this circumstance is, we may draw a
comparison with the Old Testament. Here Yahweh fights for his
people, and without making any defense they are delivered from
the pursuing Egyptians. The sea divides so that the children of
Israel can pass dry-shod, but the waves close over the Egyptians
so that none escapes. Or God permits his people to conquer a
city whose walls collapse of themselves at the trumpet blasts and
shouts of the Israelites who parade around it, so that they need
only to march in. In Homer, of course, nothing happens without the god concerned manifesting himself. But despite this
remarkable proximity of the divine, everything takes its natural course. We hear, indeed we see in lifelike imagery, how
a god whispers a saving device to a baffled warrior at the right
instant, we hear that he rouses spirit and kindles courage, that he
makes limbs supple and nimble and gives a right arm accuracy
and strength. But if we look more closely at the occasions when
these divine interventions take place, we find that they always
come at the critical moment when human powers suddenly converge, as if charged by electric contact, on some insight, some
resolution, some deed. These decisive turns which, as every attentive observer knows, are regularly experienced in an active

life, the Greeks regarded as manifestations of the gods. Not only the flow of events with its critical moments, however, but also duration itself indicated the divine. In all larger forms and conditions of life and existence the Greek perceived the eternal visage of divinity. Taken all together these essences constituted the holiness of the world. Hence the Homeric poems are filled with divine proximity and presence as are those of no other people or age. In their world the divine is not superimposed as a sovereign power over natural events; it is revealed in the forms of the natural, as their very essence and being. For other peoples miracles take place; but a greater miracle takes place in the spirit of the Greek, for he is capable of so regarding the objects of daily experience that they can display the awesome lineaments of the divine without losing a whit of their natural reality.

Here we perceive the spiritual tendency of the people destined to teach mankind to investigate nature,—both within and around man; the Greek approach, that is to say, first gave mankind the idea of nature which is so familiar to modern man.

4

From experience, history, and anthropology we learn that the world may present itself to man's mind and emotion in manifold guises. Among possible modes of perceiving and thinking, two in particular stand out and claim our attention because neither is wholly wanting in any place or age, diverse as their apparent significance may be. The one we may call the objective or—if the word be not limited to the sense of the calculating intellect—the rational. Its object is the reality of nature, and its aim is to apprehend the substance of nature in all directions and to regard its forms and laws with reverence.

The other mode of thought is the magical. It always has to do with the dynamic; power and action are its basic categories, and therefore it seeks and reveres the extraordinary. Certain primitive peoples have special names for the wonder-working aspect in man himself or in objects in the world. This feeling for the miraculous derives from a peculiar composition of human emotions,

which in some indescribable manner become aware of a power
out of which limitless, which is to say supernatural, effects may
emanate. Hence we are justified in speaking of a magical mode
of thought. To the human consciousness of power significant
phenomena of the outer world present themselves as events and
manifestations of power. Natural experience of the regular or
normal obviously takes place here also, but passionate interest
in the extraordinary denotes a very narrow conception of what is
natural. The domain of nature is interrupted by the intervention
of the tremendous, at which point the sphere of limitless powers
and effects, the domain of quivering dread or joy, takes its incep-
tion. The matter which is here offered for admiration and worship
is unintelligible and formless. It is completely sovereign in its
opposition to the world of experience, and its only correspondence
lies in the magic power of human emotions. From this point of
view nothing in the natural world is firmly fixed. The properties
of things undergo limitless change; anything may turn into anything.

This mode of thought seems to be associated with primitive
civilizations; but in itself it is by no means primitive. It is capable
of attaining grandeur and sublimity. It is so deeply rooted in
human nature that no people and no age can wholly deny it,
though differences in its effects are very considerable. In higher
religions it gives rise to belief in a deity who faces the natural
world with infinite power and whom it is impossible to comprehend. The greatest expansion of this power is to be observed
in the spiritual development of ancient India. Here the mysterious
omnipotent, the "truth of the truth" (Brahman), is made positively
equal to the psychic power within man (Atman); and it was inevitable that the world of experience should be relegated from the
rank of a lesser reality to the nothingness of mere appearance.[2]

The thing here designated and characterized as magical
thought was naturally not wholly alien to the Greeks. But anyone
with an eye for the basic traits of various conceptions of the
world must realize that the Greek attitude was hostile to magical
thought to a quite marked degree. Its position is at the opposite
pole, and is the most magnificent objectivation of the rational
mode of thought. Instead of a narrow concept of the natural,

here we have the broadest possible. Indeed, when we today utter
the word *nature* in the large and vital sense in which Goethe used
it, we are in the debt of the Greek spirit. The natural can therefore of itself stand in the glory of the sublime and divine. To be
sure, upon the intervention of Greek gods also, extraordinary
and thrilling events took place. This does not, however, mean the
appearance of a force with limitless power; it does mean that
existence manifests itself in infinitely various living expressions as
the essence of our world. First and highest is not the power that
acts, but the being that is manifested in the form of the act. And
the holiest shudder comes not from the tremendous and infinitely
powerful, but rather from the depths of natural experience.

This concept of the world which we call specifically Greek
found its first and greatest expression in the age whose monu-
ments are the Homeric poems. It is recognizable at once by the
almost complete absence of the magical element. Goethe represents Faust as uttering a wish at the end of his life:

> All magic—from my path if I could spurn it,
> All incantation—once for all unlearn it,
> To face you, Nature, as one man of men—
> It would be worth it to be human then.[3]

Nowhere but in the Greek world is this wish fulfilled; it is in the
Greek spirit that nature, before which Faust wished to stand with
nothing foreign interposed, was transformed into idea.

The Greek genius must have received the figures of its religion
and its worship in pre-Homeric times, for in Homer they are
fixed, and this book proposes to show that they remained basically
what they were for Homer. To find one's world is tantamount—
whether for a people or an individual—to finding one's self, to attaining realization of one's own character. The period whose
concept of the world we learn from Homer is therefore the
period of genius in Hellenism. Whatever notions earlier generations may have associated with the names of the Homeric gods
are of slight significance in comparison. The specifically Greek
idea which made them what they were was originated in and
belonged to the age for which Homer is our witness.

It is often said that it is the needs of human nature, and their

growth and change that are expressed in the formulation of the
gods. True enough, but surely among these needs are the requirements of thought and perception. The most significant event in
the life of a people—whether or not we detect a connection with
external vicissitudes—is the emergence of the mode of thought
that is peculiar to it, as if designed for it from the beginning of
time, by which it is henceforward distinguishable in the world's
history. This process took place when the prehistoric view was
transformed into the view which we first find in Homer and which
we never thereafter encounter with comparable clarity and
grandeur. However much we may ascribe to the poet's own rich
thought and taste in his presentation of divine manifestations, the
natural idealism or ideal naturalism which astonishes and enchants us in these manifestations remains the basic character of
this new and in a true sense Greek religion.

5

The ancient Greek religion comprehended the things of this world
with the most powerful sense of reality possible, and nevertheless
—nay, for that very reason—recognized in them the marvellous
delineations of the divine. It does not revolve upon the anxieties,
longings, and spiritual broodings of the human soul: its temple
is the world, from whose vitality and movement emanates its
knowledge of the divine. It alone has no need to seclude itself
from the evidence of experiences, for only by all the rich gamut
of their tints, light and dark, do they crystallize on the large
images of the divinities.

We shall not let ourselves be deterred by the officious judgments of zealots and pedants who charge Homeric religion with
immorality or primitive crudeness because its gods are partial and
at odds and sometimes indulge in conduct that is outlawed in
bourgeois ethics. To be sure, Greek philosophers also engaged in
this kind of criticism, but the fact that the pious sense of nature
could fade even in Hellenism does not justify such criticism. For
pious naturalism many things are true and important which may

seem foolish and wicked to theorists and moralizers. But once we have apprehended what it is that this piety reveres we shall no longer venture to condemn the things it tolerates and condones.

In ancient Greek worship there is revealed to us one of humanity's greatest religious ideas—we make bold to say *the religious idea of the European spirit*. It is very different from the religious idea of other civilizations, and particularly of those which customarily supply our religious scholarship and philosophy with examples for the origin of religion. But it is essentially related to all genuine thoughts and creations of Hellenism, and is conceived in the same spirit. Like other eternal achievements of the Greeks it stands before humanity large and imperishable. The faculty which in other religions is constantly being thwarted and inhibited here flowers forth with the admirable assurance of genius—the faculty of seeing the world in the light of the divine, not a world yearned for, aspired to, or mystically present in rare ecstatic experiences, but the world into which we were born, part of which we are, interwoven with it through our senses and, through our minds, obligated to it for all its abundance and vitality. And the figures in which this world was divinely revealed to the Greeks—do they not demonstrate their truth by the fact that they are still alive today, that we still encounter them when we raise ourselves out of petty constraints to an enlarged vision? Zeus, Apollo, Athena, Artemis, Dionysus, Aphrodite—wherever the ideas of the Greek spirit are honored, there we must never forget that these were its greatest ideas, indeed in a sense the totality of its ideas in general; and they will endure as long as the European spirit, which in them has attained its most significant objectivation, is not wholly subjugated to the spirit of the Orient or to that of utilitarian rationality.

NOTE

The birth of the spirit, of which we have here spoken in anticipation, is premised in the Homeric poems in which it finds its most definitive as well as its earliest expression. Our account is therefore based upon Homeric evidence. Evidence adduced from other sources is intended as complement and commentary for the picture of Homeric beliefs.

We can disregard wholly any difference of date between the *Iliad* and the *Odyssey* and also any diversity between individual portions of the epic, because in all essentials the religious outlook is consistent throughout.

Objections should not be taken to such expressions as "Homeric Age," which are not infrequently used for the sake of convenience. They mean nothing more than the time during which the views of the world documented by Homer were matured and established. There is no intention to delimit the scope of their validity and force either in spatial or in societal sense.

It is an unfortunate superstition of our age that thoughts concerning the world arise out of the necessities of the many, only to attain solitary heights in the minds of the few. It is rather among rare and spiritually gifted men—whether in groups or individuals—that they are born, only to be abased and to sink to the point where they become meager, dull, and crude, and are finally rigidified. Only an age spiritually poor could believe that popular religious usages and ideas have never had meaning beyond the capacities of a simple man's thought and experience. To find their living source one must ascend into the higher regions.

Every religion and every world view is entitled to be judged not by the levels where it is flattened, coarsened, and, for want of character, is like any other, but by the clear and large contours of its heights. It is only there that it is what it truly is and what others are not.

II

RELIGION AND MYTH
IN HIGH ANTIQUITY

THE HOMERIC POEMS are based upon a clear and unified view of the world. They give evidence of this view at almost every verse, for every significant thing they say is associated with it and through this association receives its peculiar character. Remote as this view of the world may be from what other peoples and ages regard as religion, we call it religious nevertheless, because for it the divine is the fundamental basis of all being and happening, and this basis shines so clearly through all things and events that the Greeks themselves must needs speak of it in connection with even the most ordinary and familiar matters. For them no part of life is wholly without the divine.

The religious outlook of the Homeric poems is clear and self-contained. It never speaks through conceptual formulization in the way of dogma, but is expressed as a vital force in everything that happens or is said or thought. And though in details there remains a residue which may be equivocal, in large and essential matters the testimony is never contradictory. It can be collected methodically and accurately, sifted and listed, and it yields specific answers to questions of life and death, man and god, freedom and fate. Unmistakably a criterion for the nature of the divine emerges. The ·images of individual divine personages are also firmly delineated. Each of them possesses its special character, clearly defined in all its traits. The poet can assume that the listener has a vivid idea of the being and essence of every god. Whenever he introduces a god he characterizes him in a few strokes; these are always set down with the mastery which for millennia has been admired in Homer but which has not generally been recognized in scenes where gods figure. Yet it is just such scenes that must have given perceptive audiences special pleasure by their aptness. But for us the few strokes by which the god is vividly presented to our eyes are a precious index to his essence, and from all such strokes taken together his complete figure is articulated.

The divine, presented with such clarity in the Homeric poems, is manifold in form and yet everywhere consistent. A lofty spirit, a noble content, is expressed in all of its forms. It is not the purpose of the poems to communicate any religious revelation, to give force to any religious doctrine. They desire only to behold, and in the joy of beholding to fashion forms; before them lie all the riches of the world, earth and heaven, water and air, trees, animals, men and gods.

The view of the world which speaks out of these poems breathes a spirit which we must call specifically Greek. We may not overlook the fact that succeeding ages produced many views and aspirations of a quite different orientation. But if we observe the large and decisive lines of Greek genius we cannot doubt that it is the Homeric direction that they followed. The Homeric mode of seeing and thinking is continued, despite all temporal and individual variations, in the representative works of Greek genius, whether in poetry, plastic art, or philosophy. It possesses all the marks of what we call Greek, in contradistinction to other species of humanity, especially the oriental; and it possesses this character as a thing natural and obvious. Its world view and its mode of thought must therefore have made their appearance in the centuries before the completion of the Homeric epics. For the spiritual process that then transpired we unfortunately have no direct evidence; only the end result stands before us in its power. Nor can we determine the duration of the epoch in question. Tempting as it may seem to bring the change and transformation of thought into connection with the succession of cultural eras, such as the Mycenean and post-Mycenean, we must abstain from any such attempt because we do not possess the necessary documentation. But even though the historical course must remain dark, the development of the spiritual process is clear and plain. The Homeric poems exhibit the new view of the world, which is decisive for Hellenism, in its mature and fixed form. And there are enough remains and echoes, not least in Homer himself, from which we may formulate some notion of earlier thought and belief.

The old faith was earth-bound and as much constricted by the
elemental as ancient existence itself. Earth, procreation, blood,
and death are the great realities which dominated it. Each of
these had its own sacred sphere of images and needs, and the
rigor of their here and now could be abated by no freedom of
reason. Kindly and benevolent to those who remained loyal to
them, terrible to any who—whether out of willfulness or necessity
—disregarded them, they enclosed the life of the community and
of the individual by their unalterable ordinances. They are a
multiplicity but belong to the same realm, and they are not only
related to one another but all flow together into a single large essence. This we can see in the divinities in which they are represented: all belong to the earth, all have a share in life as in death;
whatever their individual traits may be, all may be designated
as deities of earth and of death.

This marks the sharpest of distinctions from the new gods,
who belong neither to the earth nor to the elemental in general
and have no dealings with death. But the ancient world of gods
was not forgotten even in later times and never wholly lost its
power and its sanctity. The Olympian religion displaced it from
its primacy, but it allowed it to subsist in the background, with
that magnanimous liberality and truth which distinguish it. Greek
faith underwent no dogmatic revolution, as did the Israelite or
Persian, which reduced the older worship to superstition or re-
belliousness against the sole domination of the new lord. Even in
Homer, the purest witness to the Olympian religion, the elemental
retains its ancient character of sanctity, and the divine spirits
which derive from it come forward meaningfully at their appropriate times. We are therefore still able to obtain a reasonably
precise picture of the nature of the ancient world of gods.

It is remarkable to see how the two realms of the divine collide
in Aeschylean tragedy, as if the Olympian masters had but just
triumphed over the ancient forces. The plaints and scorn of the

Titan Prometheus pierce the Scythian solitude where he is chained to the cliff as an opponent of the new king of the gods. As witnesses to the tyrannical violence he suffers he calls upon the divine primal elements—the heavenly ether, the winds, rivers, waves of the sea, earth the mother of all, and the eye of the sun;[1] the chorus of sea-nymphs weeps for his lot and in the end sinks into the abyss with him. But here, at least in the extant play, only the opposition and its partisan position finds expression. In the *Eumenides*, on the other hand, we have a formal discussion of the two realms of the divine and their respective rights. The old powers and their protest against the "new gods" are, to be sure, represented only by the Erinyes, and it is only upon a single issue that they come into conflict with one another. But the issue is of such great significance and the attitude of the divine litigants so revealing that it enables us to discern, if not all the aspects, at least the basic character of the ancient earth-religion with greater certainty than we could otherwise do.

The Eumenides call themselves daughters of Night,[2] the mighty primal divinity who is mentioned with respect even in the *Iliad*. Their sisters are the Moirai,[3] "the revered," who, as powers of birth, marriage, and death, determine the lot of every human life. From their hands come the blessings of the earth—health, fertility, wealth, and peace.[4] Hence the Athenians made offerings to them at weddings.[5] There was nothing terrifying about their cult images at Athens[6] and in most of the names by which they are variously invoked, not horror but awe is expressed; at Athens they are called Semnai, "the revered," and elsewhere Eumenides, "the kindly minded," or Potniai, "the mistresses." Thus they are related to other divinities of the earthy realm, such as the Charites. As Demeter Erinys, the ancient earth-mother Demeter bears their name, and Gaia ("earth") itself is designated as their mother.[7] The verses of Epimenides[8] give unmistakable expression to their relationship with the earth and the ancient race of gods; Cronus, the pre-Olympian king of the gods, the chief of the Titans, begot them upon Euonyme, the earth-goddess, and in addition to them Aphrodite and the Moirai. But the blessings of the earth-divinities are controlled by the great ordinances of which the Erinyes are guardians. Woe to him who transgresses them! In an instant the amiable benefactresses turn into spirits of execration from whom there can be no escape, for they are inexorable. This zeal in supervising the holy ordinances of Nature, this grim wrath against any one who fails to respect them, this horrible consistency with which he is brought to a reckoning and retribution is exacted to the last drop of blood, regardless of whether his intentions were honorable or whether he has repented and sues for mercy—this rigorous and menacing character of the elements is sharply and specifically expressed in the Erinyes, and hence they obtain their title of Furies.

The Aeschylean tragedy presents them as prosecuting a violent crime against the sanctity of blood: Orestes has shed the blood of his own mother. They are, as it were, the spirits of spilled blood that cries out to heaven. They drink of the blood of the victim[9] and pursue the perpetrator like a wild beast that is hunted to death. Madness comes over him. At his every step and turn they are near and stare at him with gruesome eyes. He has forfeited his own blood, and they wish to suck it from his living limbs and then draw him down to the night of terror like an exhausted shadow.[10] But Orestes did not commit his deed with wicked intent. He had to avenge his father, King Agamemnon, whom this woman who was his mother had beguiled and slain on the very day of his homecoming in a most degrading manner. And behind him there stands one greater: the god Apollo, who had required this vengeance of him. Now too Apollo stands by him at the trial which, under the presidency of Athena, is to condemn or acquit him. The persecutors are the Erinyes. Thus the old gods and the new here encounter one another. The primal divine law of the earth protests against the new Olympian spirit.

Two worlds are locked in struggle. Each presents its case fully, each asserts the validity of its motivation. And as they dispute with one another their inmost natures are revealed to us.

Apollo, the Olympian god, is utterly repelled by the ghastly ghouls who gorge on human gore and celebrate their grisly rites at sites of torture and savagery.[11] The Erinyes are one with blood. Brute and blind as the will of blood are their purpose and procedure. To the spiritual freedom of the Olympian god they defiantly oppose their intransigence; for the softness of unspiritual nature turns stony hard in defending itself. They know only deeds, and if the fact of commission is established, words are useless. The deed must be followed by the consequence ordained for it from eternity. Their argument is the simplest possible, and a mockery of the autonomy of the spirit. They ask the accused, "Have you slain your mother?" and his admission decides the issue. It shall not profit him that Apollo had commanded the terrible deed, Apollo whose sayings all emanate from Zeus himself. He had avenged the murder of his father Agamemnon. Is it right for the avenger of a father's murder to shed the blood of a mother? According to the law of blood the answer can only be No, and the Erinyes must maintain the law. Deed of blood is weighed against deed of blood, and Orestes' is incomparably heavier because he shed his own blood whereas the husband whom Clytemnestra murdered was not related to her by blood.[12]

Out of a world of wholly different values and ordinances Apollo introduces a psychological differentiation which the Erinyes can only regard as arrogant caprice. The issue, says he,[13] is not that blood has been shed; in that case Orestes' deed would be as grave as Clytemnestra's, who had paid for it with her life, or indeed graver, because it was his own mother he had slain. The worth of the victim and the indignity visited upon him determine the gravity of the deed. Here a noble lord, a king by grace of god, was murdered on the day of his glorious return from a campaign, and at that by a woman who had cunningly entrapped him and had cut him down when he was alone and helpless. From all this all that the Erinyes glean is that higher claims are made for a father than for a mother and that a mother's blood may remain unavenged. Who is to decide?

We feel with horror that these two world orders are in conflict and that their opposition is insoluble. It must be counted as a magnificent aspect of Greek thought, which Aeschylus here represents, that it left this opposition unresolved. No declaration of an external power places the right upon one side and the wrong upon another. The goddess Athena herself declares that it is not for her to speak the deciding word in this dispute.[14] She installs the jury, who in future are to pronounce judgment in cases of murder, and retains only one vote for herself; this she casts for

Orestes, because she herself stands on the side of the masculine and of her own father, and the death of a woman who had slain her lord and husband could have no overwhelming importance in her sight.[15] Without Athena's ballot Orestes would have been lost. He is acquitted, but only by a tie vote. The avenging goddesses are eventually reconciled by Athena who promises them high honors, and pronounce their blessing instead of their curse over land and people. These events are of paramount significance. The Aeschylean tragedy celebrates the institution of the Athenian court for cases of murder, by means of which the law and authority of the state supplants the bloody expiation of the old order. But for the Greeks this event has a meaning which extends into the realm of the gods. When a matter is to be decided among men a clarification of it must first take place among the gods. Here the new Olympian gods stand opposed to the ancient deities; the bright and free spirit of the Olympians comes face to face with the brutish, narrow, earth-bound spirit of the primal forces. And the Olympians justify their new dominion by achieving reconciliation with the old forces. The new truth does not extinguish reverence for the old.

The Erinyes of Aeschylean tragedy present a living picture of the ancient earth-powers. Athena's decisive acknowledgment of masculinity is significant, for it may also be said that the masculine and feminine concepts of existence are here opposed. The Erinyes themselves are feminine, as are most divinities of the terrestrial domain. Thoroughly feminine is the question by which they wish to establish guilt: "Have you slain your mother?" Yea or Nay must decide. Woman's feeling for the actual has never been set forth more truly and at the same time more fearfully. It is this which gives us understanding of the narrowness, the severity, and at the same time the kindliness of the ancient divinities. The preponderance of the feminine is one of the most important determinants of its character, whereas in the Olympian divinity the masculine temper is triumphant.

Here is a maternal realm of forms, tensions, and ordinances whose holiness penetrates the entire human existence. At the center stands earth itself, as primal goddess, under many names. Out of her bosom well forth all life and all abundance, and into it they sink again. Birth and death both belong to her, and in her they close the sacred circle. But inexhaustible as is her vital buoyancy, rich and kindly as are her gifts, so holy and inviolable are her regulations, all being and all happening must yield to her fixed ordinances. Again it is the Erinyes whose wrath is roused when these ordinances are transgressed. Wherever anything takes place contrary to nature, there they cry their Nay! They seal the mouth of Achilles' steed whom goddess Athena had suddenly endowed with human speech.[16] Heraclitus calls them "Dike's police"[17] and says that for dread of them "even the sun does not exceed its bounds."

Associated unmistakably with belief in natural ordinances and their rigor is the fear of what the ancients called "envy" of the gods. This concept, which is one of the many that were handed down from high antiquity to the classical religion—and which is still current among ourselves, albeit in a different form—is naturally hard to reconcile with belief in deity as a spiritual personage. The fact that it could nevertheless never be wholly abolished proves how deeply belief in eternal ordinances is rooted in human temperament. We find it most powerfully developed among primitive civilizations, and a controlling factor in formulating their views of the world. It is repeatedly betrayed in the ineradicable anxiety lest a certain level of prosperity provoke the ill-will of higher powers as being excessive.

This lively awareness of fixed norms and systems is characteristic of religions that conceive of the divine not as form and person but rather as a dark force. Here again we discern the great distinction between the old world of the gods and the new. Not merely is the old divinity associated with belief in the holiness of the order of nature, it is actually one with this holiness. In it the order presents itself as the sacred will of the elemental world. This order is anything but mechanical. It can be violated. But always the sacred will rises again, menacing and crying halt. Human life too is wholly interwoven with this order. And here where willfulness is so often at work its essence is most clearly revealed: its power is summoned out of the darkness by curses and conjurations.

And now we have suddenly reached magic. Magic is in fact

associated to the same high degree with the sphere of thought which we are here attempting to describe, as it is alien to the Homeric.

Today magic is usually conceived of in a rational and mechanistic sense as a practice whose effectiveness rests exclusively upon its own power. This is a very short-sighted view. All genuine magic assumes human consciousness and concentration of thought on the one hand, and on the other the existence of a strict but not a mechanical order of nature. Only in a condition of special excitement is the genuinely magical act possible. This excitement takes its rise when the mind discovers with horror that the revered rule of nature has been disregarded. This distinguishes true magic from willfulness, which is nowadays customarily regarded as the point of departure for explaining it. One must never overlook the fact that it is most intimately connected with consciousness of generally valid norms which limit the personal will of the individual. It is not willfulness when an unhappy man calls imprecations upon his oppressor, an insulted father or abused mother upon a son, an elder upon a ruthless younger. These are the very cases where, according to the old view of the world, the wrathful deities rose up.

In their own abode underground they are called "spirits of curse" (Arai).[18] The curse of a man violently oppressed and the demonic vengeance of a violated world order are basically one and the same thing. So the pauper and beggar is a person to be revered, and when he is pitilessly repelled from the table of the rich or even roughly handled, then the vengeance of the Erinyes who stand at the beggar's side is visited upon the proud miscreants.[19] A related matter is the sanctity of the hospitable board; if it is outraged the higher powers grow exceeding wroth.[20] As is the case with much of the ancient law, the care of strangers and suppliants was later taken over by Zeus himself,[21] whose famous title "Protector of Strangers" (Xenios) gives clear expression to this aspect of his functions.

Much more serious, however, are the rights of blood and kinship. The story of Althaea and Meleager shows that concepts of the sanctity of these bonds and of the fearful wrath visited upon violators of them were shaped in a period which regarded degrees of relationship differently than they were regarded in the historical period. Althaea devotes her own son to destruction because he had killed her brother in combat.[22] Bathed in tears she kneels to the ground, smites the earth with her hands, and calls upon the subterranean powers to give death to her son, "and Erinys who walks in gloom, of heart pitiless, heard out of the dark places." Meleager had killed his mother's brother in battle. The deed was not one he himself had willed; he might as likely have been killed by his adversary. Even less guilty, according to modern feeling, is Oedipus, who, without suspecting what he was doing, transgressed against his own mother, by taking her to wife after he had unknowingly killed his father. The enormity, as the *Odyssey* tells the story,[23] did not long remain hidden. The mother hanged herself, and upon Oedipus there descended measureless woe which the "Erinyes of mothers" called down upon him. An excess of woe is all the more natural when a son's hard-heartedness drives his mother to utter a curse to which the depths respond. Telemachus cannot force his mother to leave the house as the wife of another; the higher powers would surely punish him, for as she departs the unhappy woman would call upon "the awful Erinyes."[24] A father too can invoke "the awful Erinyes" against a son if he affronts him instead of paying the honor due him: so Phoenix asserts in the *Iliad*.[25]

Thus in the maternal deities of the earth we see the guardians and representatives of those revered ordinances which constitute a bond between parents, children, and siblings. The various birthrights of children are also hallowed in them. Even in the *Iliad* Poseidon, when he is unwilling to yield to Zeus's orders, is reminded that the Erinyes always stand at the side of the elder,[26] and he is at once ready to conform.

It is not merely the spirit of family blood that speaks out of these earth-goddesses: human blood, which obligates every man to his neighbor, cries out to them and obtains their response. This obligation has nothing whatever to do with charity or selflessness. It is based on no philosophy or doctrine; it results from life's powerful need to convince and unite. The objective order to which it belongs is precisely coextensive with the primal revolt of the human soul when in fear and affliction it unburdens itself of its preternatural pressure by a curse and appeals to the obligation.

The ancient group of sanctities thus also includes obligations to the needy, the unprotected, to those astray. The feeling that the eternal powers must be angry with failure to sympathize receives lively expression in the *Iliad* also. Dying Hector utters it and on his lips it is tantamount to a curse. He had adjured Achilles by all that is sacred not to cast his body out for dogs to devour but to deliver it to his parents for decent burial in return for a rich ransom. But in vain. Now with his last breath he says,[27] "You have a heart of iron. Take care that I be not made the gods' curse upon you." And in fact Apollo, to whom Hector's last words allude, threatens with the anger of the gods the pitiless man who drags his victim's body behind his chariot, and he does so because Achilles "dishonors the dumb earth in his fury."[28] In ancient thinking this is frightful wickedness, for Gaia, "the eldest of the gods, the eternal and inexhaustible earth," as the chorus in Sophocles' *Antigone* calls her,[29] is basically one with Themis,[30] goddess of what is valid and needful. The important place which man's primal obligations held in the ancient earth-religion we can clearly discern in the curses called down upon, among others, those who would not show the way to a man astray, by the priest of the clan of the Buzyges ("ox-yokers") in Athens when the ritual plowing was performed.

The deity of earth and fertility in whose name these primal obligations were sanctified is not merely mother of the living. The dead belong to her also. A matricide, as the Erinyes threaten Orestes,[31] will have no peace even in the nether world. They list the primal offences which are punished in Hades: sins against deity, against hospitality, against parents. Against deity the gravest sin is forswearing, and it is very noteworthy that the *Iliad*, which in other respects ignores the possibility of bliss or suffering after death, knows the solemn formula of oaths in which, besides Zeus, the sun, the rivers, and the earth, those powers are invoked as witnesses "who under earth take vengeance on dead men, whoever among them has sworn to falsehood."[32] Triptolemus, whom Demeter of Eleusis had sent forth with the blessing of the fields, is said also to have promulgated those basic rules to which respect for parents belongs. And Eleusis was the site of Greece's most famous mysteries, which Cicero praises for having taught men not only "to live in happiness but also to die with high hope."[33]

In the earth-religion death does not separate a man from the community of the living. He becomes only the more powerful and respected. He dwells in maternal earth—in Athens he was anciently called Demetrius, that is, belonging to Demeter[34]—and there he receives the prayers and offerings of the living, and from there sends blessings up to them. On certain days when the earth loosens up and new life sprouts, the dead all return and are festively received until their visit is terminated.

This belief presupposes interment, by which the body returns to the bosom of the earth whence it came. Of this usage the civilization of the Homeric epic is no longer aware. In it cremation of the dead is assumed. This doubtless involves the difference in thought concerning the dead—one of the most characteristic distinctions of the new religion from the old; the dead do not, indeed, cease to be, but their being is no longer that of the living and there is no longer any connection between the two spheres. Furthermore the sphere of the dead has lost its sanctity; the gods belong wholly to life and are by their essence separated from all that is death's. The Olympian deities have nothing to do with the dead; indeed it is expressly said of them that they shudder before the dark realm of death.[35] In Homer, indeed, they do not fear contact with the dead, for their existence belongs wholly to the past; but later ages, which did not confront the problem of death with the same freedom, shunned the proximity of the dying and the dead in order to avoid pollution.[36] So broad is the interval that separates the Olympians from the ancient divinities. Whatever individual forms these latter may take, they are almost without exception also gods of the nether world and the dead.

All of them communicate the spirit of the earth, from which derive all blessings and obligations of earthly existence, the spirit which itself gives birth to all living, and again, when life's span is over, receives it back into itself. The maternal, the feminine, occupies the prime position in this earth-bound religion. The masculine is not wanting, but it is subordinate to the feminine.

That is true even for Poseidon, whose power indubitably extended over the whole world in primitive times; his name[37] describes him as the husband of the great goddess whose aspects we have dealt with in the foregoing section.

In Homer the dominion of Poseidon is wholly limited to the sea. He does participate in battles as a friend of the Greeks, but we need only compare him with other Olympians to realize his limitations. Whereas the others impinge upon human life in manifold ways, he is thought of only in connection with the sea and with horses. And yet he alone ventures to protest against the overlordship of Zeus and would have Zeus confined to heaven as his only rightful domain.[38] He must once have been much more powerful than he appears in the *Iliad*. In numerous ways, and not least by acute characterization, the Homeric poems indicate that his true greatness belongs to the past. Occasionally they confront him with the younger deities, and upon each occasion he appears to be somewhat awkward and old-fashioned before the bright and buoyant spirit of an Apollo.[39] According to the view of the *Iliad*[40] Poseidon is the younger brother of Zeus. But as we shall see, Hesiod was doubtless preserving an older view when he represented Zeus as the youngest scion of Cronus.[41]

The primal might of Poseidon is suggested by the sons whom myth ascribes to him; they are gigantic and unrestrained manifestations of strength such as Orion, Otus and Ephialtes, Polyphemus, and many others. His own true nature is clearly revealed by his name. The second part of this name, which points to the earth-goddess, contains the same ancient word whereby Damater (Demeter) is called "Mother Da." The cults of Arcadia retain very ancient myths of Poseidon's connection with that goddess. Demeter Erinys, who was worshipped there, was impregnated, as a mare, by Poseidon in the shape of a stallion, and gave birth to a daughter and to the curse-steed Arion, of whom it is also said that earth itself brought it forth.[42]

Related to this myth is another according to which Poseidon espoused Medusa.[43] Medusa too bears a name of the earth-goddess. Her name means "She who sways." Here the ancient earth-divinity brings her children forth in the monstrous ways characteristic of early myth: Medusa is decapitated by Perseus, and immediately there spring to light Chrysaor, "the man with the golden sword," and Pegasus, the lightning steed. The fact that the earth-goddess and her husband couple in equine form bespeaks the ancient notion that the horse belongs to the earth and the nether world. Poseidon figures as creator, father, or giver of the horse, bears the equine epithet Hippios, and is worshipped by sacrifice of a horse and by chariot races. According to Arcadian legend Rhea gave Cronus a filly to swallow instead of Poseidon. His son Neleus is said to have been brought up in a herd of horses. With Neleus, "the pitiless," we have arrived in the realm of the nether world, and many things go to show that Poseidon himself was once at home there. If we look for the action by which the strength of earth's consort is revealed, we find that the most important is the shaking of the earth, from which he received and retained many epithets. He is always the fearful god of the earthquake. In the *Iliad* he so shakes the earth that the mountains tremble and the horrible realm of the abyss threatens to burst open.[44] He not only cleaves the earth but causes salt water and fresh to bubble forth out of it, and thus he is the god of springs and rivers. But his most majestic manifestation is in the sea, whose uproar is related to the earthquake.

The notion that Poseidon is the ruler of the sea, which in Homer is the only relic of his formerly much wider activity, also undoubtedly belongs to his original image, as does his figure as an earth-shaker. A trait to which belief clings so long must have been very strong from the beginning. But we cannot avoid the impression that in Homer, and also in post-Homeric belief generally, Poseidon retained only fragments, albeit very important ones, of his sometime lordliness. This shrinkage is proof of a greater change in thought, inasmuch as Poseidon was formerly not merely a great god, but an all-embracing one; specifically, as his name suggests, the masculine figure associated with the feminine earth-deity. In this role we could compare him only to Zeus, hurler of the lightning; he himself had also hurled lightning, and his familiar trident was originally nothing else than a lightning bolt.

This Poseidon appears in myth, as we noted, in the figure of a horse, and his partner Demeter of a mare. This is characteristic of the way gods were imagined in remote antiquity, and any later manifestations of gods in animal form or of animal attendants upon gods of human form point back to that period of religion. Legends of the gods still contain abundant evidence that once the gods preferred to manifest themselves in animal form. For the newer mode of thinking this could only signify that they assumed animal form at specific moments and for specific purposes, and thus a large proportion of the well-known and well-loved stories of transformations came into being. But originally the animal body must have been wholly appropriate to the god who bore it, and so even under the altered conditions of existence characteristic of the new period individual gods could not give up their connection with specific animals, which was typically expressed in epithets, sacrificial usages, and legends.

It is difficult if not impossible for a modern to acclimate himself to this peculiar mode of thought, and it would be better to let the myths stand upon their own terms than to falsify them through the persistent intrusion of one's own categories of thought. It is falsification of this sort to say that the early period imagined the gods as animals just as the Homeric and post-Homeric periods imagined them as men. The Olympian religion countenances only the human form in deity. This positiveness is evidence for a basic transformation of thought whose meaning we shall have to examine in the sequel. For the old-fashioned religion, on the other hand, the lack of positiveness is equally characteristic. Ideas of god in animal form by no means exclude the human form. From primitive peoples today we can learn how preposterous it is to assume what we call "simple" ideas for early eras of human thought, for in point of fact the primitive is usually the least simple. In that world of thought and belief it is perfectly possible for one to be that specific man or superman in human guise and at the same time an animal or plant or anything else completely incongruous to our way of thinking; and if scientific investigation takes concrete and unequivocal aspects as its point of departure, understanding is frustrated from the start. Even in the historic religions wherever anything of antiquity or primitiveness has been retained, whether in cult or legend or popular belief, we find the same fluidity of ideas, in contrast to which our approach, controlled by a determination to master nature, seems stiff and mechanical. The divine river is this concrete water which I see flowing, hear murmuring, and can draw with my hand; but at the same time it is also a bull and a being in human form besides, precisely as a primitive clan consists of men who can simultaneously be eagles or the like. Plastic art represents this abundance of being by mixed forms, and the fact that such representations are avoided for the great deities from a certain period on is a significant sign of the transformation in thought. Here too the change in the direction of thought is perceptibly away from the elemental. The Protean variability of its conceptions is characteristic of its earthy objectivity. This sounds like a contradiction, yet it is quite natural. Where thought and reverence are bound to elementary being, they cannot at the same time possess the freedom and clear simplicity of spiritual form. Hence Asiatic modes of thought and belief have always remained at the stage which the spirit of the Homeric world definitely left behind. Its own early stages, on the other hand, must have been strongly dominated by elemental thought, in the degree of their remoteness. Hence the gods were manifested in animal form; their being was intimately connected with trees, plants, bodies of water, with earth and formations of earth, with wind and clouds. They dwelt not in the heavens like the Olympian gods, but on and in the earth.

3

We saw that in prehistoric religion the feminine essence was dominant. It was women too who held the highest divine rank. Even in the case of Poseidon, whose power must once have been so large and inclusive that comparison with Zeus was feasible, it is obvious that he did not approach the earth-goddess in dignity. As her husband he was, as the name shows, invoked in prayer. The same style of address is applied to Zeus in Homer[45] as an antique ceremonial form. This primal world of gods is pervaded by a maternal strain, which is as characteristic of it as is the paternal and masculine strain in the Homeric world of gods. In the antique stories of Uranus and Gaia and of Cronus and Rhea, to which we shall address ourselves presently, the children are wholly on the side of the mother, and the father seems to be a stranger with whom they have nothing to do. Things are very different in the realm of Zeus; there the outstanding deities describe themselves emphatically as children of their father.

But the distinction of the pre-Homeric religion from the Homeric is not comprised in the fact that the male is of less weight than the female. In pre-Homeric religion the masculine divinities themselves are fashioned differently than we are accustomed to imagine them from Homer and classical art. Here they are Titans, of whom it is told that they were overthrown by the Olympian gods and incarcerated in the abyss. Tradition has thus preserved the memory of a strenuous conflict which ended with the victory of the new gods. What was it that they overcame on that occasion? Surely not merely names, but essences.

We know enough of the nature of the Titans to realize that they were basically different from the Olympians for whom they had to make way. The first of the Aeschylean tragedies mentioned previously introduces us to one of them with overwhelming grandeur—Prometheus.

Prometheus is a god, son of the great earth-goddess, whose obduracy the new lord of heaven is unable to crush. He mocks the youthful race of gods, which abuses him only because he preserved mankind from destruction. As witnesses to the injustice which he has suffered he invokes the primal divine elements, the ether, the air, the streams, the sea, mother earth, and the sun. About him are the daughters of Oceanus, and the old god of the earth-stream himself comes to show his sympathy. This Prometheus who takes his mighty secret with him into the abyss has been imagined by Aeschylus with the grandeur that has impressed the spirit of humanity ever since. But there is no doubt that Prometheus was originally not so eminent a figure. Like Hephaestus he was a god of fire and handicraft to whom human existence owed much, indeed nearly everything. But *how* did he bestow his benefactions on the human race? Hesiod applies the designation "crafty" (*ankylometes*) to him.[46] In Homer, Cronus, the chief of the Titans, and only he, is often so designated, and Hesiod's account gives him the same epithet.[47] For both deities the epithet must have carried special significance; and in fact the myths that deal with them show their strength as consisting in cunning and in secret ambushes. Homer therefore ignores their prowess, and we must resort to Hesiod for information. The poet who was enthralled by the proud and wonderful masculinity of the Olympians must have found such characters and the peculiar myths in which they appeared distasteful. It was by theft that Prometheus procured the fire that is useful to man;[48] the myth of the theft of fire, which is extremely widespread, was applied to him. His second achievement was the deception by means of which he brought it about that the gods themselves chose the worse portion of the sacrifice as their share and left the better portion for men.[49] Cronus too is a robber. To mutilate his father Uranus he fell upon him in the dark, out of ambush. His misdeeds against wife and children are also depicted as thieving attacks.[50] He lurked to spy upon the pregnant mother, and it was only when she was on the point of giving birth to Zeus that she succeeded, with her parents' help, in hiding from him and in bringing her youngest son into the world surreptitiously. He himself was overreached by similar cunning: instead of the children he wished to swallow he was given a stone, and further guile brought him to disgorge first the stone and then all the children he had previously swallowed.[51]

When we read these stories, up to the establishment of the lordship of Zeus, we feel ourselves in a different, one may almost say, an un-Greek world. Memories of mythical tales of primal civilizations are aroused. In many respects the principal personages are like the inventive heroes and deliverers of primitive peoples. As in the case of the latter, the human and divine are marvellously intermingled. This spiritual kinship is given very characteristic expression in a peculiar trait of the stories: the hero, the deliverer of his people, the one called to lordship, is the youngest. This is true of Cronus,[52] of Zeus,[53] and, to cite only a single example, of Maui, the divine deliverer of Polynesia, who was the last-born child of his parents. The mere fact that in Homer

Zeus is no longer the youngest but rather the eldest son of Cronus is in itself evidence of the great transformation in thought.

The impression which the myths give of the masculine deities who were suppressed by the Olympians seems to fit in admirably with what we learn of their names and forms. The name Titan is said to have denoted "king."[54] Nor did the word designate a specific kind of god but more properly the great gods in general, like *deus* among the Romans and *theos* among the Greeks. This is consistent with the suggestion lately advanced by Paul Kretschmer:[55] in the name Titan he recognizes a "Pelasgian" forerunner of the Greek (or Latin) word for heavenly gods which inheres in such names as Zeus, Diespiter, and the like; Tinia, the Etruscan name for Jupiter, would be a similar forerunner on Italian soil. It appears then that in "Titan" we have the name which comprehended the pre-Olympian gods and by which they were invoked. There are many indications that it acquired the connotation of "wild," "rebellious," or even "wicked" by opposition to the Olympians, to whom the Titans yielded only after a struggle.

Now it is to be noted that these Titans are frequently characterized as Priapean deities. Kaibel[56] regarded this as the principal and original conception; latterly it has been held that nothing more than a joke is implied. But the evidence justifies Kaibel, inasmuch as it compels us to believe that there must have been a remarkable similarity between the ithyphallic deities and the picture in which the Titans were imagined. Nevertheless we must not attribute to the emphasis on the sexual in the case of the Titans the significance that attached to phallic beings in historical times. The little wooden idols of primitive cultures can teach us how the idols of Titans must have been fashioned to remind men in later centuries, who may have encountered such wooden images frequently, of Priapus and his peers. In these small and quite simple figures masculinity was markedly emphasized. This characterized them as virile deities capable of reproduction, but not as wanton, and it was thus that they stood beside the maternal deities and their epitome, Mother Earth, whose feminine and maternal powers far transcended them in grandeur and dignity.

In one single case the concept of the masculine divinity rises to true grandeur, and that is the union of divine heaven and divine earth in wedlock. Even Aeschylus[57] sings of the amorous glow of "holy heaven" and the nuptial yearning of Earth, who is impregnated by the rain from above. The myth represents the embrace as a mighty event, at the very beginning of the world. The remarkable account in the *Theogony*[58] tells how "great Uranus came, bringing on night and longing for love, and he lay about Gaia, spreading himself full upon her."

The high significance of this picture is proven by its survival in famous myths. In these, however, it has been disguised, for the conjugal pair do not bear such transparent names as "heaven" and "earth"; Zeus appears in the rôle of heaven, and in that of earth appear Danaë, Semele, or other human women. But upon closer examination it becomes clear that these are recurrences of the same primal motif under various names and in various conceptions. Yet lofty as the heavenly god appears in this picture, and although he is little inferior to the earth-goddess in grandeur, the fact that the masculine divinity is secondary to the feminine in the religious thought of the early period remains unalterable. The god of heaven in particular must have played only a slight part in early religion, however persistent the myths concerning him may be. So in the religions of primitive peoples, of which there is much to remind us here, the masculine divinity of heaven often remains in the background.

But the figure of the god of heaven draws our attention to one of the most significant phenomena of the prehistoric world, the myth. We must understand that great myths in the proper sense were done with when the new view of the world came to prevail. In the latter period, interest was centered upon the sharply delineated personal figure. But myth is always a happening in which the magnitude and importance of the individual agents or victims are swallowed up. The hugeness of the happening so dominates them that their images may easily appear monstrous, grotesque, and comic to the tamer taste of later generations. Thus we see that the Homeric poems disdain their characteristic creations with well-bred silence, as though they were ignorant of them, though they knew them well enough, and that Plato who was himself gifted in mythic thought—though in a new mode —makes no secret of his disgust for them.

One such myth, filled with the spirit of the primal period, is that of Cronus and Uranus.[59] Uranus does not suffer the children whom Gaia is on the point of bearing to him to reach the light but hides them in her depths. In her affliction Earth groans. Her children are horrified at the thought of attacking their father; only the youngest son, Cronus, "the crafty," shows courage, and with the sharp weapon which his mother had given him falls upon his father from ambush just as, at nightfall and yearning for love, Uranus is spreading himself full over the earth. Cronus amputates his father's male member and flings it into the sea.

This remarkable myth bears unmistakable kinship with the famous Polynesian story of the primal parents, heaven and earth, and of their enforced separation by one of their sons.[60] Long ago Bastian pointed the kinship out.[61] It is not as if some historical connection between the two could be made plausible; aside from other considerations, the divergences are considerable. At the beginning of all things, says the Polynesian legend, everlasting darkness prevailed, for Rangi and Papa, that is, heaven and earth, lay locked together. Their sons considered what was to be done and determined to separate their parents from one another by force. Various attempts to do so proved futile, until Tane, the god of trees, insinuated himself between them and raised heaven high above earth. But differences in detail are of no consequence. The meaning and the character of the conception as a whole are obviously the same in the Hesiodic and the Polynesian account, and the Greek myth, spatially so far removed from the barbarian, must teach us that the Hesiodic report on Uranus and Cronus bears the authentic stamp of genuine mythic thought. In one by no means negligible detail the Polynesian fancy seems to coincide almost exactly with the Greek. Uranus hides his children, instead of suffering them to come to light, in the earth's depths (*Gaies en keuthmoni*); the Polynesian myth concludes (ac-

cording to Bastian) with the words: "Immediately upon the separation of heaven and earth the people who had previously been
hidden in the hollows of their parents' breasts, became visible."

The myth of Cronus and Rhea[62] repeats the myth of heaven
and earth with other fancies and other names. Just as Uranus did
not suffer his children to come to light but hid them in earth's
bosom as soon as they were born, so Cronus swallows his immediately after birth. Again it is the youngest, Zeus, from whom deliverance comes. In this connection it is impossible not to think
of the famous myth of the birth of Athena. It is Hesiod, again, who
first tells the story.[63] Athena's mother is said to have been Metis,
the goddess "Intelligence," but before the child came into the
world Zeus the father swallowed the mother. Here too, then, the
father prevents the child from issuing forth from its mother; here
too he swallows it, as Cronus had done, but together with the
mother; here too he acts to forestall the destiny foretold by Uranus and Gaia that a son of this union would cast him from his
throne.[64] But here we have added the new motif that the child
is born of the father himself, and in very peculiar fashion—from
the head.[65] This reminds us of the birth of Dionysus, whom Zeus
caught up into his own thigh as an incomplete embryo from his
burning mother and himself gave birth to at the appropriate
season.

It is quite remarkable that all these myths could latterly have
been considered as relatively late creations of speculation or exe-
gesis. With full regard to the caution that is here called for it
may still be positively asserted that of all possible interpretations
this is the least probable. Whatever the original meaning of these
stories may have been, their astonishing, romantic, and gigantic
qualities are proof of their validity as creations of genuine and
original mythic thought, or rather, viewpoint. They are quite
analogous to the first rank growth of myths among primitive civilizations and strike us with the same sense of strangeness. Even
the remarkable birth of Athena has a Polynesian parallel, at least
in the circumstance that there too the mythical personage was
born out of the head. Of Tangaroa it is related that his mother
Papa bore him not in the usual manner but through her arm, or,
according to another version, "straight out of her head."[66]

To us they sound strange, these myths, and so they did to the Homeric age also. Homer knew well enough that Athena sprang from her father's head; the honorific epithet *obrimopatre*, "daughter of the mighty father," is a clear enough indication. The goddess herself declares, in Aeschylus, that she is "wholly her father's" and knows of no mother; she is equally her father's in Homer. But concerning the romantic myth of her birth from his head Homer is silent, and it is as little conceivable that he could speak of it as it is that he could speak of the monstrous myths of Uranus and Cronus. We realize that the age of the fantastic narrative myth is over. In the new age, which conceives the essence of the world and of human life in lofty figures, myth no longer enjoys the sovereign independence and capacity for the fabulous which it had possessed in the prehistoric period. The distinction between the two will become clear in the sequel.

Along with ancient myth, magic also perished, and though both may have survived here and there in Greece in one form or another, the main line of the Greek spirit proves that it had once and for all decided against them. And this decision was made in the period for which the Homeric poems are the great document.

We can classify the world-view of peoples according to the degree by which they are preoccupied and controlled by magic thinking. None has so completely overcome magic in its characteristic world of thought as has the Greek. In the Homeric world, magic possesses no importance, whether we look at gods or men, and the few cases where knowledge of magic is indicated only go to show how remote it had become. The gods do not practice enchantment, even though at times they bring things to pass in a manner reminiscent of ancient magic. Their might, like their essence, is based not on magical *power*, but on the *being* of nature. "Nature" is the great new word which the matured Greek spirit opposed to ancient magic. From here the path leads directly to the arts and to the sciences of the Greeks. But in the age when the ancient myths were still vital, magic (which is related to ancient myth in spirit) appears to have possessed no slight importance; for in mythical narratives the miraculous, which has grown alien to the Homeric spirit, occupies a large place.

A genuine miraculous hero in early myth is Perseus, whom his mother Danaë conceived in the depths of the earth from the golden rain of the god of heaven; as an infant he was fished out of an ark in the sea, and later experienced adventures most astonishing. To reach the horrid Gorgons at the western extremity of the world, beyond Ocean, he first visited the Old Women and forced them to show him the way to the Nymphs, from whom he received winged shoes, a cap of invisibility, and scrip. Thus equipped he flew to the end of the world and hewed Medusa's head off, whereupon there sprang from her trunk Chrysaor, "the man with the golden sword," and Pegasus, the lightning steed, whom Medusa had conceived from Poseidon.

How different is the world to which this heroic myth belongs from the world of Homeric gods and men; how different is this hero from a Heracles or from the heroes of Homer! Here adventure and marvel is everything, and nothing is left of the personage involved. All that happens has a marvellous, fairytale quality, and is extraordinary to the point of monstrosity. When the head of Medusa is severed from her body and man and horse spring forth, one feels that something powerful and profoundly significant is going on, expressed in peculiar imagery—but who can now interpret such an image? Guile and enchantment are the qualities by which the hero brings the incredible to pass. The Old Women he robs of their most precious possession and thereby forces them to show him the way to the Nymphs; and from these he receives the magic articles by which alone he can reach his goal in the extreme west beyond Ocean and perform his adventure—winged shoes and the cap that made him invisible. One is reminded of "crafty" Cronus and of the deed he achieved with his sickle—the same weapon that one imagines in the hands of Perseus.

Perseus is not a god, but he stands very near the gods and perhaps once was one. Kinship with Hermes is very striking, and extends precisely to those traits in the picture of Hermes which, as we shall see, belong to the oldest mode of conceiving the world. And thus it becomes possible for us to recognize clearly what it is that distinguishes the earlier conception of the gods from the Homeric, and in the fullest sense Greek, conception.

The most miraculous happening in the world and the most astonishing and magical capacity of higher beings—such are the images and thoughts by which the spirit was at one time filled. But the new spirit looks into existence with different eyes. For it, not happening and capacity are most important, but *being*. The divinities become figures of reality in which the manifold being of nature finds its perfect and eternal expression. With this step ancient myth is abolished, magic overcome, and the gods are finally separated from the elemental.

III

OLYMPIAN DEITIES

T HE SERIES OF GODS to whom we shall devote special attention should begin with Hermes if it were desired to connect this section closely with what precedes, for he is without doubt next in order to the ancient divinities, and our investigation of pre-historic thought inevitably leads up to Hermes. But it is precisely because of this connection that Hermes is the least distinguished phenomenon in the new circle of gods, and if his figure were given first place, false notions concerning him might arise. Athena and Apollo will therefore be treated first. Artemis is connected with Apollo. Aphrodite and Hermes will be reserved for the conclusion.

The basic idea of this book provides the explanation of why only such divinities as are important in Homeric religion are given special and extensive treatment. But even of the Homeric gods only the greatest and most representative are considered. Of the others, who were less important in active worship or who are not regarded in Homer, a word will be said at appropriate junctures in later chapters.

Zeus, the greatest of the gods, indeed the epitome of the divine, is not dealt with separately because all lines converge in him and no problem can leave him out of consideration.

ATHENA

1

Worship of Athena can apparently be traced back to the early period. Her name itself points to a source outside the Greek range, to which neither its root syllable nor its word-form can belong.

The likeness of an armed goddess with body almost wholly covered by a shield occurs frequently in Mycenean art. A familiar painted stucco relief from Mycenae shows this goddess, almost wholly hidden by her huge shield, at the center, with two women worshipping her at right and left.[1] It has been believed that this figure represents the Mycenean Athena, and no one can deny the plausibility of this interpretation. But this tells us very little about the early history of our goddess; Cretan and Mycenean statuary is for us, unfortunately, virtually mute. We see a goddess covered by her shield, ready to attack or to guard. But is this all that her figure suggested when belief in her was a living thing? Should we call her maiden of the shield, maiden of battles? We are given no answer to this question. For the Homeric Athena, at least, such designations are not appropriate, joyous and mighty in battle as the goddess may appear. She is much more than a goddess of battle; she is, in fact, the sworn enemy of the wild spirit whose sole delight is the rush of combat. First of all we are inclined to think of the so-called Palladium and the many famous statues of armed Athena, although we are aware that the city of Athens, which bore the goddess's name, worshipped in the old temple on the Acropolis a carved wooden image which was not of this type.[2] The ancient heroic legend in which Athena is so much involved exhibits her as a goddess of vigorous but by no means exclusively military action. Very few of the deeds of Heracles, at which her presence was an inspiration and a help, were of such a sort that his divine patroness could be called the maiden of battles. She does stand by Achilles, Diomedes, and others of her favorites in battle, but she also helps Jason build

his ship and Bellerophon tame his horse. She stands at Odysseus'
side in all manner of difficult situations. None of these operations
can be assigned, unless by sheer caprice, to an earlier stage in
the development of belief in Athena. If we do so assign them, we
disrupt the unity of the Homeric and post-Homeric picture of
Athena even before we have attempted to understand it. But it is
very easy to understand if we do not, out of stubborn insistence
on seeing a product of accident, close our eyes to the consistent
and meaningful entity.

2

The goddess reveals her true identity by the mode of her epiph-
anies and her interventions.

In the poetic accounts of her birth she is represented as mighty
in battle. "Zeus himself," we read in Hesiod's *Theogony*, "gave
birth from his own head to owl-eyed Tritogeneia, the awful, the
strife-stirring, the host-leader . . . who delights in tumults and
wars and battles."[3] Pindar's lines with reference to the island of
Rhodes are majestic:

> Where once the high king of the gods drenched their city in a gold
>   snowfall,
> when, by the artifice of Hephaestus,
> at the stroke of the bronze-heeled axe Athena sprang
> from the height of her father's head with a strong cry.
> The sky shivered before her and earth our mother.[4]

The twenty-eighth *Homeric Hymn* presents a truly grand picture of her nature and her first appearance among the gods: "I
begin to sing of Pallas Athena, the glorious goddess, owl-eyed, inventive, unbending of heart, pure virgin, savior of cities, courageous, Tritogeneia. From his awful head wise Zeus himself bore
her arrayed in warlike arms of flashing gold, and awe seized all
the gods as they gazed. But Athena sprang quickly from the immortal head and stood before Zeus who holds the aegis, shaking
a sharp spear: great Olympus began to reel horribly at the might
of the owl-eyed goddess, and earth round about cried fearfully,
and the sea was moved and tossed with dark waves, while foam

burst forth suddenly: the bright son of Hyperion stopped his swift-footed horses a long while, until the maiden Pallas Athena had stripped the heavenly armor from her immortal shoulders. And wise Zeus was glad."[5]

Her effects upon the world of men and her manifestations in it are celebrated by poets and artists. First of all it is the warriors whose courage she kindles. Before battle begins they sense her inspiriting presence and yearn to perform heroic deeds worthy of her. In the *Iliad* she sweeps, brandishing her fearful aegis, through the armed companies of the Greeks, urging them to battle; only a little while ago they were jubilant at the thought of returning home—now all that is forgotten; the spirit of the goddess causes all hearts to thrill with battle glee.[6] Or again she moves through the tumult and is present wherever the Greeks begin to flag.[7] So the Athenian phalanx felt her presence in the Persian War:

> Hah! their arrows hail so densely, all the sun is in eclipse!
> Yet we drove their ranks before us, ere the fall of eventide:
> As we closed, an owl flew o'er us, and the gods were on our side.[8]

Once the poet sees her, swathed in a darkling cloud, descending from heaven in order to urge the warriors on.[9]

Particularly significant is her appearance at the battle of the suitors in the *Odyssey*. Odysseus has shot his bolts at the suitors and now stands ready-armed with his son and two faithful servitors at the threshold. Before he begins the decisive battle Athena suddenly appears at his side in the guise of Mentor and urges him to strike out. She is barely seen and heard before she disappears— the poet himself sees her soaring aloft like a swallow[10]—and perches invisible on a rafter. Now spears fly on both sides and the suitors fall, one after another. But when the time comes for the final struggle, the goddess raises her aegis high and the terrified suitors stray through the hall until the last has fulfilled his fate.[11] In all these descriptions Athena's presence alone is effective; she does not actively participate. So she is shown in the famous pediment reliefs of the temple of Aphaia in Aegina: she stands fully armed but in attitude of repose in the midst of the warriors. On the shield of Achilles she was shown along with Ares in super-

human stature at the head of an army marching out to battle.[12]
One of her Homeric epithets (*ageleie*) designates her as "driver of
booty"; later she was called "destroyer of cities" (*persepolis*). But
the Trojan women invoked her as "guardian of cities" (*erysip-
tolis*),[13] and in many cities she was worshipped as goddess of the
citadel (*polias, poliouchos*); so especially in Athens, which took its
name from her. Perhaps it is this warlike and protective Athena
whom we should recognize in the picture of the Mycenean
shield-divinity with which we began.

But it is not merely over armies and cities that she holds sway;
even more significant is her bond with the strongest personalities.
She is the divine sister, friend, and companion of the hero in his
undertakings; always her heavenly presence kindles, illuminates,
and blesses him at the right instant. Ancient songs knew of many
men who were thus favored. To the mighty Tydeus who fell
before Thebes she was so devoted that she even petitioned the
supreme god to grant him immortality. His son Diomedes, whose
prowess is recounted in the fifth book of the *Iliad*, inherited this
friendship. Everyone knows of her love for Odysseus. When he
and Diomedes embarked on their perilous venture at night, she
aroused their confidence by the omen of a bird, and Odysseus
prayed: "Hear me, daughter of Zeus of the aegis, you who always
stand beside me in all my tasks and always remember me wherever I go: be thou friendly to me now more than ever, grant that
I come back to our ships covered with glory, having achieved
some great deed that shall bring sorrow to the Trojans." The
goddess helped them fall upon the enemy in their sleep and admonished them to return at the proper moment, so that the heroes
came back to their camp in safety.[14] On Diomedes' day of glory
she appeared to him in the flesh and gave him courage to confront
Ares himself, the hated madman, face to face; in place of his
charioteer Sthenelus, whom she thrust away, she sprang up on
his chariot, so that the axle creaked, and it was through her power
that the hero's spear pierced deep into the body of the god.

Her enmity towards Ares, which breaks out repeatedly in the
Iliad, permits us to understand something of her own nature. In
the famous battle of the gods in the twenty-first book (where ac-

tually no real battle other than this occurs) she crushes the war-
god down to earth with little effort.[15] Ares' partisanship for the
Trojans is alleged to be the cause of this hatred, but we feel
plainly that there is a deeper cause, rooted in the opposition between their natures. Ares is sketched as a bloodthirsty, raging
demon, whose confidence in victory is nothing more than brag-
gadocio compared to the rational power of an Athena. "Mad" and
"insane" the gods call him;[16] he does not know "what is right,"[17]
and turns, with no character, "now to one and now to another."[18]
To Zeus himself "no Olympian god is so hated" as he, for "he
thinks only of strife and wars and battles."[19] Against this grim
spirit of slaughter and bloodshed the bright form of Athena stands
in admirable contrast, and this contrast is intentional on the part
of the poet. She is much more than merely a warrior. This is most
memorably expressed in her affectionate care for Heracles, whose
prowess goes far beyond delight in battle and the strength to
challenge any opponent. The grandeur which ennobles the deeds
of Heracles and makes them the paradigm for the heroic course
that conquers heaven is the expression of Athena's spirit. In
poetry as in plastic art we see her ever at his side; she accompanies him upon his journeys, she helps him to encompass the superhuman, and finally she leads him into heaven.[20] For us, sculpture
and vase-paintings show the bond between the goddess and the
great champion most significantly and most beautifully. Always
she appears at the right moment as the true counsellor and helper
of the mighty hero who proudly challenged monsters and paved
his own path to the gods by glorious struggle. The nearness of
the divine at the moment of severest trial is perhaps nowhere presented to our eyes more compellingly than by the creator of the
Atlas metope of the temple of Zeus at Olympia. The arch of
heaven rests heavily upon the neck of the hero, threatening to
crush him; but unnoticed the bright and noble figure of Athena
has stepped up behind him, and with the indescribable dignity of
posture which is the hallmark of Greek divinity she gently touches
the burden—and Heracles, who cannot see her, feels that his
strength is gigantic and is able to perform the impossible. Other
reliefs of the same temple show the hero during or after some

superhuman feat, and the presence of the goddess, who instructs him with royal gesture or accepts the booty, leaves us in no doubt that the deed was performed in a spirit of magnanimity.

Not furious onset but prudence and dignity are pleasing to Athena. This is shown by her care for wrathful Achilles.[21] At the insulting words of Agamemnon the mighty hero is angered and has already laid his hand upon his sword; he reflects for a moment whether he should cut the offender down or make the effort to control himself; at this moment he feels himself touched from behind, turns his head, and encounters the flaming eyes of the goddess. She makes it plain to him that if he retains his composure for the present the offender would later offer him threefold recompense. Achilles thrusts his sword back into its sheath. Reason has prevailed. No one but himself saw the goddess.

With this we may compare the story of the death of Tydeus, which was told in a lost poem.[22] To this hero too Athena was a faithful companion,[23] and at the end of his lifespan she even wished to make him immortal. As he lay fatally wounded, she approached him with the potion of eternal life, but he was on the point of wrenching open the skull of his slain opponent, to gulp the brain out of its pan in his cannibalistic rage. The goddess was repelled by this sight and turned back, and the protégé for whom she intended the supreme distinction sank into the common lot of death, for he had degraded himself. It is a mistake to believe that the Athena known to the *Iliad* was oblivious to such regard for moral factors. Conduct like that of Tydeus is unthinkable for any friend of Athena in the *Iliad*. The goddess who recalls Achilles to reason and dignity at the right moment is none other than she who is revolted by and turns away from a Tydeus dehumanized in dying.

And she is not merely the admonisher: she herself is properly the decision, specifically on the side of reason against mere passion. Achilles himself pondered whether he should strike or restrain himself. "Even as he pondered and was drawing the sword from its scabbard"[24] Athena suddenly touched him. The sense of her coming is the victory of reason. This describes her better than long discussions of her nature can do. Thus she presents herself to her protégé Odysseus as victorious thought in a

2. Athena

moment of great tension, where not energy alone but above all
shrewdness was required to save a desperate situation. The invitation to return home by which Agamemnon intended only to
test his soldiery was accepted with wild enthusiasm, and in a
moment all were rushing to the ships. Then Athena approached
Odysseus, who was sunk in sad thought, and admonished him to
restrain the disintegrating mass by argument and deft intervention.
Just as she suddenly looked Achilles in the eye in the midst of his
pondering whether he should attack Agamemnon or control himself and made him choose the more intelligent and dignified
course, so the goddess appeared to Odysseus as he stood sad and
anxious, and spoke the thoughts which a psychological narrator
would represent as passing through his head and heart. The poet
does not tell of her departure, but only of the well-calculated and
energetic action to which Odysseus proceeded immediately after
her words. But later, when he rose up as the first speaker in the
restored assembly, she stood beside him in the guise of a herald
and commanded silence.[25]

In this and other ways Athena is always at Odysseus' side, to
counsel and assist, as the stories in the *Odyssey* show best of all.
Among Homer's heroes Odysseus is the man "of many counsels"
(*polymetis*). In the *Iliad* the word serves as a stereotype characterization for him, and for him alone. It recalls the praise of the
god who possesses the highest "intelligence" and "counsel"
(*metis*), of Zeus who alone among the gods is called "master of intelligence" or "of counsel" (*metieta, metioeis*). Not only is it said of
Odysseus that his intelligence and counsel are the most excellent
in the world of men,[26] but he is not infrequently compared with
Zeus himself in this respect.[27] One such passage is that discussed above,[28] and it is significant that his "counsel" (*metis*) is
made equal to that of Zeus at the moment when his heavy heart
receives saving counsel from Athena. It is she whose inspiration
arouses his famous ingenuity and alertness. In the beautiful
Homeric Hymn to Athena she is called "of many counsels" (*polymetis*), exactly as Odysseus is in both epics, and indeed at the
very opening of the *Hymn*, before her warlike qualities are
praised.[29] And in the *Odyssey*[30] she herself tells Odysseus what it
is that distinguishes them and binds them together: "Of all man-

kind thou art easily foremost, both in counsel and speech, and
among all gods I win fame for my wit (*metis*) and cleverness." In
Hesiod's *Theogony*[31] she is described as "equal to her father in
strength and in wise understanding." This excellence of "intelligence" or "counsel" constitutes an essential trait in the Homeric
picture of Athena. When she "schemes" (*metioōsa*) the homecoming of Odysseus she betakes herself to sleeping Nausicaa, who is to
be her instrument.[32] "Now she bethought her of another thing,"[33]
a stereotype verse says, when at a decisive moment she introduces a device to serve her plans. With this acute perception, with
ever-ready inventiveness, she stands by the heroes' side, builds
the first great ship with Jason and with Danaus,[34] and with
Epeius the wooden horse with which Troy would be taken;[35] she
helps Bellerophon master Pegasus by giving him a golden bridle.[36]
This shrewd device for breaking a horse is perfectly in keeping
with her spirit, and in many places she was worshipped as mistress of horses, in Corinth with the epithet Chalinitis,[37] and elsewhere with the epithet Hippia. This and much like it is the sense
of the ancient poetry when it praises the "intelligence" and "counsel" (*metis*) of the goddess. The attribute "of many counsels"
(*polymetis*) which characterizes Athena's favorite Odysseus in
both epics and Athena herself in the *Hymn* is once applied in the
Iliad[38] to the masterly fire-god Hephaestus; and a verse of the
Odyssey[39] describes the assuaging effect of a remedy as "of much
counsel" (*metioeis*).

3

The importance and antiquity of the notion that "intelligence"
and "counsel" (*metis*) manifest themselves in Athena are demonstrated by the famous myth of her begetting and her birth.

No mother bore her. She knows only of a father and belongs
wholly to him. This limited and unilateral allegiance is a fixed
premise for Homer whenever he writes of the gods. Aeschylus has
the goddess speak in express terms of her motherlessness and of
her exclusive connection with her father.[40] As a daughter who
issued solely from her father she must reflect the image of Zeus'

special distinction—"intelligence" or "counsel" (*metis*). The twenty-eighth *Homeric Hymn*, which praises her in its opening as "of many counsels" (*polymetis*), says, two verses later, that "the master of craft (*metieta*) Zeus alone bore her out of his holy head." Homer himself does not reveal how the birth of the goddess is to be thought of, and we can understand his reticence. But he very significantly calls her "daughter of the mighty father" (*obrimopatre*), and in these words we detect the echo of the marvellous myth which Hesiod is the first to tell us.

The daughter sprang from the head of her father—a fabulous picture, which is given monumental representation in the east pediment of the Parthenon at Athens. But it is not enough that she issued directly from her father, and at that from his head; a more astonishing myth knows of a goddess Metis who was properly her mother. Upon this mistress of intelligence and counsel Zeus begot her, but before she travailed he swallowed the pregnant mother in order to retain her forever as counsellor in his own entrails. When the appropriate time came, he himself brought his daughter into the light of the world through the top of his head. Such is the account of Hesiod's *Theogony*.[41] Latterly this double myth has been strangely interpreted as a late addition, and the part concerning Metis even as an absurd theological invention.[42] The god's skull, it has been held, must have been in the oldest myth the peak of the divine mountain out of which the young goddess climbed, just as we see other goddesses ascend out of the earth. It was only later that this event was transferred to the head of a god thought of in human form. But the enlightened age to which the transformation of the original description is ascribed did not create any such image as parturition from the head of a god. The monstrousness of the notion corresponds wholly to the primal mode of mythic conception, and the mythology of primitive peoples offers us a close parallel.[43] How alien such a story was to the spirit of the new age we can see in Homer's avoidance of it; he surely knows the story, but passes it over in silence, as he does the wild myths of Cronus who emasculated his father Uranus and swallowed his own children. Such notions had become intolerable to the new spirit. Hence there is all the less reason to doubt their antiquity and genuineness.

If the picture of Athena's birth from the head is really to be regarded as derivative, we must hold that an early myth from some source or other has been transferred to Athena. But it is much more natural to accept the story as tradition has transmitted it, as the true myth of the birth of Athena. It is incomparably well suited to the character of the masculine and clever goddess. This applies equally to the antecedent of this myth—namely, that Athena did nevertheless have a mother, the goddess Metis, who was swallowed up by Zeus, however, in her pregnant condition. This story has been explained as an invention of later theology, and Hesiodic authorship of it has been denied; careful examination of Hesiod's text is said to indicate that the passage is a later interpolation. But this text, which enumerates the wives and children of Zeus—lines 886-929—is a meaningful unity as it stands, despite all that has been said about it; no portion can be removed without doing willful and disruptive violence to it. Concerning this there is no need for further analysis here; for on the point to which chief exception has been taken, the introduction of Metis as mother of Athena, clarification is easy. This thought, it has been held, was possible only after the warlike maiden had been transformed into the "goddess of wisdom."

It is true that in later times the nature of Athena was explained as "mind and thought" (*nous kai dianoia*).[44] But her old connection with Metis has a quite different meaning. The word *metis* always signifies *practical* understanding and thinking through, which is more valuable than physical strength even in the life of one whose desire is battle and victory. Before the beginning of the foot-race at the funeral games[45] Nestor calls his son's attention to the inestimable worth of good counsel (*metis*) and says: "Through counsel (*metis*) a man is a better cleaver of wood than through strength; through counsel (*metis*) the pilot steers his swift ship through the storms in the dark; through counsel (*metis*) the charioteer gains the upper hand over his fellows." It is just such counsel which distinguishes Athena from a "shield-maiden" and marks her superiority.

If, then, a myth makes this power, as a thing divine, Athena's mother—Metis—and connects this motherhood with birth from her father through the primal images of swallowing and birth from the head, we have every reason to regard it as genuine and ancient.

The time has now come to penetrate deeper into the nature of Athena. Together with the being of the goddess, something of the spirit and the ideal of Hellenism will be revealed to us, for where should they be shown more clearly than in the manifestation of the divine?

What Athena shows man, what she desires of him, and what she inspires him to, is boldness, will to victory, courage. But all of this is nothing without directing reason and illuminating clarity. These are the true fountainheads of worthy deeds, and it is they which complete the nature of the goddess of victory. This light of hers illumines not alone the warrior in battle: wherever in a life of action and heroism great things must be wrought, perfected, and struggled for, there Athena is present. Broad indeed is the spirit of a battle-loving people when it recognizes the same perfection wherever a clear and intelligent glance shows the path to achievement, and when no mere maid of battle can be adequate. Athena is the splendor of the serene and powerful moment to which consummation must fly, just as the winged Victory flies to the victor with its wreath from the hands of the goddess. She is the ever-near whose word and whose lightning glance encounter the hero at the right moment and summon him to his most intelligent and manly prowess. Here our thoughts inevitably turn to Apollo, Hermes, and Artemis, and we are compelled to compare them with Athena.

Just as Apollo is the god of distance and as such the god of purity and of cognition, so is Athena the goddess of nearness. In this she resembles Hermes. Like him she acts as guide to her favorites, and at times both she and Hermes accompany the same hero. And yet there is a world of difference between their modes of guidance. In Hermes we recognize divine presence and direction as the wonderful windfall of sudden gain, finding, snatching, and irresponsible enjoyment. Athena, on the other hand, is the heavenly presence and direction as illumination and inspiration to victorious comprehension and consummation. To Hermes belongs what is clandestine, twilit, uncanny; Athena is bright as day.

Dreaminess, yearning, languishing, are alien to her. Of the tender
raptures of love she knows nothing. "All creatures in heaven and
on earth," says the *Homeric Hymn to Aphrodite*, "pay homage to
the goddess of love, but with Athena her power ceases." In
Homer and Hesiod she is called Pallas, "the maid,"[46] and in
Athens she bears the famous name "the Virgin" (*Parthenos*). Her
disinclination to love and marriage suggests a likeness to Artemis,
but here again the greatest profit in the comparison is that it
underscores the essential difference. In Artemis maidenhood has
a tart, shy, disdaining character which fends love off; in Athena
maidenhood is the spirit of action. It is in her nature to associate
with men, to think of them always, always to be near them, in
order to reveal herself to them in moments of life which differ
from the erotic not by shy aloofness but by the strength and
clarity of energetic action. There is a great difference between
this goddess of the near and the spirit of distance which we must
recognize equally in Apollo and in his sister Artemis. Athena's
inclination and involvement are in the nature of the friendship
that man feels for man. To this the lives of many heroes testify.
In poetry the clearest case is her love for Odysseus; in plastic art,
her love for Heracles. She shares in everything—advising, helping,
encouraging, and rejoicing in success. The Homeric description of
her meeting with Odysseus in his homeland which he has at long
last regained but not yet recognized is deeply stirring: she reveals
her identity to him, smilingly strokes him, is not at all angry that
he will not believe even her, the goddess, but rather takes the
occasion to assure him how firmly they two are eternally bound
together because of their clear minds.[47] In all this there is not a
breath of feminine grace in the goddess, not a trace of service
to a lady in the man. Athena is a woman, and yet it is as if she
were a man. She lacks even that feminine feeling which binds
daughter to mother; she really never had a mother, and is "the
daughter of the mighty father" (*obrimopatre*). It is established
from of old—the *Iliad* is our oldest evidence—that she belonged
to her father, always and wholly. In Aeschylus she gives unequivocal utterance to her masculine temperament: "No mother bore
me," she says in the *Eumenides;*[48] "in all things my heart turns to
the male, save only for wedlock, and I incline wholly to the
father." And yet her sex is feminine; what does this signify?

One opinion holds that there is no reason for seeking special significance. Athena was already a goddess before her worshippers felt such keen inclination to war that they required a divinity of battle. There was thus nothing left for her but to assume warlike—that is, masculine—qualities.[49] Another approach attempts deeper penetration: Athena is a woman because the proud heroes who accepted her guidance would not so readily have yielded to a man, even if he were a god.[50] But genuine divinities do not spring from a caprice or whim. Only the significance of the sphere in which they manifest themselves can give decisive evidence for their character, and hence also for their sex. Athena's sphere of action, which extends far beyond the battlefield and includes the entire realm of clear-sighted action, must itself supply us with a clue to her femininity.

Here too a comparison is useful. In Apollo we recognize the wholly masculine man. The aristocratic aloofness, the superiority of cognition, the sense of proportion, these and other related traits in a man, even music in the broadest sense of the word, are, in the last analysis, alien to a woman. Apollo is all these things. But perfection in the living present, untrammelled and victorious action, not in the service of some remote and infinite idea but for mastery over the moment—that is the triumph which has always delighted woman in a man, to which she inspires him, and whose high satisfaction he can learn from her. The divine precision of the well-planned deed, the readiness to be forceful and merciless, the unflagging will to victory—this, paradoxical as it may sound, is woman's gift to man, who by nature is indifferent to the momentary and strives for the infinite. So we understand the femininity of a divine being who nevertheless stands wholly on the side of man. She does, in addition, denote the conquest of coarseness and barbarity by the nobility of the beautiful, but there is never any admixture of softness and gentleness. In the prosecution of her will, woman, for all her charm, is more strenuous and unyielding than man. This too is implied in Athena's appearance. The modern, and particularly the northerner, must accustom himself to the lightning clarity of her form gradually. Her brightness breaks into our foggy atmosphere with almost terrifying harshness. She is oblivious to what we call tender-heartedness. Neither wisdom

nor vision, neither devotion nor pleasure is her will. Consummation, the immediate present, action here and now—that is Athena.

5

What the goddess meant to exceptional men she meant also to the
multitude who needed clarity and strength to master a task. The
Homeric Hymn to Aphrodite says of Athena, after mentioning her
warlike proclivities, that it was from her that joiners learned how
to build wagons. So we read in the *Iliad* that the shipwright who
knows the art of shaping timbers with skillful hand is her favorite[51] and has attained his mastery through her instruction.[52]
The deft metal-worker who can fashion beautiful vessels of silver
and gold is also Athena's disciple,[53] and Hesiod calls the smith
who constructs a plow-share her servant.[54] The potters too
claimed her for their own. "Come to us, Athena," a familiar
Homeric epigram[55] says, "hold your hand over our oven!"

So it comes about that the spirit of the goddess who so definitely
acknowledges masculinity holds sway over the artistic work of
the women's apartment also, and hence becomes a guide of girls
and women without being false to her basic character. She herself, when she makes herself visible to Odysseus, "is like a tall
and handsome woman who understands artistic handicraft."[56] The
highest praise for a young woman, on the lips of Achilles,[57] is
to rival Aphrodite in beauty and Athena in craftsmanship. She
gives young girls skill in handiwork.[58] Penelope she endowed
with marvellous skill in weaving, and moreover with clear understanding and wit, like no other Greek woman.[59] Athena herself
weaves her garments with her own hands,[60] and the handsome
robe which Hera puts on to seduce Zeus was worked by Athena's
fingers.[61] She also clothes Pandora.[62]

A disciple of Anaxagoras who explained the Homeric gods as
allegories saw Athena as craftsmanship (*techne*), and there is an
Orphic verse which suggests that if she lost her hands it would
be all over with Athena "of many counsels" (*polymetis*).[63] In all
works of craftsmanship, for which Athena was worshipped as
Ergane and linked with Hephaestus, intelligence and counsel,

which are a manifestation of her nature, were dominant. One or another handicraft may be of later origin or may have become attached to Athena relatively late, but the goddess had no need to change her nature in order to receive new protégés. On the other hand, when it was not a great man but an industrious artisan who was inspired by her, the manifestation of her nearness was also diminished in stature, power, and brilliance.

6

No more than other genuine divinities can Athena be understood from a single and particularly striking activity. The powerful mind which made her the genius of victory extends to a breadth far beyond the range of the battlefield. Only the "bright-eyed intelligence" capable of discerning the decisive element at every juncture and of supplying the most effective instrumentality is an adequate characterization of her ideal with its multiplicity of vital functions.

Epic customarily gives its gods fixed attributes which designate their nature as well as the outward impression they communicate. Thus Hera is called "cow-eyed." This epithet is said to derive from her sacred animal, whose form, apparently, she herself was formerly imagined to have borne, and this explanation is surely correct. But what is the significance of the association of the goddess with this specific animal? The question recurs in the case of all deities with attributes derived from animals or plants which were once the forms in which they themselves appeared. Students of religion are often satisfied with superficial or accidental connections to explain this phenomenon. But we must remember how remote we are from the mythic age in our apprehension of existence and of the world, and how slight a probability there is, in many cases, that we can ever divine the meaning of the relationship. But sometimes, even to us, animals and plants may communicate an impression which approaches that of the divine figures. What seems more natural than that the peacock should become the bird of Hera? This connection, to be sure, belongs to a relatively late period. But would not a cow seem similarly appropriate, if we appreciate the royal serenity and beauty of that motherly creature properly? And it is precisely that element by which this serenity and power are most effectively expressed, the glance of the large eyes, which serves as a designation for Hera in the epic.

So the owl (*glaux*) was felt to be the bird of Athena, indeed the manifestation of her presence. However old the notion may be, by its use of an expression which had long ago become a stereotype the epic emphasizes that aspect of the owl which is most striking —its bright eyes. Athena is called Glaukopis, which is to say "bright-eyed." In the old language the word *glaukos* serves as an attribute of the sea,[64] and recurs in the name of the old sea-god Glaucus and of the Nereid Glauke; the aspect of the moon is also so described,[65] and later stars, dawn, and ether also. The word must therefore have denoted a bright glow, and this is confirmed by the usage that applies the same epithet to the olive tree to denote its sheen.[66] If the word is intended to express a manner of looking, it is appropriate for the glittering eye of a lion about to charge[67] or for the eye of a dragon,[68] but in general the word cannot denote the frightful or repulsive. The goddess's eye can indeed be terrible, and she is therefore occasionally called not Glaukopis but Gorgopis.[69] That Glaukopis does not denote a terrible aspect is shown not only by its use with reference to sea and stars but also by the fact that the beauty of Athena's eyes is emphasized.[70] If Athena is associated with an animal which is called *glaux* because of its sharp and bright eyes, as she herself is called Glaukopis, there can hardly be any doubt that, because of this remarkable look, her spirit was believed to be present in the bird. The owl is a predatory creature, but this characteristic it shares with many others. The thing that is striking and unforgettable is the acutely intelligent expression of the face and the bright, piercing eyes that gave it its name. The owl was regarded as the wisest of all birds.[71] In Athena too the eyes are emphasized. As Oxyderkes, "the sharp-sighted," she had a sanctuary in Corinth, allegedly established by Diomedes because she made him bright-eyed.[72] In Sparta she was worshipped as Optilitis or Ophthalmitis.[73] She is said to have saved one or both his eyes for Lycurgus. In the famous choral ode in *Oedipus at Colonus* Sophocles beautifully joins Glaukopis Athena with all-seeing Zeus when he says of the shining (*glaukos*) olive tree that "the sleepless eye of Zeus Morios beholds it, and Athena of the bright eyes (*glaukopis*).[74]

When we imagine the presence of the goddess, this spirit of brightest vigilance which grasps with lightning speed what the instant requires, which always and with serenity never troubled devises counsel and encounters the most difficult tasks with poised and ready energy—we can think of no better mark and symbol for such a being than the bright and luminous glance of the eye. There can be no more grievous misunderstanding of this beautiful image than to regard it as a relic of primitive divine or demonic terror. Where a spiritual explanation is so ready to hand, why persist in a predilection for explanations based on the coarse and the crude? They were no terrifying eyes that looked upon angry Achilles, as Homer describes it,[75] "shining mightily," when he suddenly looked into Athena's face and was by her admonished to prudence and restraint.

7

The true Athena is neither a savage nor a contemplative being; she is equally remote from both dispositions. Her fighting spirit is no impulsive drive, her bright mind no pure reason. She represents a world of action, not, however, unconsidered and brute, but reasonable action which through her clear awareness will most surely lead to victory.

It is victory, indeed, which makes her world perfect. In the city which bore her name she herself was called Nike, and Phidias' famous statue of the Maid bore an image of the goddess of victory on its right hand. Nike, "the giver of sweet gifts who on gold-gleaming Olympus at Zeus' side determines for gods and men success in noble endeavors,"[76] heeds Athena's nod. In Hesiod's *Shield of Heracles* she herself springs up to Heracles upon his chariot, "holding victory and glory in her divine hands."[77]

Thus she is present at every manly struggle that possesses greatness. But man must know that greatness and triumph are manifestations of the divine. Whoever rejects the goddess and relies only upon his own strength will fall miserably through that same divine power.[78]

Belief in Athena arose from no individual need or individual longing of human life. She is the meaning and actuality of a complete and self-contained world—the clear, hard, glorious masculine world of design and fulfillment whose delight is in struggle. This world includes the feminine also. Not, however, as lover or mother, not as dancing girl or Amazon, but as a knowledgeable and artistically constructive nature does woman belong to Athena. But in order to understand the meaning of her nature completely, we must be perfectly clear on what she is *not*.

In course of time and at individual cult-sites she was associated with various undertakings and needs. Thus in Athens we find her as patroness of the art of healing, of agriculture, even of marriage and the rearing of children. But all of this is not essential and need not be pursued further. Finally she became patroness even of the arts and sciences. This late picture of Athena derives from the brilliance and intellectual leadership of her city Athens. But it is far removed from the ancient picture. The bright spirit of the genuine Athena has nothing to do with pure cognition or any aspect of the Muses. The calmness of objectivity, the detachment of contemplation, which are the prerequisites for the higher forms of the creative process, are alien to her. She is without music, either in the proper or the broad sense of the word. She is reputed to have invented the flute, indeed, but it is said that she discarded it at once. On the other hand, the invention of the war-trumpet is in perfect keeping with her nature.

Thus many qualities that distinguish other deities, and especially Apollo, she does not possess. But what is wanting in her, as in any complete figure, are those aspects which are excluded by her essential meaning. For she is spirited immediacy, redeeming spiritual presence, swift action. She is *the ever-near*.

APOLLO AND ARTEMIS

APOLLO

> Description of Apollo demands the highest style—
> an exaltation above everything human.
>
> WINCKELMANN

1

Next after Zeus, Apollo is the most important Greek god. Even as early as in Homer there can be no doubt of this fact.

Apollo cannot be imagined as making any appearance without demonstrating his superiority, and in more than one case his epiphany is truly grandiose. His voice resounds with the majesty of thunder when he bids raging Diomedes halt.[1] His encounters with the mighty and the proud become a symbol for the perishability of all beings earthly, even the greatest, before the presence of deity. As long as humanity retains a feeling for the divine, no reader will fail to be stirred by the picture of Apollo striding into Patroclus's path and shattering him in the midst of his charge.[2] We have the premonition that it is he before whom the most brilliant of all heroes, Achilles, will be crushed. It is with reference to both those great dooms that the speaking horse Xanthus calls Apollo "the mightiest of the gods."[3]

The greatness of this Homeric Apollo is ennobled by loftiness of spirit. And so artists in the post-Homeric centuries strove emulously to make his likeness a vivid representation of what is loftiest, most eminent, and at the same time brightest. A man who has once seen the Apollo of the temple of Zeus at Olympia can never forget it. The artist has perpetuated a moment of overwhelming magnificence. In the midst of the wildest tumult the god has suddenly appeared, and his outstretched arm enjoins calm. Loftiness shines out of his countenance; its wide eyes command merely by the superiority of his look; but about the strong and noble mouth there is a delicate, almost melancholy suggestion of superior knowledge. The manifestation of the divine amidst the desolation and confusion of this world cannot possibly be represented with greater forcefulness. Apollo's other statues also characterize him through nobility of attitude and movement, through the power of his glance, through the illuminating and liberating effect of his bearing. In the lineaments of his countenance virile strength and clarity are combined with the splendor of the sublime. He is youth in its freshest bloom and purity. Poets praise his flowing hair, which even the earliest lyric calls golden. Plastic art represents him almost without exception as beardless, and not seated but standing or striding.

In many respects his image recalls that of Artemis, in whom all these traits have only been made feminine. Since early times these two have been so closely connected that we shall first consider them together.

2

Myth calls Apollo and Artemis brother and sister. We do not know how they came to be associated, but their historical figures resemble one another as closely as only brother and sister can, and the deeper we penetrate into their character the more significant this resemblance becomes. What appeared to be disparateness soon proves to be the necessary diversity between the sexes, and in the end there is revealed a divine being in twofold expression, whose agreements and oppositions in some marvellous and ingenious fashion constitute a complete world.

Apollo and Artemis are the most sublime of the Greek gods. That is shown by their presence as seen in poetry and plastic art. Their particular position in the circle of heavenly beings is indicated by the attribute of purity and holiness which is peculiar to them. According to Plutarch and others, Phoebus means "pure" and "holy," and they are indubitably right. So Aeschylus and other poets after him understood the name, for they employed the same word to characterize the rays of the sun or water. Even in Homer

the name is so current that he can call the god not only Phoebus
Apollo but merely Phoebus. Artemis is the only one of the heavenly deities whom Homer honors with the epithet *hagne*, which
means "holy" and "pure." The same attribute is given to Apollo by
Aeschylus and Pindar. In both deities there is something mysterious and unapproachable, something that commands an awed
distance. As archers they shoot unerringly and unseen from afar,
and he that is struck is painlessly extinguished, with the smile of
life upon his lips. Artemis is the ever-distant. She loves the solitude of woods and mountains, and plays with the wild beasts. He
that is devoted to her plucks garlands for her "from a virgin
meadow, where no shepherd presumes to pasture his flock, nor
has iron ever come there; virgin it is, and in summer the bees
frequent it, while Purity waters it like a garden."[4] Her whole
quality is unfettered being, raised above all bonds.

Withdrawal is in the nature of Apollo also. In Delphi, Delos,
and other cult sites it was believed that he always abode for part
of the year in a remote and secret place. At the onset of winter he
goes forth, only to return in the spring, when he is greeted by
pious chants. According to the Delians he sojourned in Lycia
during the winter months.[5] The Delphian myth makes his resort
the fabulous land of the Hyperboreans, of which, from early
times, much was said in Delos also. "No ship and no traveller
can reach that land."[6] There dwell the holy people that know
neither sickness nor old age, for whom trouble and struggle do not
exist. In their sacrificial festivals Apollo takes delight; everywhere
there is the music of maiden choirs, lyres, and flutes, and glisten-
ing laurel crowns the heads of the celebrants.[7] To that place
Athena once conducted Perseus, when he was to slay the Gorgon;[8]
otherwise only those Apollo had chosen saw that fabulous country. The prophet and wonder-worker Abaris came from there as an
emissary of Apollo, and carried the god's bolt through all lands.[9]
Aristeas of Proconnesus declared in his own poem[10] that "seized
by Apollo" he arrived at the country of the Issedones, and that
beyond the Issedones lived the one-eyed Arimaspeans, next the
gold-guarding griffins, and finally the Hyperboreans.

Concerning the Hyperboreans most could be learned, according to Herodotus,[11] in Delos, where stories were told about sacred

embassies and missions from that remote and wonderful place. The Hyperboreans are not mentioned in Homeric epic, but (according to Herodotus[12]) only by Hesiod and the epic of the Epigoni. But no argument is needed to show that the notion of this blessed land of light must be very old. There "Phoebus's ancient garden" was located, as Sophocles said in a lost tragedy.[13] Thither he vanished each year, and thence returned, when all was in bloom, with his swans. Alcaeus has sung of this in a *Hymn to Apollo* which is unfortunately lost, but whose contents we know through Himerius:[14] When Apollo was born, Zeus gave him a chariot with swans, upon which he rode not to Delphi but to the Hyperboreans; the Delphians summoned him with chants, but he remained with the Hyperboreans for a whole year. But when the time came, he permitted his swans to take the road to Delphi. It was summer, and the nightingales sang to him, and the swallows and cicadas as well; the fount of Castaly bubbled forth silvern, and Cephisus swelled with darkling waves. Thus Alcaeus. And as the god came on that occasion, so he came regularly with the warm season of the year, and brought song and prophecy.

His remoteness is uncommonly illuminating for the nature of Apollo. If we compare him with Athena, the great difference between them becomes clear instantaneously. Just as she is the ever-near, so is he the withdrawn. He accompanies no hero as faithful friend, as ever-ready helper and counsellor. He is not, as Athena is, a spirit of immediacy, of clever and energetic mastery over the moment. His chosen ones are not the men of action.

3

Who is this god whose eye greets us from afar and whose presence is bathed in such enchanting brilliance?

On quite respectable grounds it has been conjectured that his home is to be sought not in Greece but in Asia Minor.[15] He appears to have derived from Lycia, where his mother Leto also originated. But with this hypothesis, in itself attractive, other and bolder conjectures have been ventured: that as an Asiatic deity Homer puts him wholly on the side of the Trojans; and that his original character, still obvious at the opening of the *Iliad,* is that of a terrible death-dealing god. Between such a picture of terror and the god of Delphian wisdom the distance is so great that it could only be explained by some profound religious reform.

But careful examination of Homer indicates that his Apollo is no other than the god later worshipped at Delphi. The peculiar idea of the divine which bears the name of Apollo and comprised so important a spiritual force in Greece must have made its appearance long before the Homeric epic and must be counted among the manifestations that constitute the substance of Olympian, that is to say, Greek, religion in its proper sense. But how the likeness of the god was conceived before this epoch we have no means of knowing. No one will doubt that the bow and the lyre belonged to him even in the earliest period, and it is more than probable that prophecy was associated with him also. But we must be aware of the illusion that the living substance of a prehistoric deity and the significance he had for his worshippers can be deduced from merely factual data. We shall therefore leave such questions aside, and direct our attention solely to the belief as it first emerges clearly in Homer.

If we read Homer under the preconception that contemporary religion could have possessed nothing more than is explicitly stated of it, then indeed Apollo could have become the god of purity only at a later period, and his sharp clarity, his superior spirit, his will that enjoins insight, moderation, and order, in short all that we call Apollonian to this day, must have been unknown to Homer. But Homer has no intention to indoctrinate. He lets the gods appear and act and speak in modes familiar to himself and his audience. As in the case of other gods, so for Apollo too a few strokes suffice him for presenting a vivid picture. But if we listen attentively we recognize the masterly delineation of a character which must have been familiar to every hearer, and often we can learn more from figures thus fleetingly sketched than from many assertions concerning the power and purposes of the god.

In the famous battle of the gods in the twenty-first book of the *Iliad,* two gods refuse to participate in the struggle, and each indicates his own motive for abstaining. Hermes, the arch-rogue,

the spirit of good luck and favorable opportunity, has no intention
of coming to grips with great Leto and has no objection to her
boasting among the gods that she has got the better of him. Apollo
behaves very differently. In a vigorous speech, Poseidon had challenged him to a duel, and with noble pride he calmly replies:
"You would have me be without measure and without prudence,
if I am to fight for insignificant mortals, who now flourish like
leaves of the trees and then fade away and are dead." And when
his sister Artemis, with true feminine temper, reproaches him as a
coward, he steps aside in silence.[16] Is this not the god of Pindar,
the promulgator of insight, of self-knowledge, of measure, and of
intelligent order? "What are we?" says Pindar in Apollo's spirit;
". . . The shadow of a dream is man, no more. But when the
brightness comes, and God gives it, there is a shining of light on
men, and their life is sweet."[17] Nothing so clearly defines that attitude whose ideal the post-Homeric Apollo made present to
men's eyes as does the notion of *sophrosyne*, with which his
speech in Homer begins.[18] "Know thyself," he calls out to the
visitors at his Delphian temple. This means,[19] know what man is,
and how great is the interval which separates him from the greatness of the eternal gods; consider the limitations of humanity.
Can we doubt that it is this Apollo who appears in the epic scene
just cited? But surely not in that scene alone. The poet keeps his
character consistent. In the fifth book of the *Iliad*, Diomedes
brings Aeneas down, wounds the goddess Aphrodite who had put
her protecting arms about her son, and again falls upon his victim
though he knows that Apollo himself has a hand in the matter.
Then the majestic god thunders forth: "Take care, son of Tydeus,
give back; measure yourself no longer against the gods, for not
of the same breed are the gods immortal and men who walk on
the ground."[20] And in the last book of the *Iliad,* Apollo rises with
the pathos of restraining reason and magnanimity in order to put
a stop to the inhumanity of Achilles who for twelve days has been
abusing the corpse of Hector. Before the gods he charges him
with ruthlessness and hardness of heart: he lacks respect for the
eternal laws of nature, and the self-restraint which is seemly for
the noble even after grievous bereavement. "Great as he is, let

him take care not to make us angry, for in his fury he does dishonor to the dumb earth."[21] The gods approve his words.

Such is the Homeric Apollo; manifestation of spiritual loftiness is part of his essence and not a later addition to his picture. The same is true of the individual traits later characteristic of him. Just as at Delphi he proclaimed the thoughts of the highest god of heaven, so in Homer he stands nearer that god than does any other deity. Only prejudice could regard his functions as guardian of purity and master of purifications as properties of later belief. It is true that Homer regularly and cavalierly ignores this whole sphere, but he frequently designates the god as Phoebus, that is, the pure. Only when we appreciate what purity and purification can mean in the Apollonian sense, will the true character of his spiritual stature become intelligible. We realize at once that to this spirituality belongs Apollonian music, knowledge of right and of the future, institution of higher ordinances. All these qualities characterize the Homeric Apollo. We sense that these properties and perfections radiate from a single basic quality and are manifold manifestations of a single divine being which the Greeks had worshipped as Apollo even before Homer. But we must examine them in detail if we wish a nearer approach to the sense of the whole and the one.

4

We begin with purity.

An eminent function of the post-Homeric Apollo is care for purifications and expiations. Of this the Homeric poems say nothing, but it does not follow that Apollo assumed this function only at a later period. In the Homeric world scruples concerning pollution had almost entirely disappeared, and hence there was no need to seek Apollo's protection against it. But we can easily conceive that this power in particular belonged to his genuine and early character. As is well known, the art of healing, according to ancient notions, included also a capacity to ward off the dangers of impurity. Apollo was, and had always been, the most important god of healing. It was in this capacity that Italy and Rome

came to know him. The purifier is the healer, the healer the purifier. As Agyieus, as he was called according to an ancient conception (he also bears other epithets, such as Thyraios), he cleanses
paths of all evil, and his stone pillars stand in front of houses as a
symbol of security. Though for Homer Apollo's connection with
purifications and expiations may have grown remote, the figure of
Apollo as presented by Homer provides a valuable finger-post
for the proper understanding of Apollonian purifications.

For us it is strange to find ideas of purification associated with
a god to whom spiritual quality is attributed, because modern
religious scholarship has accustomed us to understand ancient
ritual in a wholly materialistic sense. From this prejudice we must
resolve to free ourselves, for it only transfers our own mode of
thought to the situation of more primitive humanity whose peculiarity it is our purpose to explain.

Apollo purifies the guilty person of the pollution that adheres
to and menaces him. The homicide to whom the fearful blood of
the slain man cleaves is freed from the curse by Apollo's intervention and is made clean again. In this and similar cases pollution
comes from bodily contact and a material stain. The ritual that
restores the unclean man to a state of purity is therefore also com-
posed of corporeal acts. From such measures, which recur with
remarkable similarity among all ancient peoples, the conclusion,
believed inevitable, was drawn that by uncleanliness religion at
one time meant merely a material state, namely, being burdened
with dangerous matter which could be removed by physical measures. But a mode of thought that is of natural growth and not yet
theoretical knows of no corporeality that is nothing more than
merely material. Upon everything corporeal it bestows a regard
that is virtually lost upon us, and hence it is very difficult for us
even to surmise the meaning of its attitude. It does not sever the
corporeal from what we call spiritual or psychic, but always sees
the one in the other. If, according to this conception, contact and
pollution are more than merely material, their operation affects
the whole man and not only imperils his physical nature but may
also burden and corrupt his mental state. By the act actually carried out—and not by mere thought of it—the homicide falls into
a terrible tangle. His external existence is uncannily surrounded

by lurking threats, and more terrifying still is the constraint that weighs upon his inward being. This conviction, which springs from immediate experience, is no less serious and profound if the cause of the evil is conceived as material and its removal is effected by a physical procedure. In any case, the necessity for purification was by no means limited to acts of blood; it extended over every contact with the uncanny, as for example with death when it occurs naturally. Here there can be no thought of moral guilt, and therefore it has been deemed just to assume that the entire nature of expiation in its specific sense had to do only with the outer, not with the inner, man. But such judgment only reveals how completely the character of naïve modes of thought has been misunderstood. Direct illumination should come at least from the fact that the tangle into which the unclean man falls must be conceived of quite differently, depending upon whether it is the result of a passive encounter or of an act of violence—even though our ancient witnesses are, as was to be expected, silent on the subject. In the second alternative, just as he was the attacker, so must he be attacked differently than in a case of mere accident. To be sure, in one important point this primitive conception diverges sharply from our own reasonable mode of thought. For the consequences of the deed it makes no difference whether it was intentional or involuntary, whether it was committed under duress or was self-willed. Everywhere, according to ancient belief, man must suffer for things he did not intend. Who shall say that this is untrue? Who shall make bold to call it unjust?

It is easy to see how the ritual of purification with its rules and practices is liable to degenerate into the petty and superstitious, but that is no reason for failing to realize its profound meaning. It points to the sphere whose representatives are demonic powers of a kind similar to the Erinyes. We have become acquainted with their realm, with the primal sacred bonds and the inescapable responsibilities over which they keep watch.[22] The gloom and melancholy of this ancient world is now confronted by the Olympian deities. There is no intention of effacing it, for it abides forever, forever nourished by the heavy breath of the earth. But by the new divine light its omnipotence is broken. We must remember the *Oresteia* of Aeschylus, which was discussed in Chapter 2.

The god who there ventures not merely to purify the matricide but, in the name of a higher justice, to defend the deed, which he himself enjoined, against the frightful cry of vengeance for spilled blood is Apollo. He undertakes the purification, which is to say, he acknowledges the grim actuality, but is able to point to the proper liberation from its curse. Life is to be freed of such uncanny barriers, of demonic entanglements over which even the purest human will has no power. Apollo therefore advises men in distress what is to be done and what left undone, where atonement and submission may be necessary. Once on a time, it is said, he himself required purification of the blood of the Delphian dragon.

In Homer's world men no longer took thought of demonic dangers. But the Homeric Apollo reveals a higher mode of purity, the mode which he so impressively promulgated from Delphi along with prescriptions for atonement, and this should warn us against understanding Apollonian purification in too superficial a sense. It is through clarification of inward being that man should guard against the dangers he can avoid. More than this: the god sets up an ideal of outward and inner attitudes which, quite apart from consequences, may have validity as purity in a higher sense.

Visitors to his Delphian shrine Apollo hails not with ordinary forms of greeting but with "Know thyself!"[23] This and other dicta the Seven Sages were said to have bestowed upon Delphi as the tribute of their spirit.[24] Their celebrated wisdom set down in such maxims as "measure is best" (*metron ariston*) correspond perfectly with the spiritual cast of the Delphian god, with whom they were also associated in tradition. One of the sages, the great Solon, declared that not Croesus with his royal pomp but a simple Athenian citizen was the happiest man, because he had led an untroubled life, blessed with children and grandchildren, had ended it fighting gloriously for his country, and had been honored by a public funeral. The king who regarded himself as the happiest of men Solon earnestly admonished not to be self-assured but in all earthly matters to look to the end.[25] Of the same nature were the decrees of the Delphian oracle,[26] which, according to Pliny, "were delivered as a reproach to human vanity."[27] When the great king Gyges asked who the happiest man was, he was given the name of a humble peasant in Arcadia who had never gone beyond the limits of the little property which supported him.[28] The rich man who honored the god with costly offerings and wished to discover who was most pleasing to the god was referred to a poor country-man who had strewed upon the altar a handful of grain out of his sack.[29] But the most memorable instance is the god's naming Socrates when he was asked who the wisest man was. According to Plato's account, Socrates himself interpreted this saying to mean that he must devote his life to seeking for knowledge and examining himself and his fellow-men. This was the form of worship to which no earthly power could make him prove faithless. Fear of death could not affect his decision, for no one could know whether death is a blessing or an evil. His superiority over other men, Socrates said, consisted in the fact that he did not believe that he had knowledge where in fact he had none; but this he did know, that doing injustice and disobeying higher powers was bad and wicked.[30]

5

The god who induces such a declaration of faith is also the founder of the ordinances which give human society its proper form. Upon his authority states establish their legal institutions. He shows colonists their way to a new homeland. He is the patron of young people entering into manhood, the leader in the stages of adult life, the guide of noble and manly athletics. At his most important festivals it was mainly the boys and youths who made their appearance. To him the boy attaining manhood dedicated his long hair. Himself the lord of gymnasia and palestra, he once loved young Hyacinthus and in a contest unluckily slew him with a discus. At the celebrated Lacedaemonian Gymnopaedia the choristers representing the age groups divided into three choirs, and the high solemnity of the Carnean festival was characterized by systematic divisions reminiscent of military discipline. We can understand why Pindar, at the foundation of a city, prays Apollo to populate it with vigorous men.[31] But all of this recalls the Homeric Apollo to our minds. According to the poet of the *Odyssey*, it was his favor which enabled Telemachus to become so manly a youth,[32] and Hesiod too says of him that he develops boys into men.[33]

Accurate perception is a portion of knowledge of the true essence of things and their interrelationship. Apollo also reveals what is hidden and what is yet to be. According to the *Odyssey*, even Agamemnon before he set out for Troy made inquiry of Apollo at Delphi,[34] and the treasures of that sanctuary are known to the *Iliad*.[35] "The lyre and the curved bow shall ever be dear to me, and I will declare to men the unfailing will of Zeus"—these, according to the *Homeric Hymn to the Delian Apollo*, were the first words of the new-born god.[36] To him the great seers owe their gifts. This is said of Calchas, for example, at the very beginning of the *Iliad*.[37] Women like Cassandra or the Sibyls on whom the spirit of the god descended, often with terrible violence, were especially celebrated. But we shall not linger over individual phenomena, nor over the numerous oracular sites, some very famous, that existed beside Delphi. Nor shall we here inquire into the form of prophecy which originally characterized Apollonian worship. Occult knowledge, by whatever procedure it is communicated, is always associated with special exaltation of spirit. And this calls poetry and music to mind.

Surely music stands at the very center of Apollo's manifold perfections; surely it is the source out of which these perfections flow. Other gods too take joy in music, but with Apollo his whole nature seems to be musical. In the *Iliad* he plucks the lyre at the table of the gods,[38] and the poet knows that he had once done the same at the marriage of Peleus and Thetis.[39] Homer nowhere says that Apollo himself sings, which plastic art later represented him as doing; in the epic only the Muses sing. But Apollo inspires the singer, and if his song hits the mark he must have been taught by the Muses or Apollo.[40] "From the Muses and far-darting Apollo derive all singers and players upon the lyre," says Hesiod.[41] The *Hymn to the Pythian Apollo* magnificently describes how, upon his entry to Olympus, all the gods were stirred by the ecstasy of music: "All the Muses together, voice sweetly answering voice, hymn the unending gifts the gods enjoy and the sufferings of men, all that they endure at the hands of the deathless gods, and how they live witless and helpless and cannot find healing for death

3. Apollo

4. Artemis

or defense against old age. Meanwhile the rich-tressed Graces
and cheerful Horae dance with Harmonia and Hebe and Aphrodite, daughter of Zeus, holding each other by the wrist. And
among them sings one, not mean nor puny, but tall to look upon
and enviable in mien, Artemis who delights in arrows, sister of
Apollo. Among them sport Ares and the keen-eyed slayer of
Argus, while Apollo plays his lyre stepping high and featly and a
radiance shines around him, the gleaming of his feet and close-
woven vest."[42]

Once he moved into Delphi, making music as he went.[43] At his
arrival "nightingales, swallows, and cicadas sang," as Alcaeus
declared in his hymn. Callimachus sensed the god's nearness: the
laurel trembled, and the swans in the air uttered song.[44] Even in
Claudian we are moved as we read how, at Apollo's approach,
the voices of the forests and the grottoes were awakened.[45]

In Apollo's music there resounds the spirit of all living forms.
It is hearkened to with delight by friends of the lucid and well-
ordered world, which is governed by the lofty thought of Zeus;
but to all immoderate and monstrous beings it is strange and
disagreeable. So Pindar sings of the heavenly power of Apollonian
music:

> Golden lyre, held of Apollo in common possession
> with the violet-haired Muses: the dance steps, leaders of festival,
>   heed you;
> the singers obey your measures
> when, shaken with music, you cast the beat to lead choirs of dancers.
> You have power to quench the spread thunderbolt
> of flowing fire. Zeus' eagle sleeps on his staff, folding his quick wings
>   both ways to quiet,
> lord of birds; you shed a mist on his hooked head,
> dark and gentle closure of eyes; dreaming, he ripples
> his lithe back, bound in spell
> of your waves. Violent Ares even, leaving aside the stern pride
> of spears, makes gentle his heart in sleep.
> Your shafts enchant the divinities by grace of the wisdom of Leto's
>   son and the deep-girdled Muses.[46]

Moderation and beauty are the essence and the effect of this
music. It restrains all that is wild; even predatory beasts of the
wilderness are charmed by it.[47] Nay, even stones follow the sound

of the lyre and take their place in masonry walls.[48] That is why herds prosper when Apollo is their shepherd.[49] Making music Apollo pastured the flocks of Admetus,[50] and, according to Trojan legend, kept the kine of Laomedon.[51] The life of men is also fashioned by Apollo's music. Through it he becomes man's first and best educator, as Plato sets forth with wonderful insight: "The gods, pitying the toils which our race is born to undergo, have appointed holy festivals, wherein men alternate rest with labors and have given them the Muses and Apollo, the leader of the Muses, and Dionysus. . . . Men say that the young of all creatures cannot be quiet in their bodies or in their voices; they are always wanting to move and cry out; some leaping and skipping, and overflowing with sportiveness and delight at something, others uttering all sorts of cries. But whereas the animals have no perception of order or disorder in their movements, that is of rhythm and harmony, as they are called, to us the gods, who, as we say, have been appointed to be our companions in the dance, have given the pleasurable sense of harmony and rhythm, and so they stir us into life, and we follow them, joining hands together in dances and songs."[52]

"Verily," says Plutarch in his Life of Coriolanus, "among all the benefits which men derive from the favor of the Muses none other is so great as that softening of the nature which is produced by culture and discipline, for by culture nature is induced to take on moderation and cast off excess."[53] It is this thoroughly Greek thought which suggested to Horace his truly magnificent prayer to the Muses.[54]

6

> Who tempers the zither with strings,
> and with strings the bow.
>
> OVID, *Metamorphoses* 10.108

And now we finally come to Apollo's attribute which, next to the lyre, is the most celebrated and most important, and which, though it is so often named together with the lyre, appears at first blush to have no connection with it—the *bow*.

"The lyre and the curved bow shall ever be dear to me," the new-born god cries in the *Homeric Hymn to the Delian Apollo*,[55] and at the beginning of the *Hymn* we are given a mighty picture of Apollo entering the hall of Zeus with bow drawn taut while all the gods spring trembling from their seats. Numerous epithets, in Homer and in later authors, characterize Apollo as a mighty archer. At the opening of the *Iliad* he discharges his destructive bolts into the Greek camp and slays beasts and men in heaps. All that are expert in archery owe their skill to him and pray to him before shooting.[56] His festival, incidentally the only regular festival of the gods expressly mentioned in the Homeric poems, is the day upon which Odysseus returns home, performs his feat of archery, and lays the suitors low—both with Apollo's assistance.[57] The mighty marksman Eurytus paid with his life for having challenged Apollo to a contest in archery.[58] With his bow Apollo slew the Delphian dragon;[59] by it Achilles sank into the dust before Troy.

But the most remarkable thing is that his arrows also cause a wonderful drifting away in slumber. They fly unseen and produce a gentle death which falls upon a man suddenly and preserves his appearance as fresh as that of a man asleep.[60] The god's shafts are therefore called "gentle." Of a blessed island the *Odyssey*[61] tells that no evil sicknesses occur there; when people grow old Apollo and Artemis end their lives with their gentle arrows. For it is only to men that Apollo sends this fair death; women are struck by the arrow of Artemis.

From descriptions like that of the angry Apollo at the opening of the *Iliad*, where he causes baneful destruction among men and descends to his fearful task from Olympus "with a face as dark as night,"[62] justification has been claimed for the inference that Apollo must originally have been a god of death. But how could the figure of Apollo have developed out of a god of death? The mythic images point to a quite different direction. A god before whom even the mightiest fall when their hour strikes is not for that reason necessarily a god of death. He is certainly not that when he destroys dangerous giants and monsters, like the Aloadae[63] or the dragon at Delphi. At the opening of the *Iliad* he comes in order to punish, and his dark look is compared to night just as Hector's is when he bursts into the Greek camp,[64] or Heracles', when he draws his bow even in Hades.[65] But if he strikes other men, against whom he does not proceed as an avenger, with "gentle" arrows, so that they are suddenly and wonderfully extinguished and seem merely to slumber—that is certainly *not* the style of a god of death. Rather does this bitter-sweet process, which produces its effect from a mysterious and unseen source and reflects the iridescence of a fairy-land, recall the god of distance, who comes to man out of a remote land of light and always disappears into that same land again. This brings us back to our point of departure.

Is not the bow a symbol of distance? The arrow is sped from a place unseen and flies to its mark from afar. And the lyre? Is it mere coincidence that Apollo loves it as well as the bow, or does the connection have some deeper meaning?

Kinship between the two instruments has often been felt. The likeness is not limited to outward form, which, for Heraclitus, makes bow and lyre a symbol for the harmony of opposites.[66] Both are strung with animal sinews. The same verb which is used for striking the strings of a musical instrument (*psallo*) is frequently applied to the snapping touch of the bowstring. Furthermore both give off a sound. "The bow twanged and the string sang aloud,"[67] we read in the *Iliad*, when Pandarus discharged his arrow at Menelaus. Pindar calls the string of archer Heracles "deep-sounding."[68] The liveliest picture is presented by a celebrated scene in the *Odyssey*. When the efforts of the suitors to string the mighty bow had proved vain, Odysseus strung it "as a man who is skilled with the lute and practiced in singing easily stretches the string on a new-made peg of his lyre." Then he tested the string with his hand, and "full sweetly it rang under his touch, as the song of the swallow."[69] Perhaps we shall some day learn that bow and stringed instruments actually derive from the same source. Anthropology is familiar with the so-called musical bow, and we hear that in ancient times even the archer's bow was used for producing musical tones. Firdusi tells us that the Persians of old so used it when they marched out to battle. But for our understanding of Apollo it is of the highest importance that the Greeks themselves felt an essential kinship between what the bow and the lyre produced. In both they saw a dart speeding to its goal, in one case the unerring arrow, in the other unerring song. Pindar sees the true singer as a marksman and his song as an arrow that never misses. He lets his "sweet" bolt fly to Pytho, the goal of his song[70]—and immediately we recall that other bolt which brings death and which Homer calls "bitter." ". . . strain the bow to the mark now!" the poet of the Olympian festival sings. "Whom shall we strike in gentleness, slipping merciful arrows? . . ."[71] He sees the Muses drawing the "bow" of song, and in praise of the bow applies to it the epithet which has always been Apollo's distinguishing mark, "far-shooting."[72]

We know that the Greeks habitually pictured recognition of what is right under the image of an accurate bow-shot. The simile is directly illuminating. But we find it strange to equate music and song with the art of hitting the mark, for in the latter case we do not think of what is right and of recognition. That then is the point where the nature of Apollonian music must be made accessible to us.

The song of the most alert of all gods does not arise dreamlike out of an intoxicated soul but flies directly towards a clearly seen goal, the truth, and the rightness of its aim is a sign of its divinity. Out of Apollo's music there resounds divine recognition. In everything it perceives and attains form. The chaotic must take shape, the turbulent must be reduced to time and measure, opposites must be wedded in harmony. This music is thus the great educator, the source and symbol of all order in the world and in the life of mankind. Apollo the musician is identical with the founder of ordinances, identical with him, who knows what is right, what is necessary, what is to be. In this accuracy of the god's aim Hölderlin could still recognize the archer, when, in his *Bread and Wine,* he lamented the vanished Delphian oracle:

> Where, oh where do they shine, the oracles distantly striking?
> Delphi slumbers, and where does the glorious destiny sound?[73]

7

But what can be the higher meaning of that distance which we have noticed from the beginning and for which the bow is so expressive a symbol?

Apollo is the most Greek of all gods. If the Greek spirit found
its first formulation in the Olympian religion, then it is Apollo
whose form most clearly manifests it. Although Dionysiac enthusiasm was once an important force there can nevertheless be
no doubt that the Greek temper was inclined to subdue this and
all other forms of intemperance, and that its great representatives
unhesitatingly embraced the Apollonian spirit and nature. Dionysiac nature desiderates intoxication, and hence proximity; Apollonian desiderates clarity and form, and hence distance. The first
impression this word gives is of something negative, but implied
in it is the most positive thing of all—the attitude of cognition.

Apollo rejects whatever is too near—entanglement in things, the
melting gaze, and, equally, soulful merging, mystical inebriation
and its ecstatic vision. He desires not soul but spirit. And this
means freedom from the heaviness, coarseness, and constriction of
what is near, stately objectivity, a ranging glance. Apollo's ideal
of distance not only puts him in opposition to Dionysiac exuber-
ance: for us it is even more significant that it involves a flat contradiction of values which Christianity later rated high.

Just as Apollo himself never emphasizes his personality and
never, by his Delphian oracles, claims praise and honor for himself beyond all others, so he is oblivious to the eternal worth of the
human individual and the single soul. The sense of his manifestation is that it directs a man's attention not to the worth of his ego
and the profound inwardness of his individual soul, but rather to
what transcends the personal, to the unchangeable, to the eternal
forms. What we are accustomed to call reality, concrete existence
with its sense of self, vanishes like smoke; the ego with its private
emotions, whether of pleasure or pain, pride or humility, sinks like
a wave. But eternally there abides, "divine among divinities, the
form." The particular and transitory, the ego with its here and
now, is only the matter in which the imperishable forms appear.
If the Christian humbles himself and is thereby assured of becoming worthy of God's love and God's nearness, Apollo requires a
different humility. Between the eternal and the earthly phenomena, to which man as an individual belongs, there is a gaping
chasm. The individual being has no part of the realm of infinity.
What Pindar, in the spirit of Apollo, impresses upon his hearers

is not a mystical doctrine of a blessed or unhappy beyond, but the thing that separates gods and men from one another. Both may indeed have the same primal mother, but man is fleeting and vain, and only the heavenly beings endure forever.[74] The life of man glides away like a shadow, and if it shine, it is a light from above that gilds it.[75] Man must therefore not presume to equality with the gods but should recognize his limitations and remember that earth will be his garment.[76] The crown of life, which even mortals may attain, is the memory of his virtues. Not his person but a more important thing, the spirit of his perfections and creations, prevails over death and soars in song, eternally young, from generation to generation. For only the form belongs to the realm of the imperishable.

In Apollo there greets us the spirit of clear-eyed cognition which confronts existence and the world with unparalleled freedom—the truly Greek spirit which was destined to produce not only the arts but eventually even science. It was capable of looking upon world and existence as form, with a glance free alike of greed and of yearning for redemption. In form the elemental, momentary, and individual aspects of the world are cancelled, but its essence is acknowledged and confirmed. To attain it requires distance, of which no denial of the world has been capable.

8

The image of Apollo "who shoots from afar" is the manifestation of a single idea. Its substance does not belong to the sphere of simple necessities of life, and in this case the much-favored method of comparison with primitive forms of belief is quite useless. It is a spiritual force which here raises its voice, and it is sufficiently important to give form to a whole humanity. It proclaims the presence of the divine not in the miracles of a supernatural power, not in the rigor of an absolute justice, not in the providence of an infinite love, but in the victorious splendor of clarity, in the intelligent sway of order and moderation. Clarity and form are the objective aspect, to which distance and freedom are the subjective pendant. It is in this attitude that Apollo presents himself to the world of men; in it his bright, unencumbered, luminous, and penetrating divinity is given expression.

We can easily understand that since his sublime being is based neither on an element nor on a process of nature, he could relatively early be brought into connection with the sun. As early as Aeschylus, in a lost tragedy called *Bassarai*, it was said that Orpheus revered Helios as the greatest of all gods and called him Apollo. In his *Prometheus*[77] the same poet characterized the sun with the word *phoibos* which we know as an epithet of Apollo and indeed the most famous. And now there emerges the mighty picture of Apollo holding the universe in harmonious motion by the tones of his lyre,[78] and of the plectrum with which he strikes the lyre as the light of the sun.[79]

ARTEMIS

Unmistakably, the essence of Apollo is specifically masculine. Spiritual freedom and distance are qualities of the male. But it is also masculine to doubt one's self. A man who has overcome the constraint of nature has also forfeited its motherly protection, and only the strong spirit of his god can help him stand fast and abide in the light.

Here Artemis confronts us with freedom of another sort—the feminine. The mirror of this divine femininity is *nature*—not the great holy mother who gives birth to all life, sustains it, and in the end receives it back into her bosom, but nature of a quite different sort, which we might call virginal, free nature with its brilliance and wildness, with its guiltless purity and its uncanniness. This nature is maternal indeed, and shows tender solicitude, but it is of the true nature of a maiden, and as such disdainful, hard, and cruel.

1

For men of our civilization, solitary nature can be infinitely moving and healing. Here the intellectual worker, the harried slave of expedience, finds peace and wholesome air and is not troubled by the awe with which generations more pious entered the silent valleys and hills. A slight sense of strangeness, a touch of uneasiness, do not seriously disturb his pleasure. He is in firm control of his knowledge and technical skill, and in a short time can make even the wildest regions familiar, comfortable, and profitable. But though the proud victor press as far forward as he will, the secret is not revealed, the enigma not solved; without his noticing, it flies from before him and is again everywhere that he is not—the hallowed solitude of untouched nature, which he can only rend and disturb but never comprehend and build up.

Here is a teeming concourse of elements, flora and fauna, life unnumbered which sprouts, blooms, spreads its scent, bubbles, hops, leaps, flutters, soars, and sings; an infinity of sympathy and discord, pairing and struggle, rest and feverish movement, and yet all is related, interwoven, and borne by a single life-spirit, and the quiet visitor senses the higher presence with the awe of the indescribable. Here the people whose religion we begin to grasp found the divine. To them not the fearful majesty of the sinless judge of conscience but the purity of the untouched element was holiest. And they felt that man, this questionable creature that mirrors, doubts, and condemns itself, that has long lost its peace through so much distress and so much striving, could only with diffidence thrust himself into the chaste environs where the divine hovered and held sway. The divine seemed to breathe in the enveloping splendor of mountain meadows, in river and seas and the smiling limpidity that hung over all. And at luminous moments suddenly the form appeared, a god or a goddess, now like a man, now nearer the monstrous, like an animal. The solitudes of nature possess geniuses of diverse form, from the fearful and wild to the shy spirit of sweet maidenhood. But loftiest of all is an encounter with the sublime. It dwells in the clear ether of the mountain peak, in the golden iridescence of mountain meadows, in the lightning glint of ice-crystals and snowy slopes, in the silent astonishment of field and forest when the moonlight bathes them in its glow and drips glittering from the leaves. Here everything is transparent and weightless. Earth itself has lost its heaviness and the blood is no longer conscious of its dark passions. A dance of white

feet seems to hover over the ground, a chase to pass through the
air. This is the divine spirit of sublime nature, the lofty shimmer-
ing mistress, the pure one, who compels delight and yet cannot
love, the dancer and huntress who fondles cubs in her bosom and
races the deer, who brings death when she draws her golden bow,
reserved and unapproachable like wild nature, and yet, like nature, wholly enchantment and fresh excitement and lightning
beauty. *This is Artemis.* Manifold as her manifestations may be,
in this idea they possess their unity and are no longer contradictory.

2

Artemis' relationship to non-Greek Asia Minor, whence her name
seems to derive,[1] is not clear. But it is certain that she was at home
on Greek soil from very early times, and that her figure, as we
first come to know her in Homer, is wholly and genuinely Greek.

She too possesses the property of disappearing into the distance.
The Argives regularly celebrated her departure and her return.
Like Apollo she too was brought into connection with the Hyperboreans;[2] myths name other remote and fabulous regions, particularly Ortygia, which is designated as her birthplace,[3] and give the
name Ortygia to various places, preferably to one near Ephesus.[4]
Ortygia takes its name from the quail, a bird associated with
Artemis; coveys of quail return to Greek coasts and islands each
spring. The migratory bird is an appropriate symbol for the goddess of distance.

Artemis' realm is the ever-distant wilderness. With her remoteness is connected her virginity. This is not inconsistent with her
motherliness, for maternal anxiety sorts very well with the de-
mureness of girlhood. In genuine myth Artemis could only be
thought of as virgin. Other divine maidens who were her playmates and intimates might succumb to love; she herself is more
sublime than all of these. In Euripides she herself utters her irrefragable hatred for the goddess of love,[5] and the *Homeric Hymn
to Aphrodite* acknowledges that that goddess has no power over
Artemis.[6] The bold man who would approach her is struck down
by her unerring shaft. After Homer she is generally called Virgin

or Maiden; in Homer she receives the laudatory designation
hagne,[7] a word in which the meanings "holy" and "pure" merge
and which is frequently applied to the untouched aspects of nature. Besides Artemis only Persephone, the exalted queen of the
dead, is distinguished by this epithet in Homer.

Everywhere in free and untamed nature, on mountains, plains,
and in forests, are her playgrounds, where she dances and hunts
with her charming companions the Nymphs. "Her pleasure is in
the bow," says the *Homeric Hymn to Aphrodite* of Artemis, "and
in the lyre, in the round-dance, and in echoing outcries."[8] The
Homeric picture is unforgettable: "Forth upon the mountains of
Taygetus or Erymanthus goes huntress Artemis to hunt wild boars
or deer, and the wood-nymphs, daughters of aegis-bearing Zeus,
take their sport along with her; then is Leto proud at seeing her
daughter stand a full head taller than the others and eclipse the
loveliest amid a whole bevy of beauties."[9] From the mountain
heights she receives several epithets; Aeschylus calls her "the lady
of the wild mountains."[10] She loves clear waters also; it is her blessing that gives healing power to warm springs. Her splendor hovers
over untrodden fields of flowers, where her devotee plucks a garland "from a virgin meadow, where no shepherd presumes to pasture his flock, nor has iron ever come there. Virgin it is, and in
summer the bees frequent it, while Purity waters it like a garden."[11] In the bright and flowery fields she joins in the round-
dance with her maidens.[12] In honor of her, dances were introduced in many cults. It was from such a round-dance, at Artemis'
sanctuary in Sparta, that Theseus once ravished Helen.[13] The
beauty of her tall stature is beyond compare.[14] When Odysseus
beheld the tall and distinguished daughter of the king of the
Phaeacians, he could not help thinking of Artemis.[15] Girls whom
Artemis wishes well she endows with tall stature.[16] She was called
"the beautiful" or "the most beautiful," and was honored by this
title.[17]

Just as her dancing and her beauty belong to the magic and
splendor of untrammelled nature, so is she also most intimately
bound up with everything that lives in nature, with animals and
with trees. She is "the Lady of the wild beasts,"[18] and it is quite
in the spirit of nature that she cares for them like a mother and yet

hunts them down like a gay huntress and archer. The François vase, which was made in Athens about half a century before the birth of Aeschylus and Pindar, shows her lifting a lion by the scruff with either hand, as if they were cats; and again, grasping a panther with one hand and with the other holding a stag by the throat. No poet speaks so movingly of her care for wild beasts as does Aeschylus in his *Agamemnon*. Eagles have slain and gutted a pregnant hare, and holy Artemis laments the unhappy beast, "for well she loves the tender cubs of ravening lions and well the suckling of every beast of the wood."[19] She must once have taken particular joy in lions. On the Corinthian chest of Cypselus, Artemis was represented with wings (as she was on the François vase, with which this is practically contemporary), in the oriental fashion, her right hand holding a panther and her left a lion.[20] Before her temple in Thebes stood a lion of stone.[21] In the festival procession at Syracuse, of which Theocritus tells,[22] the lioness was most admired.

Next to the lion the bear was her favorite. The Arcadian Callisto, her companion and double, was said to have received the form of a bear; and in the Attic cult this animal held great importance. The stag is her standing attribute in plastic art; she is called "stag-huntress" in the *Homeric Hymns*,[23] and she acquired a number of other epithets from the stag. Her doe plays a part in the legends of Heracles and Iphigenia. Her companion Taygete, who was named from the Arcadian mountains which were Artemis' favorite hunting grounds, was transformed into a doe; and in the legend of the Aloadae she herself assumes that form. Near Colophon there was a little island sacred to Artemis to which it was believed that pregnant does swam in order to bear their young.[24] Many other animals, specifically boar, wolf, steer, and horse—in Homer she guides the horse "with golden bridle"[25]—are frequently named in connection with her. In her sacred grove on the Timavus in the land of the Eneti, it was believed, the wild beasts were tame, and deer and wolves lived together in peace and allowed men to stroke them; no game that took refuge there was hunted any more.[26] On the day before her festival at Patras in Achaea[27] there was a brilliant festal procession which closed with the virgin priestess of Artemis riding on a chariot drawn by stags. On the day following there were thrown upon the altar, which was transformed into a pyre, living wild boars, deer, roe, wolf and bear cubs, and even full-grown animals of the same species; if an animal attempted to escape from the flames it was driven back, and it was said that no one was ever injured in the process. Artemis' cult image represented her as a huntress.

Plastic art retained the figure of Artemis as huntress, and she was so characterized by numerous, and in part very old, epithets. In Homer she is called "wearer of the bow,"[28] but more frequently "the archeress."[29] Sometimes she is called "the resounding,"[30] which has been taken to refer to the noise of the chase. "To draw the bow is her pleasure, and to hunt wild beasts upon the mountains."[31] Like Apollo she is called "far-darter."[32] It is to her inspiration and assistance that the huntsman owes his skill. Thus Homer says of Scamandrius that "Artemis herself had taught him how to kill every kind of wild creature that is bred in mountain forests."[33] And the lucky huntsman fixes the heads of the game he has killed upon trees as an offering to Artemis.[34]

Her rare quality of wildness and its eerie fascination is manifested especially during the night, when mysterious lights flare up and dart about or the moonlight works magic transformation upon field and forest. Then Artemis goes hunting and brandishes "the brilliant blaze with which she storms through the mountains of Lycia."[35] She is called simply "the goddess that roves by night."[36] "Artemis smiter of the deer, goddess of the two-fold torch," Sophocles[37] calls her. At Aulis there were two stone statues of her, one with torches and the other with bow and arrow.[38] In the temple of Despoina in Arcadian Acacesion her statue was clothed with the pelt of a deer; on her back hung a quiver, one hand bore a torch, and nearby lay a hunting-dog.[39] In vases of the fifth century she is frequently represented with torches in both hands; hence her common designation of "light-bearer" (*phosphoros*). This same aspect is the source for her early connection with the moon, in which her enticing, romantic, and remote qualities are reflected. When Aeschylus speaks of the "glance of her starry eye"[40] he means the light of the moon, as whose goddess she so often appears in later times. We can understand that she could be a guide on distant roads, where she is thought of as rov-

ing with her band of spirits. Here she is like Hermes; a number
of epithets designate her as pointing the way. In legends of city-
foundings, Artemis shows settlers the way to the place where they
are to build their new city. The founders of Laconian Boiae were
led by a hare, who disappeared in a myrtle tree; the tree was regarded as sacred, and Artemis was worshipped as "deliverer."[41]
The goddess of space and distance is the good companion for
those who journey forth.

3

The queen of the wilderness enters into human life also, and
brings with her her oddities and her terrors, but also her kindliness.

Several times we hear of human sacrifices in her cult.[42] To her
Iphigenia was to be immolated as the most beautiful girl born
during the year.[43] In Melite, the westerly suburb of Athens, there
was a temple of Artemis Aristobule at the spot where, down to a
late period, bodies of capital criminals were cast away and nooses
that had served suicides were disposed of.[44] In Rhodes too, Aristobule was worshipped outside the gates, and at the festival of the
Cronia a condemned criminal was sacrificed to her at the site
of her statue.[45] It is said that she aroused madness, and, as a
gentle goddess, healed it. The fearsome huntress, in whose name
the Greeks undoubtedly detected the meaning "she who slays,"
showed her nature in battles also. The Spartans offered sacrifices
to Artemis Agrotera on the battlefield. At Athens a large sacrifice
was regularly offered to her for the victory at Marathon; her
temple was in the suburb Agrai, on the Ilissus, where she is said
to have hunted for the first time.[46] Thus she was represented as a
warrior,[47] and occasionally associated with the Amazons. As Eu-
cleia she had a sanctuary in the market-place of Athens as well as
in Locrian and Boeotian cities.

But the uncanny goddess attacks the abodes of men also. Her
shafts are called "gentle," because, like Apollo's, they permit the
victim to fall suddenly asleep, without sickness.[48] A woman in
distress prays the goddess for such an instantaneous and kindly
death.[49] For it is women whom she sweeps away, just as her

brother does men.[50] And yet her coming denotes an evil visitation
for the female sex, for the bitterness and danger of woman's most
difficult hours come from Artemis, who, like so many spirit-crea-
tures among other peoples, works her mysterious effects upon
womankind from the wilderness. "Zeus made her as a lion among
women, and let her kill them whenever she chose."[51] She causes
child-bed fever, which brings speedy death upon women. But
she can also bring help to women in travail, who therefore call
upon her in their need. "Helper in pains whom no pain touches"—
thus is she invoked in the Orphic hymn.[52] And in the hymn of
Callimachus she says of herself, "Upon the mountains I choose to
dwell, and mingle amongst city-folk only when women in the
anguish of travail call upon my help."[53] As Artemis Eileithyia
she is directly equated with the goddess of travail, who, according to the Homeric view,[54] is also an archer and by her shafts
brings birth pangs upon women. "I experienced this thrill, this
chill, in my own womb, but I cried to the heavenly archer, goddess Artemis, who presides over childbirth"—so sing the chorus
of women in Euripides' *Hippolytus*.[55] An epigram of the Hel-
lenistic poet Phaedimus thanks the goddess for an easy delivery,
"because, coming in gentle guise without thy bow thou didst hold
thy two hands over her in her labor."[56] "May Artemis, the far-
darter, look with blessing upon the child-bed of women"—so the
chorus prays in Aeschylus' *Suppliants*.[57] When Artemis is angry
with mankind, then "either the women die in child-bed, smitten
by her shafts, or if they survive, bear children that cannot live."[58]
As goddess of parturition she bears such epithets as Lecho or
Locheia. To Iphigenia, who belonged to her and whose tomb was
in the sanctuary of Artemis at Brauron, was dedicated the clothing of women who died in child-bed.[59] Because of her great importance for the life of women she is called "sovereign lady of
women,"[60] "she who holds mighty power over womankind."[61]
Athenian women swore by "Lady Artemis,"[62] young girls were
consecrated to her service at Brauron in Attica, women celebrated
her festival, and in several cults choirs of maidens danced in her
honor.

And finally Artemis' power extended also over the sphere of
life which is woman's most sacred care. Just as the fate of women

giving birth was in her hands, so she bestowed her benison upon
children new-born and growing. Did she not care even for the
youngling beasts of the wilderness? The epigram of Phaedimus
previously cited closes its thanksgiving for an easy delivery with a
prayer for the child: "And Artemis, vouchsafe to see this baby boy
of Leon's grow great and strong."[63] She teaches the nurture and
upbringing of little children, and is therefore called *kurotrophos*
("nurse of children").[64] We know other of her epithets of similar
significance. In Homer she cares, along with other deities, for the
orphaned daughters of Pandareus and bestows upon them the tall
stature without which a girl cannot be truly beautiful.[65] In Laco-
nia, the Tithenidia ("festival of nurses") was celebrated in her
honor; on that day their nurses brought little boys to Artemis. At
Athens, children's hair was dedicated to her on the Apaturia. At
Elis, there was a sanctuary of Artemis near the gymnasium, and
there she bore the significant appellation "friend of boys."[66] Armed
ephebi marched in festal procession in her honor, especially in
Athens. In a poem of Crinagoras a young man dedicates "the first
spring-bloom that clothes the cheeks of young men . . . to Zeus
Teleius and Artemis who soothes the pangs of child-bed," and
prays these gods to "lead him straight into the season of gray
hairs."[67]

Like her brother Apollo, then, Artemis watches over growing
youth, and stands in a special relationship to those who are entering upon maturity. This might suggest the gruelling trials which
were imposed upon Spartan boys in her cult. These were surely
not a surrogate for earlier human sacrifice, but here the goddess
of the wilderness does show her terrifying harshness in no ambiguous terms. Callimachus knows that she visits retribution with
her fearful bow upon cities in which citizens and strangers were
evilly entreated;[68] but in the city of just men, as the *Homeric
Hymn to Aphrodite* says, she takes pleasure.[69]

4

And so the dancer of the flower-decked meadows, the huntress
of the mountains, moves in the affairs of men also. And yet she

nevertheless remains the mercurial queen of solitude, a being enchanting and wild, unapproachable and ever chaste.

In the belief of the Ionian epic she had long been paired with Apollo, as daughter of Leto and Zeus. "Hail to thee, blessed Leto," the *Homeric Hymn* begins, "who hast borne children so stately, lord Apollo and archer Artemis, her in Ortygia and him in rocky Delos."[70] In the *Iliad,* together with Leto Artemis heals Aeneas, who has been saved by Apollo.[71] Apollo too is sometimes called "the huntsman."[72] But Homer makes the distinction that Artemis teaches the hunter, Apollo the archer in battle and in contests. Along with Apollo Artemis takes pleasure in the dances and songs of the Graces and the Muses.[73] Each has a terrifying as well as a glorious aspect, and this is made very plain in Homer. Both shoot from afar their invisible and unerring shafts, which bring sudden and painless death. On the fabulous island of Syria there is no sickness; "when men grow old, Apollo of the silver bow and Artemis strike them with their gentle shafts."[74] Each possesses purity that may never be sullied. Each exhibits a remoteness which we may call withdrawal or stately aloofness. Thus they are truly twin deities.

But how different is the sense of distance and purity in Apollo! How different the symbols by which the creative spirit has fashioned them! For Apollo freedom and distance denote a spiritual quality—the will to clarity and form; with him purity denotes release from constricting and oppressive forces. For Artemis, on the other hand, these are ideals of physical existence, just as purity in her case is understood in the sense of virginity. Her will does not pursue spiritual freedom but nature and its elemental freshness, mobility, and development. In other words, Apollo is the symbol of higher masculinity, and Artemis is transfigured woman. She exhibits a quite different aspect of the feminine than do Hera, Aphrodite, or the primal-mother earth-goddess. In her manifestation of the spirit of untouched nature there appears a primal image of the feminine whose eternal form belongs to the circle of the gods.

She is life and being, starry-bright, sparkling, blinding, mobile, whose sweet strangeness draws man on the more irresistibly the more disdainfully it dismisses him; an essence crystal-clear, which is nevertheless intertwined with the dark roots in all animate nature; a being childishly simple and yet incalculable, sweetly amiable and diamond-hard; girlishly demure, fleeting, elusive, and suddenly brusque and contrary; playing, frolicking, dancing, and in a flash most inexorably serious; lovingly anxious and tenderly solicitous, with the enchantment of a smile that outweighs perdition, and yet wild to the point of gruesomeness and cruel to the point of repulsiveness. All of these are traits of the free, withdrawn nature to which Artemis belongs, and in her the piously intuitive spirit has learned to perceive this eternal image of sublime femininity as a thing divine.

APHRODITE

Every earthly Venus arises like heaven's first,
A dark birth out of the endless sea.

SCHILLER

1

"Golden" Aphrodite, goddess of love, bears a name certainly not Greek. We know that she came to Greece from the east, but she was not only naturalized in pre-Homeric times but became wholly Greek. She was the great goddess of fertility and love of the Babylonians, Phoenicians, and other Asiatics, and is mentioned in the Old Testament as "queen of heaven."[1] Definite word of her immigration survives. According to Herodotus the mother sanctuary was that of Aphrodite Urania at Askalon; it was thence, as he says, that the Cyprians themselves derived their cult of Aphrodite, which the Phoenicians brought from Askalon to Cythera also.[2] The celebrated name Cypris, which occurs as early as Homer[3] as a proper name of the goddess, points to the island of Cyprus; and the name Cyprogenes and Cyprogeneia in Hesiod and other writers is obvious proof that she came from that island. The *Odyssey*[4] speaks of her sanctuary in Paphos on Cyprus. The name Cytherea, used in the *Odyssey*[5] and later very famous, recalls the island Cythera. It was thither, according to Hesiod's *Theogony*,[6] that the goddess went directly she arose from the sea, and it was from there that she first came to Cyprus.

But in Greece the foreign goddess seems to have found an ancient native form; this may explain why the Aphrodite worshipped "in the gardens" (*en Kepois*) at Athens was characterized as "eldest of the Moirai,"[7] and why Epimenides[8] makes Aphrodite sister of the Moirai and Erinyes and traces her descent from Cronus and Euonyme. Her ancient connection with Ares, the demonic spirit of curse and blood, to whom, according to Hesiod,[9]

she bore Deimos (Terror) and Phobos (Fear) but also Harmonia,
suggests a primitive folk-image.

But we can leave the question of historical origins open without fear that we shall miss data essential for understanding the
Greek goddess. Whatever the Orient or prehistoric Greece may
have contributed to her image, its basic character is thoroughly
Greek. The idea which the name Aphrodite denotes for us is a
genuine expression of the spirit of pre-Homeric Hellenism, and
we need direct our attention only to that idea. Through it even
traits whose oriental origin is unmistakable acquire a new aspect
and a particular sense. And on the other hand, through this idea
certain notions are once and for all excluded. The queen of heaven
as she is celebrated in Babylonian poems is utterly foreign not
only to the Homeric but even to the Orphic hymns.

2

According to the *Iliad*, Aphrodite is the daughter of Zeus and
Dione.[10] The other genealogy, which is to be found in its earliest
and doubtless purest form in Hesiod,[11] connects the origin of the
goddess with the cosmic myth of "Heaven" and "Earth" which
belongs to the prehistoric age of great myth-making. But the
deity who arises out of the foam of the sea is here no longer a
cosmic power but the genuinely Greek Aphrodite, the goddess of
rapture.

Hesiod tells the wonderful story of Uranus, the god of heaven,
who at the dusk of nightfall spread himself lovingly over Earth,
but at the moment of his embrace was violently mutilated by
Cronus. For a long while his severed male member floated in the
surging sea; white foam swirled up out of the divine substance,
and in it a young woman took form. She came to land first at
Cythera and then at Cyprus, and as she stepped to the ground,
earth bloomed under her feet. Eros and Himeros, the geniuses of
love and longing, stand at her side and conduct her to the assembly of the gods. Her portion of honor among men and gods is
"girlish babble and deceit and sweet rapture, embraces and caresses." So says Hesiod. Other witnesses usually speak only of her

birth from the sea, without mentioning what precedes in Hesiod. Who does not know the picture of eternal beauty arising out of the sea-foam with dripping locks and being greeted by the world with jubilation? The waves are said to have carried her to Cythera's shore in a sea-shell.[12] Her ascent from the sea was represented by Phidias on the base of the statue of Zeus at Olympia: Eros takes her up, Peitho crowns her with a garland, and the great gods round about are spectators.[13] The base of a statue of Amphitrite and Poseidon set up by Herodes Atticus showed Thalassa raising a childlike Aphrodite from her element, with Nereids at either side.[14] These descriptions inevitably recall the wonderful relief of the Terme Museum in Rome. The sixth *Homeric Hymn* tells us in detail what happened to the goddess after the sea gave her birth. In a billow of foam Zephyr with his moist breath drove her to Cyprus where the Hours received her joyfully and dressed her in divine garments. Upon her head they set a crown of gold, and they hung precious ornaments in her ears. Upon her throat and bosom they fixed golden chains, such as the Hours themselves wear when they go to the dance of the gods in their father's house. So adorned, the glorious one was led to the gods, who greeted her with delight and kindled with love for her.

What a picture! Beauty emerges from the monstrous element and makes it a mirror of her heavenly smile. It is noteworthy that the foam-born of myth was worshipped from of old as goddess of the sea and of navigation; but she is not a sea divinity in the sense that Poseidon and other rulers of the sea are. The same magnificence with which she fills all of nature has made the sea the scene of her manifestation. Her coming smooths the billows and causes the watery plain to glitter like a jewel. She is the divine enchantment of peaceful seas and prosperous voyages just as she is the enchantment of blooming nature. Lucretius has put this beautifully: "Thou, goddess, thou dost turn to flight the winds and the clouds of heaven, thou at thy coming; for thee earth, the quaint artificer, puts forth her sweet-scented flowers; for thee the levels of ocean smile, and the sky, its anger past, gleams with spreading light."[15] So she is called "goddess of the serene sea,"[16] and brings the voyager safe to harbor.[17] It was told of Herostratus of Naucratis that he took with him upon a voyage

a small image of Aphrodite bought in Paphos, and thereby preserved his ship from foundering: when prayer was offered to the
image, pure myrtle sprouted all around it, a sweet aroma filled
the ship, and the passengers who had already given up hope
reached land in safety.[18] Hence she was called "goddess of the
prosperous voyage," "goddess of the haven"; her oracle at Paphos
was consulted for favorable voyages.[19] She was worshipped in
harbor towns; Poseidon was often associated with her in a cult:
Rhodus, the divine personage of the island that was believed to
have risen from the sea, was regarded as the son of Aphrodite
and Poseidon.[20] Demetrius Poliorcetes was hailed by the Athenians as "son of the mighty god Poseidon and Aphrodite."[21] At
Thebes there was a carving of the goddess of which it was told
that Harmonia had it made out of the wooden prow of the vessel
that had brought Cadmus.[22]

The miracle of Aphrodite transpired in the realm of earth as
well as on the sea. She is the goddess of nature in bloom, and is
associated with the Graces, the kindly and beneficent spirits of
growth. With them she dances,[23] by them she is bathed and
anointed,[24] and they work the clothing she wears.[25] She manifests
herself in the magic bloom of gardens, and therefore sacred gardens are consecrated to her. The name of Hierokepis ("sacred
garden"), a place near Palaipathos on Cyprus,[26] is evidence of
this. Kepoi ("gardens") was the name of a place outside Athens
on the Ilissus where there was a temple of Aphrodite of the Gardens with a famous cult statue carved by Alcamenes.[27] In the
Medea, Euripides has the chorus sing of Aphrodite who "sprin-
kled the land from the fair streams of Cephissus and breathed
over it breezes soft and fragrant. Ever on her hair she wears a
garland of sweet-smelling roses. . . ."[28] The Cnossians of Crete
called her Anthia ("flower-lady").[29] She is celebrated as the lady
of spring blossoms, especially of roses in bloom, in the *Pervigilium
Veneris*.[30] The rose is called "image of Venus," by the poet Ti-
berianus.[31] We shall do no more than mention the so-called Gardens of Adonis, which played a characteristic rôle in the cult of
the oriental Adonis who was associated with Aphrodite. Spring
is therefore her great season. The poet Ibycus contrasts the spring
blossoms of quinces, pomegranates, and vines with the permanent

flame of love by which he himself is scorched by Cypris.[32] Wonderful tales are told of the sites where she was worshipped. On the great altar of Aphrodite on Mount Eryx all traces of fire disappeared each morning and dewy green grew in their stead.[33] Particular plants were associated with her; a place on Cyprus sacred to her was called Myrikai ("tamarisks").[34] On that island she is said to have planted the pomegranate tree also.[35] Myrtle was sacred to her.[36] Canachus' celebrated statue of Aphrodite in the temple at Sicyon held poppy seed in one hand and an apple in the other;[37] the significance of the apple in the symbolism of love is well known. It was from the Cyprian garden of Aphrodite that the golden apples with which Hippomenes won Atalanta were said to have been taken.[38]

But all this is trifling in comparison with Aphrodite's manifestation in the life of animals and men. She is the rapture of the love-embrace, which was early designated by the name of Aphrodite.[39] "Works of Aphrodite" means the pleasures of love,[40] and in other ways also her name serves in post-Homeric times to denote the joys of love.[41] "Muse, tell me the deeds of golden Aphrodite, the Cyprian," the *Homeric Hymn* to her[42] begins, "who stirs up sweet passion in the gods and subdues the tribes of mortal men and birds that fly in the air and all the many creatures that the dry land rears, and all that the sea: all these love the deeds of rich-crowned Cytherea." Only three, the *Hymn* continues, withstand her power—Athena, Artemis, and Hestia: "Of these three Aphrodite cannot bend or ensnare the hearts. But of all others no one among the blessed gods or among mortal men has escaped Aphrodite." Sophocles[43] and Euripides[44] both have famous lines on Aphrodite's omnipotence over the whole of animate creation, over men, and over gods. Lucretius sings of her magic power over the world of animals at the opening of his didactic poem: "When once the face of the spring day is revealed and the teeming breeze of the west wind is loosed from prison and blows strong, first the birds in high heaven herald thee, goddess, and thine approach, their hearts thrill with thy might. Then the tame beasts grow wild and bound over the fat pastures, and swim the racing rivers; so surely enchained by thy charm each follows thee in hot desire whither thou goest before to lead him on. Yea, through seas and

mountains and tearing rivers and the leafy haunts of birds and
verdant plains thou dost strike fond love into the hearts of all,
and makest them in hot desire to renew the stock of their races,
each after his own kind."[45] The effect of her presence is depicted
with striking vividness by the poet of the *Homeric Hymn.* As the
goddess makes her way to handsome Anchises there follow gray
wolves wagging their tails, lions with glittering eyes, bears, and
swift-footed panthers. "Joyfully the goddess looks upon them, and
fills their hearts with sweet longing, so that all in pairs take their
pleasure of love in shady retreats."[46] Thus she is able to impart
tenderness and rapture even to savage beasts. But the whole
brilliance of her majesty is manifested only in man.

It was natural enough for Aphrodite to be associated with mat-
rimony and the rearing of children. The *Odyssey* tells how Aphrodite facilitated marriage for the daughter of Pandareus.[47] In Her-
mione maidens and widows made offerings to her before marriage;[48] in Naupactus widows who desired to remarry made
special offerings.[49] In Sparta there was an Aphrodite Hera to
whom mothers of brides made an offering before the marriage of
their daughters.[50] So in Euripides she is called, "Aphrodite of the
maidens' marriage."[51]

But the sense of Aphrodite's essence is not conjugal union, and
she was never, as Hera was, a goddess of marriage. From her
comes that all-powerful yearning which can forget the whole
world for the sake of the one beloved, that can shatter honorable
bonds and break sacred faith only to melt into oneness with him.
And the goddess will not tolerate mockery; if a man thinks he
can resist her power, she persecutes him with horrible savagery.
She has her declared favorites, whose whole life and being
breathe the tender desire of her essence. These are men, but in
them the feminine aspects of the male triumph over the truly masculine qualities. Of these the most famous is Paris, the true type
of the friend of Aphrodite. At the contest of beauty among the
goddesses he awarded the prize to her, and in return she procured him the favor of the most beautiful woman. It is with profound significance that legend opposes him to her lawful husband, Menelaus, "friend of Ares" *(Areiphilos).* "Do but face Menelaus, friend of Ares," says Hector, mocking him, "and learn what

manner of man he is whose wife you have stolen; your lyre will
not help you, nor the gifts of Aphrodite, your comely locks and
fair favor."[52] Paris is handsome, a player on the lyre and a dancer.
When Aphrodite saved him from his unlucky duel and miraculously removed him to his house, she spoke to Helen, assuming
the guise of an old servant, in order to arouse her desire for him;
"he was radiant with beauty and dressed in gorgeous apparel. No
one would think he had just come from fighting, but rather that
he was going to a dance, or had done dancing and was sitting
down."[53] Anchises too was playing the lyre when she sought him
out.[54] The contrast between the two aspects of life could not be
more effectively presented than in the scene at the close of the
third book of the *Iliad*. From his dangerous duel Paris had happily been removed by Aphrodite into his bed-chamber, where
Helen sinks into his passionate embrace; on the battlefield Menelaus searches for his vanished opponent in vain, and Agamemnon
solemnly declares that Menelaus is victor and has won the decision for the Greeks.[55] This is the feminine man, the friend of
women. The wantonness which Aphrodite brought into his life
is designated by a word (*machlosynē*) elsewhere applied to
women.[56]

Of her gifts all ages speak with ravishment. First of all, naturally, is her beauty and her compelling charm (*charis*). She herself is of course the most beautiful of women—not maidenly, like
Artemis, and not dignified, like the goddesses of marriage and
motherhood, but pure feminine beauty and loveliness itself,
bathed in the moist glow of ecstasy, always fresh and untroubled
and blissful as the infinite sea which gave her birth. Plastic art
strove to grasp this image of love come alive. Poets after Homer
call her "golden" and speak of her as the "smiling" (*philomeides*)
goddess. Helen recognizes her by the ravishing beauty of her neck
and bosom and by the brilliance of her eyes,[57] just as Achilles
recognizes Athena by her mighty, flaming glance.[58] Her attendants and playmates are the Charites (Graces); they dance with
her, they bathe and anoint her, and they weave her garments. The
thing that their name means, amiable and winning charm (*charis*),
Aphrodite herself presents to the primal woman Pandora.[59] Her
unguent is called "beauty."[60] This she once presented to the boat-

man Phaon because he ferried her, in the guise of an old woman, from Lesbos to the mainland. Thereafter Phaon was the handsomest of men and the object of all women's longing; the poetess Sappho was said to have cast herself into the sea from the Leucadian cliff for his sake. In the *Odyssey* Athena bestows youthful beauty upon Penelope by means of this "beauty" of Aphrodite's.[61] Mention is also made of the girdle of her bosom, which makes any who possess it irresistible, for in it are "all Aphrodite's charms, love, desire, and that sweet flattery which steals the judgment even of the most prudent."[62] Hera begged this girdle of Aphrodite when she wished to arouse Zeus's love. Later it was said of a beautiful woman who won all hearts that Aphrodite herself had given her the girdle from her bosom.[63] About her, besides the Charites, are the geniuses of longing and persuasion, Pothos, Himeros, and "Peitho, the enticing one, who brooks no denial."[64] The magic of the wheel of love (*iynx*) is said to derive from her; according to Pindar she first brought it to Jason from Olympus and taught him magic incantations

> that he might loosen Medea's shame for her parents, and Hellas be all her desire,
> that her heart ablaze under the lash of longing be set in tumult.[65]

Her powerful enchantment causes oblivion of all duty and leads to resolves that later seem incomprehensible to the enchanted person himself. In Sophocles' *Antigone* the chorus sings: "The just themselves have their minds warped by thee to wrong, for their ruin . . . for the will of goddess Aphrodite is unconquerable."[66] But it is noteworthy that Aphrodite brings good fortune to men— if they do not affront her, as Hippolytus did—whereas to women she all too often causes doom. She wrests them out of a life of security and restraint and causes them distress by blind and often criminal devotion to a strange man. For this too myth has created a series of famous types. Frequently, in Homer, Helen laments the accursed passion that carried her from her dear home, husband, and child into an alien land and made her a curse for two nations. And in the *Iliad* we read how Aphrodite upbraids the unhappy woman when she makes a show of offering resistance.[67] It was through love that Medea became a criminal; Euripides

makes of her a terrifying example of love turned to hate. "May
you never launch at me, O Lady of Cyprus," the chorus in that
play sings, "your golden bow's passion-poisoned arrows, which
no man can avoid. May Moderation content me, the fairest gift
of heaven."[68] Phaedra was miserably ruined by mad love for the
young and chaste son of her husband Theseus.[69] Her mother Pasiphaë was inflamed with passion for a bull; from the *Cretan
Women* of Euripides we still possess her eloquent defense in
which she makes the goddess entirely responsible for her monstrous passion. Here as elsewhere ancient wrong followed by divine anger is given as the reason for the whole woeful situation.
In the *Hippolytus* of Euripides the nurse says to the love-sick
Phaedra, "You cannot withstand Cypris if she rushes upon you
full tilt. When she finds a person yielding she comes on gently,
but when she finds a person too high and mighty she takes him
and—what do you think?—knocks the pride out of him."[70] And
later, in the same speech, "It is pure presumption, wanting to be
better than the gods. Have the courage to love: a god has willed
it. You are sick; find some way to cure your sickness."[71] So violent and fearful can be the goddess whose nature is all rapture
and smiles. In Thebes, Aphrodite was also worshipped as Apos-
trophia,[72] surely so that she should "avert" sinful passion. So at
Rome, at the bidding of the Sibylline oracles, a cult was established for Venus Verticordia, to guard girls and women, particularly Vestals, from unchaste longings.[73]

If the passion which Aphrodite visits upon women often leads
to darkness and terror, the purchased love of the temple prosti-
tutes is glorified by the goddess, for that too belongs to her. Pindar
wrote an ode for Xenophon of Corinth, who, in gratitude for his
Olympian victory, established a company of such women: "Guest-
loving girls! servants of Suasion in wealthy Corinth! Ye that burn
the golden tears of fresh frankincense, full often soaring upward
in your souls unto Aphrodite, the heavenly mother of loves! She
hath granted you, ye girls, blamelessly to cull on lovely couches
the blossom of delicate bloom; for, under force, all things are
fair."[74]

Of real festivals of Aphrodite we know very little. But it is
worth mentioning that the goddess whose favor could disperse

the hardships of life in a luminous instant was also celebrated at the conclusion of important undertakings.[75] Celebration of Aphrodite also concluded the festival of Poseidon at Aegina, which was connected with the legend of the return of the Greeks from Troy.[76] The celebrations (Aphrodisia) which sailors customarily indulged in with wild abandon at the successful conclusion of a voyage became proverbial.[77]

3

For us the Aphrodite who comes from the Orient sharpens the lineaments of the Greek manifestation of her. In her a particular and magnificent form of existence is regarded as divine. Because she denotes a permanent reality which draws everything into her power, and bestows her spirit and impresses her character upon the whole realm of the elemental and the living, she is a world—and for the Greeks this means a divinity. And what is the quality of this eternal being? It is the ensnaring, heart-winning splendor in which all things and the whole world stand before the eye of love, the rapture of propinquity and fusion into oneness, whose magic draws the contact of limited creatures into boundless dissolution. It manifests itself as true divinity ranging from the natural up to the sublime heights of spirit.

Aphrodite imparts her loveliness not only to the living but also to the dead. Just as her "beauty" endows Penelope with the fresh charm of youth,[78] so with unguents and ambrosial attar of roses she protects from disfiguration the body of Hector which was abused by Achilles, and day and night keeps the dogs away from it.[79] The force of attraction by which she brings the sexes together also binds and preserves friendships. There was worship of an Aphrodite Hetaira, whom Apollodorus explains as the goddess of bonds between friends, male or female.[80] Everything charming, winning, and amiable, be it figure or gesture, speech or action, is named after her (*epaphroditos* in Greek, *venustus* in Latin). "Make us amiable in words and deeds" was a prayer to her[81] expressing the desire that the goddess impart her loveliness to social intercourse. And since she is the goddess of benison, good luck too comes from her. So the lucky throw at dice is named after her; and it is a familiar fact that Sulla rendered his Latin cognomen Felix into Greek by the word which denotes the favor of Aphrodite (*Epaphroditos*).

Here the realm of Aphrodite apparently approaches that of Hermes. But her favor has nothing of the luck of happy chance, of coincidence, of windfall. It is a benison, a grace, which resides in beauty and charm and wins every victory, without effort, because bliss produces bliss in others—"What is beautiful appears blissful in itself," as Mörike has written.

The gift of consummation and understanding, of conquest and rejoicing, is at its most sublime in the world of thought and of song. Unforgettable is Euripides' picture of Cypris: "Ever on her hair she wears a garland of sweet-smelling roses, and ever she sends the Loves (*erotes*) to assist in the court of wisdom (*sophia*). No good thing is wrought without their help."[82] Pindar speaks of his singing as labor in the garden of Aphrodite and the Graces.[83] Even Lucretius prays, in the proem of his poem, that she endow his words with "imperishable charm."[84]

We understand what Aphrodite denotes. It is not for naught that she is surrounded by the Graces, in whom she is to a certain degree mirrored. They are spirits of bloom, of what is charming and amiable. But they usually appear in the plural, and would therefore, according to our notions, be geniuses rather than divinities. Aphrodite, on the other hand, is singular. She is quite distinct from Eros, whom myth calls her son. That god plays an important rôle in cosmogonic speculation, but only a slight one in cult. He is not even mentioned in Homer, and this is a significant and important fact. He is the divine spirit of the desire and energy for reproduction. But Aphrodite's realm is of another sort and much more comprehensive. Here the notion of divine essence and power proceeds not from the desiring subject (as in the case of Eros[85]), but from the beloved object. Aphrodite is not the loving one: she is beauty and smiling charm; she enraptures. Not the urge to take possession comes first, but rather the magic of an appearance that draws irresistibly into the ravishment of union. The secret of the totality and unity of the world of Aphrodite is that in her attraction there is at work no demonic force which makes an unfeeling man seize his prey. The bewitching one is eager to surrender, the image of loveliness voluntarily bends towards the love-stricken with an undisguised yearning which is itself irresistible. That is the significance of Charis, who accompanies Aphrodite and ministers to her service. Charis is not merely the spirit of conquest which gains possession over another without giving of its own self; her loveliness is at the same time receptivity and echo, "lovableness" in the sense of favor and capacity for devotion. Hence the word also denotes gratitude and, in the woman, specifically granting of what the man desires. Sappho calls an immature girl, not yet ripe for marriage, a-charis ("without charis").[86] Thus arises harmony, in which the realm of Aphrodite finds consummation. In myth, Harmonia is called the goddess's daughter.[87] In Delphi she herself bears the related name Harma,[88] which points clearly to loving union. The chorus in Aeschylus' Suppliants[89] sing of Harmonia as Aphrodite's servitor and of her sway over the skirmishes and reunions of lovers. We have already mentioned the carvings of Aphrodite which Harmonia is said to have set up. Peitho, the assistant and double of Aphrodite, functions in a similar sense; according to Sappho, she is Aphrodite's mother.[90] The poetess often invokes Aphrodite in her poems, and in one of the most famous she turns to her, "the wile-weaving child of Zeus," out of her great need; the goddess comes and smilingly asks whom Peitho should persuade to her love, and promises that "even if she flees she shall soon pursue."[91]

This divine rapture, by which what was separated finds unity in love, was turned, long after the ancient world-myth had faded, into a cohesive force in a new concept of the cosmos. Thus for Empedocles it is the same Aphrodite who causes human hearts to beat for one another and who produces perfect harmony and unity in great world-periods. Just as Uranus had once passionately embraced Gaia, so the poet now sees heaven and earth yearning towards one another. In the Danaids Aeschylus[92] has Aphrodite herself speak with magnificent candor of the longing which moved "holy Heaven" to approach Earth conjugally, and of the bridelike yearning of Earth for love; so rain falls from Heaven and impregnates Earth, who bears herbs and fruit of the heavenly seed—and all this is the work of Aphrodite. There is a quite similar passage from a lost tragedy of Euripides.[93] Nor must we forget the beautiful verses of the *Pervigilium Veneris*, which belongs to a later period, in which the poet speaks of the first bridal solemnized by Ether when conjugal rain streams into the womb of his high consort.[94]

This goddess of the eternal miracle of love, says Lucretius at the opening of his poem,[95] alone has the power to bestow peace upon the world. Deeply wounded by love, the war-god himself seeks her embrace and fixes hungry eyes on Aphrodite and gluts them with love. Then must the goddess lovingly whisper in his ear a sweet prayer for peace.

But in closing we must again remind ourselves that to the breadth of this realm which is the world there belong also the horrible and the destructive. No power can cause such strife and confusion as can that whose office is the most luminous and blissful harmony; and it is only by these dark shadows that Aphrodite's magic brightness becomes a complete creation.

HERMES

1

Hermes, "the friendliest of the gods to men," is a genuine Olympian. His essence possesses the freedom, the breadth, and the brilliance by which we recognize the realm of Zeus. And yet he has properties which set him apart from the circle of the children of Zeus and which, when they are closely examined, appear to belong to a different and older conception of deity.

If we compare Hermes with his brother Apollo or with Athena we notice a certain lack of dignity in him. This appears quite plainly in the Homeric narrative whenever Hermes comes to the fore. His function as messenger of the gods is first mentioned in the *Odyssey*, and not in the *Iliad*, but we sense that this rôle suits his character perfectly. For his strength lies in resourcefulness. His works do not so much exhibit energy or wisdom as nimbleness and subtle cunning. He was scarcely born when, as the fourth *Homeric Hymn* tells at length, he achieved a master stroke by stealing his brother's cows and misleading their owner most craftily and unconscionably. The Io legend knows of him as the slayer of that Argus who watched over Io when she was transformed into a heifer; but the original plan was to steal the heifer, and Hermes would have carried it out if he had not been betrayed at the critical moment. So the Homeric epic sees him also. When the gods wished to put a stop to Achilles' cruel abuse of the body of Hector, their first thought was to have Hermes steal it.[1] He distinguished his son Autolycus among all men in the accomplishments of thieving and perjury,[2] which he himself possessed to such a high degree. Hence favorite epithets for him are "crafty," "deceiving," "ingenious," and he is the patron of robbers and thieves and all who are expert in gaining advantage through trickery. But his wonderful deftness makes him the ideal and patron of servants also. All that is expected of a diligent servant—skill in lighting the fire, splitting kindling wood, roasting

5. Aphrodite

6. Hermes

and carving meat, pouring wine—comes from Hermes, whose qualities made him so efficient a servant to the Olympians.

Admittedly, these are no dignified arts, even if, according to the ancient Greek view, a hero is free to avail himself of them on occasion. But the lifelike total picture which Homer presents, whenever he has Hermes appear in person, speaks more clearly than do scattered indications of his character. In that picture we see the gay master of happy chance, never at a loss, who is little troubled by standards of pride and dignity, but who despite all remains lovable: genius in bringing men luck would be pointless if it could not win affection. In the battle of the gods in the twenty-first book of the *Iliad* our rogue supplies the conclusion. After Ares and Athena have had their tiff and Apollo, with stately dignity, has refused to do battle with Poseidon, and after the typically feminine scene between Hera and Artemis which follows as a postlude, Hermes declares to Leto, with a joking reference to the treatment which Artemis would receive at Hera's hands, that he has no intention of fighting with her and would care not at all if she would boast among the immortal gods that she had vanquished him by might and main.[3] In the account of the love of Ares and Aphrodite, Apollo and Hermes are present as spectators, and Apollo asks his brother, with comic solemnity, whether he would not choose even the bondage of chains if so he might share Aphrodite's bed. Then, with the same comic dignity with which the question was put, the ingenious contriver of good luck answers that even if there were thrice as many chains, and all the gods and goddesses to look on, he would still be happy to languish in the arms of golden Aphrodite.[4] The Apollo whom the poet here presents us is big enough not to play schoolmaster to his rascal of a brother, and is even amused by him. And so are we, if we are capable of appreciating the spirited gaiety, by no means frivolous, with which the witty poet has informed his tale. But however much this Hermes may amuse us, his character, as we have seen, marks him as strikingly different from all the other great Olympians.

It is precisely the quality that makes him seem alien in the circle of Zeus which recalls the divinities of the early period who were dealt with in Chapter II. Cronus and Prometheus were characterized as "crafty"; resourcefulness, ingenuity, and deception were the qualities by which they achieved their great deeds. Hermes is strikingly like Perseus, with whose profile we concluded our brief survey of the earliest religious concepts. Both have winged shoes and the cap of invisibility, both use the sickle-sword, which myth also attributed to old Cronus. The cap of invisibility, if not the winged shoes, certainly involves magic. It is called the "cap of Hades," and Athena herself uses it once in the *Iliad*. But for Hermes it is characteristic, and thus brings us to the aspect of magic in his behavior. Magic played no inconsiderable part in the prehistoric world-outlook, but in Homer, except for a few traces, it has been left behind. Almost all of it that remains is attached to the figure of Hermes, whose position as archwizard and patron of magic is of long standing. In the *Odyssey* he shows Odysseus the magic herb that would counteract the enchantment of Circe. He possesses a magic wand with which he puts men asleep and awakens them. Just as he himself makes himself invisible at will by means of the cap of Hades, so his son Autolycus has the miraculous gift of changing things and making them unrecognizable. His whole character and presence stand under the sign of magic, though magic too, as we shall soon see, received a new and more spiritual meaning in the Olympian world.

The primitive element in Hermes is revealed by his very name, which points to cult usages of high antiquity. His pillar stood upon a heap of stones by the wayside, to which every passer-by piously added one. This gave him his name, for there can be no doubt that Hermes means "he of the stone heap." In later times the phallus remained as a characteristic of the stone pillars of Hermes, and this too points to a very ancient conception. The power of procreation, as shall soon appear, is by no means basic to Hermes' character. But we know of the phallic form in the sphere of the Titanic divinities, where it denotes a very massive aspect of primal ideology.

It appears, then, that the figure of Hermes can be traced far back to an age whose habits of thought and perception were overcome by the new spirit. But there is a great chasm indeed between what we surmise of the ancient figure and the Homeric Hermes with his brilliance and inexhaustible abundance.

What is the underlying thought in the concept of Hermes?

Of the spheres in which Hermes is thought of as operating, one or another has been put forward as his original realm, and then efforts have been made to show how his functions and nature were in the course of time extended until the picture we know was filled out. In the science of religion it has been accepted as fact that the configuration of a god, aside from the miraculous power with which he operates, possesses no meaningful and necessary unity, and could therefore not have manifested itself to thought and perception as an entity at one given time; rather must the concept have gradually been enriched and extended in the degree that the circumstances of its worshippers' life changed and their needs expanded. This view premises a remarkable vagueness in conceptions of gods and is patently refuted by a single glance at the configuration of a Greek god. In the case of Hermes the inadequacy of this view is particularly striking. It is as if the nimble and agile god always evaded lumbering attempts to grasp him. An attempt can indeed be made to have his history begin with participation in the life of flocks and shepherds; or one can mark his fructifying power, or his connection with the dead, as the beginning. He is active in all these realms. And not he alone, indeed, but many another deity with him. But his activity has a special style. And this style of his is so peculiar and so plainly delineated, it recurs so unerringly in all spheres of action, that we need only have observed it once to have no further doubt about his essence. Then we perceive both the unity of his functions and the meaning of his configuration. In whatever he may produce or foster the same idea is manifested, and that idea is Hermes.

Petitions are directed to all gods to give "the good," and they are praised as "givers of good,"[5] but this formula is applied to Hermes in particular.[6] He is "the friendliest of the gods to men and the most generous giver."[7] But *how* does he bestow his gifts? To understand this we need only think of his magic wand, which gives him the epithet *chrysorrapis* ("of the golden wand") in Homer; he is "bearer of the golden rod, giver of good."[8]

From him comes gain, cleverly calculated or wholly unexpected, but mostly the latter. That is his true characterization. If a man finds valuables on the road, if a man has a sudden stroke of luck, he thanks Hermes. The regular word for any windfall is *hermaion,* and the familiar expression for avidity is "common Hermes" (*koinos Hermes*). To be sure, a man must often take a good deal of trouble before he receives the gift of this god, but in the end it is always a lucky find. So the chorus of Aeschylus' *Eumenides* prays: "Ever may the rich produce of its mines pay the gods' gift of lucky gain" (*hermaion*).[9] It is Hermes in whom the merchant trusts; from him comes the art of sly calculation, but also the lucky chance without which his shrewdness is futile. As the true god of trade, later sculpture shows him with a full purse in his hand. But the favorable moment and its profitable exploitation are so much in the foreground that even thieves could regard themselves as his special protégés.

Even in infancy he proved himself master of the art of thieving, by stealing his brother Apollo's cattle and foiling pursuit. This is recounted in the *Homeric Hymn,* amusingly and at length. He is even said to have spirited Apollo's bow and quiver away at the very moment that Apollo was upbraiding him for the theft.[10] Similar tricks were added on in later times. The *Hymn* is unsparing of epithets in praise of his ingenuity, cunning, and deceit. Some of these recur in his cult. Perhaps the Homeric epithet *eriounes* or *eriounios,* applied to Hermes but of uncertain meaning, is one of these; at least the ancients so interpreted the word. In the epic he is so much the master thief that, as we have noticed, the gods thought of employing him to steal the body of Hector from Achilles.[11] It was by thievery that he once freed Ares from imprisonment.[12] His son, the arch-thief Autolycus, has already been mentioned; whatever Autolycus touched passed from sight.[13] Of the knavery of his other son, Myrtilus, we shall speak presently. In the *Homeric Hymn* Apollo says to the infant Hermes, "I most surely believe that you have broken into many a well-built house and stripped more than one poor wretch bare this night."[14] Thus he is the true patron of all robbery, whether perpetrated by heroes in the grand style or by poor devils. "Lord of those who do their business by night," he is called by Euripides.[15] Hipponax calls him

"companion of thieves,"[16] and in the *Homeric Hymn* he "ponders
deeds such as knavish folk pursue in the dark night-time."[17]
From him one may learn to commit perjury with the most guile-
less face, if the situation demands it; as a little boy he himself
swore falsely to his brother Apollo to clear himself of suspicion
of cattle-lifting.[18] And so Autolycus says that as favorite of
Hermes he is preeminent over all in the arts of thievery and perjury.[19]

This then is the "good," in Hermes' manner of giving it. A
number of gods are expressly called "giver of joy" (*charidotes*),
as for example Dionysus and Aphrodite. Hermes too has this
epithet, but what it means in his case we can see from the festival of Hermes Charidotes in Samos, where thievery and robbery
were permissible.[20] But Hermes protects not only palpable
knavery but also every kind of craftiness and deception, even the
much deplored arts of womankind by which even a clever man
is victimized. When the gods endowed and decked woman, who
was to cause man's fall, it was Hermes who "contrived within her
lies and crafty words and a deceitful nature."[21] Everything lucky
and without responsibility that befalls man is a gift of Hermes.
He is the god of jolly and unscrupulous profit. But this involves
an obverse: profit and loss belong together. If one man becomes
rich in a twinkling, another becomes a pauper in a twinkling. The
mysterious god who suddenly puts a treasure trove in a needy
man's way, as suddenly makes treasure vanish.

3

Hermes is the friend of flocks and the bestower of fruitfulness.
But not at all in the same fashion as other gods; if we look closely
we see the same familiar Hermes.

"No god shows such care for flocks and their increase," says
Pausanias,[22] and this is confirmed by innumerable witnesses. In
the *Homeric Hymn* care of herds is expressly attributed to him.[23]
In Ithaca the shepherd makes offerings to the Nymphs and
Hermes.[24] His association with Hecate in Hesiod's praise of that
goddess[25] is very significant: "She is good in the byre with Hermes

to increase the stock. The droves of kine and wide herds of goats and flocks of fleecy sheep, if she will, she increases from a few, or makes many to be less." The *Iliad* tells that Phorbas possessed rich flocks of sheep, for Hermes loved him best of all Trojans and blessed him with wealth.[26] The name of Hermes' beloved, Polymele, means "rich in sheep"; she bore him a son whose name, Eudorus, which means "goodly giver," recalls his father.[27] The invention of the shepherd's pipe is ascribed to Hermes in his *Hymn*.[28] A series of epithets, which recur in the cult also, characterize him as shepherd and god of flocks. On vase paintings we see him driving a herd before him. The famous statue of Hermes Criophorus shows him carrying a ram on his shoulders; he was so represented by Calamis in the temple at Tanagra. Legend told how he had once averted a pestilence which was raging in the city by striding around its walls with a ram on his shoulders; to commemorate this the handsomest of the ephebi did the same at the festival of Hermes.[29]

What was the nature of the favor for which the shepherd prayed to Hermes? How did he care for the flocks?

There can be no doubt that he is their guide. This is clear from the verses of Aeschylus' *Eumenides* as interpreted by Wilamowitz.[30] Apollo sends his ward Orestes to Athens, and as he is about to leave the Delphian sanctuary, he requests his brother Hermes to "keep watch over him; true to thy name be thou his conductor, as a shepherd guiding this my suppliant." But the gruesome goddesses of vengeance he drives from his temple with imprecations: "Begone, ye herd without a shepherd! Such flock is loved by no one of the gods." Hermes, then, is the kindly spirit who leads the flocks from their folds in the morning and faithfully guides them on their way.

But here too this kindly service is only one side of his activity. The guide can also lead astray; the watcher can also allow treasures to vanish and be lost. None of his deeds is so famous, none was repeated so often and with such pleasure in the rogue's resourcefulness, as his appropriation of the cattle of Apollo and his trick in turning the direction of their footprints so as to baffle all pursuit. Here again we recognize the master of secret power,

who causes both finding and losing. This also explains his rôle in
the increase of herds. He is not, in the proper sense, a god of generation and fertility. In its effect his blessing amounts to the same
thing, but its operation is quite different. We find confirmation
everywhere that the world of other powers is his world also, but
that it always stands under his particular sign, that is, under the
sign of deft guidance and sudden gain. He brings about the wonderfully rapid increase of herds, and this gives him the illusory
character of a god of fertility. But he betrays himself quickly
enough, for his activity has a dubious obverse in the no less
astonishing diminution of herds. The shepherds in the mountain
glades know him as a dangerous worker of mischief.[31] In the
above-mentioned passage of Hesiod where Hermes appears as a
companion of Hecate, it is said that she increases herds "from a
few, if she will, or makes many to be less."[32]

4

In the realm of love too Hermes is at home, and again we encounter the same rogue whom we have learned to know in other
departments. To connect his eroticism with that of the true gods
of love involves a basic misunderstanding. Love too has a share in
luck; indeed, it may entirely hinge on the favor of the moment,
on lucky snatches, on knavery—and that is the realm of Hermes.
Thus he is drawn by Homer, with admirable mastery, in the famous
story of Ares and Aphrodite. He does not find Ares chained and
ridiculed in so painful a situation but that he himself would not
gladly accept exposure three times as disgraceful for the pleasure
of lying in the arms of golden Aphrodite.[33] This is the pleasure of
love regarded as a "windfall" or "theft."[34] Simple folk in Attica
worshipped a god called Tychon, in whose name we recognize a
spirit of luck.[35] His effectiveness may have extended as widely
as the meaning of his name, but he played an especially important part in the erotic sphere. He was equated with Priapus
and counted in the circle of Aphrodite. Now Hermes too bears the
name Tychon, and it fits him admirably.

He appears as a lucky lover of the Nymphs in the *Homeric Hymn to Aphrodite*.[36] The account of Eudorus' mother in the *Iliad* tells how Hermes spied the fairest out and secretly embraced her: "He saw her among the singing women at a dance in honor of Artemis . . . went with her into an upper chamber, and lay with her in secret."[37] Hermes' son is the charioteer Myrtilus who, for the sake of a night of love, perpetrated the unconscionable trick of putting waxen linch-pins in the chariot axles and so caused the death of his master Oenomaus in a chariot race. His tomb was in Arcadian Pheneus behind the temple of Hermes and received annual offerings to the dead, presented by night.[38] In Euboea, Hermes of the bridal chamber bore the epithet Epithalamites. Frequently we find him associated with Aphrodite. Herbs and medicaments whose object was to procure healthy and handsome offspring bore his name. In this connection we should remember that the pillars of Hermes were regularly ithyphallic in form. In Cyllene in Elis, Hermes was worshipped in the shape of a phallus which, like the Hermes pillars, was set up on a base.[39]

But whatever the early age which saw the creation of such cult objects may have thought, in the new religion which is our present concern Hermes is no god of generation and fertility, though he may appear to be such because his miraculous power leads also to unions in love and the begetting of children. Always it is uncanny guidance that constitutes the essence of his activity, leading to desirable gain. He ravishes a beauty from a company of dancers and leads her safely, distant and dangerous though the journey may be, to her lover. So he once conducted Aphrodite to the arms of Anchises.[40] Often we see him in plastic art as a guide of three divine maidens, or as leading the three goddesses to their youthful judge of beauty.

But here too we have the obverse. Just as Hermes leads, secretly and miraculously, to the place of fulfillment, so, in reverse, he is a watchful guide for one who wishes to steal away. A bowl from Corneto[41] shows a young man leaving his sleeping love—perhaps it is Theseus forsaking Ariadne—with Hermes attentively leading the way.

And finally, Hermes is the guide to whom the dead are entrusted.
He even conducted Heracles to the underworld when he went to
fetch the hound of hell.[42] Just as he leads the Nymphs in plastic
art, so, in the last book of the *Odyssey*,[43] he precedes the souls
of the slain suitors, after he had summoned them forth, to accompany them to the place assigned them. This is Hermes Psy-
chopompus, guide of souls, of whom we hear a great deal in
later times. In Homer he appears in this rôle only this one time;
elsewhere when the dead go to the underworld there is no mention of a guide. Nevertheless there can be no doubt that the notion
is very old, for it is abundantly documented in cults and myths.

Of people dying it is said that Hermes seizes them.[44] Ajax, as he
falls upon his sword, calls on Hermes the guide to lay him to
sleep without a struggle.[45] Hermes leads the blind Oedipus on
the way to the spot where he is to depart.[46] The woman of the
island of Ceus who wished to take her own life in the presence of
Pompey poured a libation to Hermes before she drank the poisoned potion and prayed that he lead her by an easy path to
some friendly region in the lower world.[47] His connection with
the dead is proven by the Hermes pillars which stood over
graves.[48]

In this gloomy sphere also Hermes' activity has two directions:
he not only leads downward but also upward. So, in the *Homeric
Hymn to Demeter,* he brings Persephone back from the realm of
the dead. In Aeschylus' *Persians* he is invoked, along with the
earth-goddess and the ruler of the dead, to dispatch the spirit
of the Great King up to the light.[49] In a well-known vase painting in Jena, Hermes, with staff raised, stands before a huge vessel
protruding from the earth from which winged souls flutter forth.
On the last day of the Anthesteria, in which, as an all-souls festival, returning dead were honored and then dismissed with a solemn formula, offerings were made only to Hermes of the Underworld—Hermes Chthonius. As guide of the dead he has been
depicted most beautifully and compellingly by the master of the
Orpheus relief: Hermes is shown leading liberated Eurydice

from the realm of shadow, and as Orpheus turns back towards her, Hermes gently takes her by the hand to lead her back to the darkness. Dead Protesilaus, who languished for love of his wife Laodamia even in the nether-world, Hermes led back to his house, if only for a few hours, as we know from the unfortunately lost *Protesilaus* of Euripides.[50]

6

The Hermes who is linked to the nether-world by the significant epithet Chthonius may often enough appear to be a genuine god of the dead. But always he reveals himself again as guide, and he is therefore the same here as in his other spheres of action. In the favor of guidance the true essence of the god is manifested.

He is the lord of roads. By the roadsides lay the heaps of stones (*hermaion*) from which he received his name; the passerby threw a stone upon them.[51] One such "hill of Hermes" is mentioned in the *Odyssey*;[52] it lay above the town. Upon the stone heap there rose the familiar square pillars of the god with human head, the "herms,"[53] which, in any case, had to have a substructure. These herms stood conspicuously at roadsides, at the entrances of cities and houses, and at the boundaries of markets and districts. A series of epithets honor Hermes as god of ways and entries, as conductor and guide. He is the natural protector of travellers, including, of course, merchants. In older works of art he himself often appears as a traveller, wearing the traveller's hat. His pace is always rapid, indeed flying. The speed which distinguishes him is indicated by the wings on his hat. He possesses "golden" sandals "with which he could fly like the wind over land and sea."[54] This is an apt picture of his nature.

Wherever an entry is made, wherever a road is travelled, there the wonderful companion is at hand. Myth tells of him that he received the infant Dionysus upon its birth, to bring it to its foster mother[55]—a famous subject for plastic art. The throne of Amyclae showed Hermes leading the young Dionysus to heaven.[56] He is present too at the ascent of Persephone; a vase painting[57] shows her emerging slowly out of the earth, with her glance directed to Hermes, who is awaiting her. It is a trait characteristic of his nature that he is suddenly and magically present. At the opening of Aeschylus' *Eumenides*[58] he is suddenly present, with no announcement, in order to accompany Orestes, who is to leave the temple of Apollo at this instant, passing through the band of sleeping goddesses of vengeance and on to Athens. In the *Homeric Hymn* he returns from his knavish adventures, all unnoticed, and slips into the room like a breeze through the keyhole.[59] There is something of a ghostly quality about his arrival and his presence. When a silence fell upon a company it was said "Hermes has come in."[60] The sense of the extraordinary which these words imply is familiar enough to us; in such cases we say, "An angel is passing through the room." It is as if nocturnal mysteries were stirring in broad daylight.

The nocturnal aspect of his nature is revealed by the cap of Hades, by means of which he can make himself invisible. It is by night that he carries out his masterpiece of cattle-lifting, the fame of which is spread over the *Homeric Hymn*. Apollo deems his young brother capable of breaking into rich houses by night and doing his business there noiselessly.[61] In the *Hymn* he is called "spier of the night,"[62] as he is elsewhere called "the good look-out."[63] In the field, men knew how difficult and dangerous it was to "spy upon the enemy alone in the dead of night."[64] It is to this context of thought and experience that the story of the peasant Battus, who worked at night, seems to belong. Battus promised Hermes to say nothing of his cattle-lifting, and when he babbled nevertheless the god transformed him into a stone. The site where this took place was called "Battus' watch";[65] the stone itself into which Battus was transformed was called "the pointer."[66] Hermes' nocturnal sway was honored by the Phaeacians, who poured the last libation in the evening to him, immediately before retiring.[67] With his magic staff he put the wakeful to sleep and roused the sleepers.[68] Thus as guide to Priam he caused a marvellous sleep to fall over the Greek gate-warders who were busy preparing the evening meal.[69] "Gaiety, love, and sweet sleep" are the ravishments which flow from his playing of the lyre,[70] and he is himself called "guide of dreams."[71] For this reason he was remembered with reverence after a significant dream.[72]

Demonic night can be either kindly protection or dangerous leading astray. Its wonderful guidance is nowhere represented with
greater beauty and truth than in the Homeric account of Priam's
night journey. The aged king is about to undertake the fearful
venture of entering the enemy's camp in his own person and
throwing himself as a suppliant before the knees of the most relentless of men, Achilles, who had been daily abusing the corpse
of his favorite son Hector. Zeus sends Hermes to guide him.
"Hermes," he says to his son,[73] "since it is your dearest task to be
a man's companion and you give ear to whom you will, go now,
and so lead Priam to the hollow ships of the Achaeans that none
of the Danaans may see or notice him before he reach the son of
Peleus." Hermes obeys at once and gives the pathetic king divine
assistance, but gives it in the manner usual to the Homeric gods:
no miracle ensues, but a windfall such as the old man had not
even ventured to hope for occurs in a manner apparently quite
natural. At the river where the wagon stops to water the horses a
young man suddenly appears in the road. The hair on Priam's
bent limbs stood straight up and he thought he was doomed. But
the stranger took his hand in friendship and bade him have no
fear. He introduces himself as a squire of Achilles and offers to
conduct Priam safely to his master's door. He can even assure
the troubled father that the corpse of his son has continued uncorrupted despite the abuse it has received. Could any encounter
have been luckier? Joyfully Priam acknowledges the protecting
hand of the deity.[74] But that it was Hermes himself who had
joined him in the figure of a young man he discovers only at the
goal of his journey, at Achilles' door, when his kindly guide
vanishes.[75] Everything had prospered miraculously. The strange
young man had himself leapt upon the wagon, had taken the reins
in his hand, and it was astonishing how mightily the animals
pulled. When they approached the fortifications of the naval encampment, he put the guards to sleep and opened the gate. So
Priam arrived at the abode of Achilles, where Hermes revealed
his identity, imparted advice, and vanished. Achilles dealt hu-

manely with the unhappy king. He delivered his dead son to him
and offered him lodging for the night. But the danger was not
wholly past. If on his departure in the morning he should be
recognized by Agamemnon and the Greeks, it would be all over
with him. Again Hermes took his part. He awakened him before
break of day, reminded him of his peril, and guided him unnoticed out of the camp to the river, where he disappeared. Thereupon the rosy dawn came up.

It is the nocturnal aspect of his activity, the guidance along
ways that are dark, that enables us to appreciate the connection
of Hermes with the spirits of the dead, the realm of death and its
gods. Upon the roads the dead rambled during the night, and they
gathered at crossroads; by the side of the road were graves, and
not infrequently a heap of stones was a tomb.

But it is a mistake to believe that Hermes ever belonged to
the dead more than to the living. It is in his nature not to belong
to any locality and not to possess any permanent abode; always
he is on the road between here and yonder, and suddenly he
joins some solitary wayfarer. In such activity is manifested the
genius of night which, in addition to its mysterious quality and
often in the very midst of it, communicates benison to man. Many
of the things which the Greeks say of the night inevitably suggest Hermes to our minds. "The nights belong to the blessed
gods," says Hesiod,[76] and the traveller should show proper respect to the night. The third *Orphic Hymn* addresses Night as
"the friend of all," and prays her to dispel nocturnal terrors. She
is called "helper" in the *Homeric Hymn to Hermes.*[77] Poetry
after Hesiod and the prose of Herodotus use "the kindly one"
(*euphrone*) for "night." She is the confidante and protector of
lovers. In the *Orphic Hymn* mentioned above her epithet is the
name of the love goddess (Cypris). In Hesiod[78] her child is Friendship (*philotes*)—but, significantly, another of her children is Deceit (*apate*); both belong to the character of Hermes also.

8

But the marvellous and mysterious which is peculiar to night
may also appear by day as a sudden darkening or an enigmatic

smile. This mystery of night seen by day, this magic darkness in
the bright sunlight, is the realm of Hermes, whom, in later ages,
magic with good reason revered as its master. In popular feeling
this makes itself felt in the remarkable silence that may intervene
in the midst of the liveliest conversations; it was said, at such
times, that Hermes had entered the room, as we have mentioned
before. The strange moment might signify bad luck or a friendly
offer, some wonderful and happy coincidence.

The *Odyssey* describes an occurrence of this kind, and incidentally brings the mysterious friend of solitary travellers before
our eyes with the most convincing verisimilitude. Odysseus had
set out alone to find his companions who had remained behind
in the house of Circe. Unfamiliar with the locality, he was walk-
ing through the valleys, when, quite near Circe's dwelling,
Hermes—it could be no other—accosted him, in the guise of a
young man.[79] From him Odysseus learned what a dangerous enterprise he had embarked upon. Within, there lived a sorceress
who had already bewitched his companions and would now hold
him fast also. But it was possible for him to get the better of the
uncanny woman if he would take with him the magic herb, which
Hermes himself pulled out of the soil. Armed with this charm
Odysseus could knock at the strange door without fear.—So
Hermes manifested himself in the midst of wild solitude. We
sense the peculiar twilight mood, and though the time is daylight, we think of the uncertainties of the night which may suddenly be transformed by the sense of some secret kindly presence into a feeling of reassurance and deep happiness.

The night is a world in itself. Only through it can we fully
understand the realm whose divine figure is Hermes.

9

A man who is awake in the open field at night or who wanders
over silent paths experiences the world differently than by day.
Nighness vanishes, and with it distance; everything is equally far
and near, close by us and yet mysteriously remote. Space loses
its measures. There are whispers and sounds, and we do not know

where or what they are. Our feelings too are peculiarly ambiguous. There is a strangeness about what is intimate and dear, and a seductive charm about the frightening. There is no longer a distinction between the lifeless and the living, everything is animate and soulless, vigilant and asleep at once. What the day brings on and makes recognizable gradually, emerges out of the dark with no intermediary stages. The encounter suddenly confronts us, as if by a miracle: What is the thing we suddenly see—an enchanted bride, a monster, or merely a log? Everything teases the traveller, puts on a familiar face and the next moment is utterly strange, suddenly terrifies with awful gestures and immediately resumes a familiar and harmless posture.

Danger lurks everywhere. Out of the dark jaws of the night which gape beside the traveller, any moment a robber may emerge without warning, or some eerie terror, or the uneasy ghost of a dead man—who knows what may once have happened at that very spot? Perhaps mischievous apparitions of the fog seek to entice him from the right path into the desert where horror dwells, where wanton witches dance their rounds which no man ever leaves alive. Who can protect him, guide him aright, give him good counsel? The spirit of Night itself, the genius of its kindliness, its enchantment, its resourcefulness, and its profound wisdom. She is indeed the mother of all mystery. The weary she wraps in slumber, delivers from care, and she causes dreams to play about their souls. Her protection is enjoyed by the unhappy and persecuted as well as by the cunning, whom her ambivalent shadows offer a thousand devices and contrivances. With her veil she also shields lovers, and her darkness keeps ward over all caresses, all charms hidden and revealed. Music is the true language of her mystery—the enchanting voice which sounds for eyes that are closed and in which heaven and earth, the near and the far, man and nature, present and past, appear to make themselves understood.

But the darkness of night which so sweetly invites to slumber also bestows new vigilance and illumination upon the spirit. It makes it more perceptive, more acute, more enterprising. Knowledge flares up, or descends like a shooting star—rare, precious, even magical knowledge.

And so night, which can terrify the solitary man and lead him astray, can also be his friend, his helper, his counsellor.

10

This picture falls short of a true likeness of Hermes, but it does have something of all of his characteristics. We need only transpose it to a more masculine and saucier pitch and the spirit of what is peculiarly Hermes will stand before us.

Danger and protection, terror and reassurance, certainty and straying—all of these night conceals within herself. Her domain is the rare and unexpected, the sudden presentiment, unfettered by place and time. She guides and prospers the recipient of her favor, and enables him, without his expecting it, to come upon some great windfall. To all who require her protection she is even-handed; she offers herself to all, and permits all to savor her benevolence. Such too is the world of Hermes. Like every world it has its lofty and its humble sphere. Both depend on good opportunity, the favor of the moment, the luck of the road; in both, mobility, ingenuity, briskness are the highest virtues, and the goal is the treasure that suddenly bursts into light.

Broad indeed was the view that surveyed this world, lively indeed the eye that perceived its configuration to be that of a god and was able to recognize the profundity of the divine even in roguery and irresponsibility. It is in the full sense a world, that is to say, a whole world, not a fraction of the total sum of existence, which Hermes inspirits and rules. All things belong to it, but they appear in a different light than in the realms of the other gods. Whatever happens comes as on wings from heaven, and entails no obligation; whatever is done is a master stroke, and its enjoyment involves no responsibility. A man who chooses this world of gain and the favor of its god Hermes must accept loss also, for there cannot be the one without the other.

11

The Vedic Hindus worshipped a god whose qualities must inevitably recall Hermes to our minds. His name is Pushan, and

Oldenberg writes of him: "The ever recurrent characteristic of his actions lies in the fact that he knows the way, leads the way, that he saves a man from straying, that he can guide one that has gone astray back to the way and can find one that is lost. He has been regarded as a god of agriculture and husbandry, but in fact he protects agriculture and husbandry only insofar as he guides the furrow made by the plow in the right direction, and insofar as, equipped with a goad, he follows the cattle on their way to prevent their getting lost. . . . He conducts the bride on a sure way from the house of her parents to the house of her husband. . . . He also conducts the dead into the beyond. . . . A man who is starting on an enterprise makes an offering to Pushan. In the offerings distributed to all gods and spirits morning and evening, Pushan, who prepared the way, receives his at the threshold of the house. He drives evil from the path, the wolf and the highwayman. . . . He performs missions for the sun in a golden ship, both on the sea and in the air. This knower of roads who guards from being lost can also find what is lost or hidden, and causes men to find the same. . . . His manner of giving treasure to men is that he permits them to find it. . . ."[80]

All this applies to Hermes, word for word, and one is tempted to regard the two gods as doubles. But with all their similarity they are in fact very dissimilar. The Hindu god possesses power over roads and all that moves and happens upon them, and he employs this power for the advantage and benefit of men who worship him. He is thus the special god of a specific section of this world, and there his sway is what the class of peaceable and righteous men would have it; he guides them truly and protects them from all possible danger. "He drives evil from the path, the wolf and the highwayman."

But Hermes protects highwaymen and thieves, and even though he conducts pious wayfarers safely past them, it is the thieves who seem particularly close to his nature and heart. This signifies a huge expansion of the divine sphere of operation. Its compass is no longer delimited by human wishes but rather by the totality of existence. Hence it comes about that this compass contains good and evil, the desirable and the disappointing, the lofty and the base. Men did hope for Hermes' favor in making their way through danger successfully; he is said to have been the first to "cleanse" the roads, and the stone mounds seem to be an evidence of this.[81] But the *Homeric Hymn* which closes with the statement that Hermes "accompanies all men and gods" is not oblivious of the other side when it adds, "Often, indeed, he bestows benefits, yet beyond measure he deceives mortal men in the dark of night."[82]

This Hermes is not a power who provides assistance in specific needs of life; he is the spirit of a constellation which recurs in most diverse conditions and which embraces loss as well as gain, mischief as well as kindliness. Though much of this must seem questionable from a moral point of view, nevertheless it is a configuration which belongs to the fundamental aspects of living reality, and hence, according to Greek feeling, demands reverence, if not for all its individual expressions, at least for the totality of its meaning and being.

12

The world of Hermes is by no means a heroic world. An Odysseus and a Diomedes invoke Athena at their nocturnal enterprise, and the goddess comes.[83] But Dolon, who is setting out upon a quite similar adventure during the same night but whose reliance is not on the spirit of heroism but rather upon craftiness, slyness, and above all luck, recommends himself, in Euripides' *Rhesus*,[84] to Hermes, who is to guide him safe to his destination and back.

Hence Hermes is also the right god of the aptness that makes a servant indispensable to his master. Odysseus, in the guise of a beggar, boasts to Eumaeus that "by the blessing of Hermes . . . there is no one living who would make a more handy servant than I should—to put fresh wood on the fire, chop fuel, carve, cook, pour out wine, and do all those services that poor men have to do for their betters."[85] According to the *Homeric Hymn*[86] Hermes invented the kindling of fire, and he is worshipped and depicted along with Hestia, the goddess of the hearth.[87] He is also regarded as the prototype for offering sacrifice. Little wonder that this master of handiness and diligence himself became servant in Olympus, and in particular the servant and messenger of Zeus.[88] Alcaeus and Sappho already know him as cupbearer to the

gods.[89] Of this the *Iliad* knows nothing; there the messenger of
the gods is Iris, and when Zeus sends Hermes to give Priam safe
conduct,[90] he calls upon him as one "most disposed to escort men
on their way"—which indicates that he regards him no more a
servant or messenger than other gods, to whom he also might
assign missions on occasion. In the *Odyssey,* on the other hand,
Hermes is accepted as the messenger of Zeus.[91] But at whatever
period this concept gained currency, for us the important thing
is that it is thoroughly in keeping with the basic character of the
god. None could seem better suited to run errands for the god of
heaven than Hermes, who flies away quick as lightning and mysteriously bobs up everywhere. Among the accomplishments which
he found useful in his capacity as herald his vigorous voice must
be reckoned; according to legend[92] this gave him the victory in a
contest with the redoubtable Stentor. Later he often appears as
master of speech, and is already such for Hesiod, for it is Hermes
who gave Pandora her voice.[93]

But though the world of Hermes is not dignified, and indeed
in its characteristic manifestations produces a definitely undignified and often enough dubious impression, yet—and this is truly
Olympian—it is remote from vulgarity and repulsiveness. A spirit
of gaiety, a superior smile, hovers over and illuminates it, and
absolves even its boldest knaveries. And this easy laughter enables
us to understand, provided our approach is unbiased, that this is
a capacious world and that there is no life that does not at some
time share in it and require its benison. Every man has something
of the soldier of fortune and freebooter and is more bounden to
this aspect than he can himself possibly be aware. To that same
degree Hermes must be his god. Nor is his realm lacking in the
sublime. The victory of success of whatever sort stands under the
banner of his luck and his love of booty. Love itself has plenty of
craft and trickery, and yet these too are lovable.

The favor of Hermes lends charm to the works of men.[94] He
himself consorts much with the Graces, called Charites. In
Homer he appears with the winning beauty of the first bloom of
youth.[95] At the festival of Hermes in Tanagra the handsomest
ephebe was assigned the rôle of playing the ram-bearing god.[96]
The blessing in Aristophanes' *Peace* combines "Hermes, the
Graces, the Hours, Aphrodite, and Pothos."[97]

Hermes the young, handsome, nimble, and deft, the amiable and beloved, is also the right tutelary spirit of athletic contests and gymnasia. His festivals are marked by games of boys and youths. That this may also involve the god's stark mischievousness is suggested by the story of his son Myrtilus, the charioteer, mentioned above.

And finally we again recognize the essence of the god, transfigured and infinitely exalted, in his music. The *Homeric Hymn* tells how he invented the lyre and then gave it to Apollo. On Mount Helicon there were to be seen statues of Apollo and Hermes striving for the lyre.[98] In Megalopolis there was a common sanctuary to the Muses, Apollo, and Hermes.[99] The famous musician Amphion was said to have been instructed by Hermes himself in playing the lyre.[100] The invention of the shepherd's pipe also is ascribed to him in the *Homeric Hymn*. Here we have the master of ingenuity, the guide of the flocks, the friend and lover of the Nymphs and Graces, the spirit of night, sleep, and dreams. Nothing can give better expression to the gay and at the same time darkly mysterious, enchanting, and tender elements in Hermes than the magically sweet tones of lyre or flute. In the *Homeric Hymn* Apollo says of Hermes' newly invented instrument, "Truly, here are three in one to be had for the asking—gaiety, love, and sweet sleep."[101]

13

In a concept of deity of such a sort there can be no purpose in differentiating between earlier and later qualities and in seeking for some line of development to connect one with the other. Despite their multiplicity they are in fact only one, and if a single trait actually did come to the fore later than others, it still remains the same basic meaning which has found a new expression. Whatever may have been thought of Hermes in primitive times, a splendor out of the depths must once have so struck the eye that it perceived a world in the god and the god in the whole world.

Such is the origin of the figure of Hermes which Homer knew and which later ages retained.

IV

THE NATURE OF THE GODS

SPIRIT AND FORM

1

A PROCESSION OF brilliant figures has passed before us, and we stand and reflect. Who are they, these powers that carry the wealth of the world in their hands? Each severally has presented himself to us in his particular mode: but what is the essence that is common to them all and makes gods of them? It is easy to pronounce the word "god," but what can its meaning be here, among Homer's Greeks? The question has surely been often posed, but never in earnest, and that for no other reason than that the huge difference of ancient Greek religion from our own has made it inconceivable to us that it could merit complete earnestness. But should not the difference rather challenge us, indeed engage our closest attention? To be sure, for complete earnestness in penetration it is essential that we be ready and able to disregard the premises of the Judeo-Christian conception of the world and admit a wholly new viewpoint from which to regard being and happening. But nothing could be more interesting than to inquire what a human society like the Greek in its early period of genius understood by divinity or what the nature of the beings might be to whom it directed its most exalted and reverent regard.

2

Despite very great diversity in character and temperament, these gods all possess the same nature. Hence they are regularly contrasted to the human race as a unity; it is "the gods" who determine the human lot, and frequently enough the poet says simply "god" or "the deity," as if, in the final analysis, it were only a single power that affected earthly existence from above.

Common to all of them is immortality, and they are called the eternal ones who exist forever. But this must surely not be hardened into the dogma that they were never born; in view of the immeasurableness of their life such a detail is insignificant. Nevertheless they could never be imagined save in the most radiant

h. For the Hellenic idea of god this is very signifies as a symbol of their peculiar essence. Other
lt no compunction in thinking of their deity as
ry ancient; no image could more forcefully sug-
e wisdom they possessed. But for the Greek his
_eelings resisted such a notion. For him old age was a con-
dition of the weariness, impoverishment, and darkening of nature,
that vital and holy nature from which he could never at all separate the spirit. Even the highest wisdom must belong not to a
region beyond life but to life's most buoyant energy, and knowledge must dwell not on the hoary countenance turned away from
the world but on the bright and youthful brow and the blooming
lips of Apollo.

"Undying and ageless"—that is the mark of everything divine.
In the *Homeric Hymn to Aphrodite*, in her farewell to the mortal
to whom she had granted her love, the goddess complains that
soon—and he was a quite young man—old age would pitilessly
overtake him, "sorrowful and troublesome age, which is hated of
the gods."[1] If one is worthy of dwelling with the gods he must
receive eternal youth as well as immortality. So it befell "fair
Ariadne, daughter of Minos" whom "golden-haired Dionysus"
won to be his wife.[2] Loving Calypso offered Odysseus the same
fortune, but he was impelled to return home to his faithful wife,
though he knew that she could not be compared with the goddess,
"she a mortal woman with one immortal and ever young."[3] Beauty
as well as the freshness of youth belongs to the image of the gods.
And beauty could not be perfect, in the Greek view, without tall
stature. Beautiful indeed were the Nymphs with whom Artemis
played, "but she herself stood a full head taller than the others."[4]
When Demeter made herself known to dwellers on earth she suddenly stood before their terrified eyes in radiant beauty and
stature.[5] But a reverent awe of nature forbade imagination to en-
large tallness of stature into hugeness. Not as giant or monster
but in the handsomest proportions of bodily form with which nature produced its supreme works must deity manifest itself.
Eternal youth, beauty, and in addition power and knowledge,
which often seemed limitless—possession of these qualities made

the gods' existence blessed. They are expressly called "the blessed."
Their dwelling is in eternal radiance on high, never visited by
winds, rain, or snow; there they live in daily pleasure,[6] high above
men, whose need and suffering can never reach their height.

Should these perfect beings allow their blessedness to be
troubled by too serious involvement with mankind and its distress? Not only Hephaestus finds it intolerable for gods to wrangle
about mortals and be disturbed in their pleasures;[7] Apollo himself finds it inconsistent with his dignity as a god to fight with
another god for the sake of a human.[8] These are after all but poor
creatures who after a brief bloom wither and vanish.[9] The Muses
in the hall of the gods above sing of the eternal majesty of the
heavenly ones and contrast the toil and helplessness of mankind,
for whom there is no deliverance from death and no protection
against old age.[10] Thus it is only by contrast with mankind that
the gods become fully aware of their grandeur and their oneness.

We ourselves are accustomed to think of the divine being as
preoccupied with man and his needs and are little concerned with
his existence beyond humanity. But here the spiritual eye seeks
a higher world which is no longer troubled for man's sake; and it
stands enthralled before the vision of its perfection. Only in a
remote reflection are we still able to grasp this vision, but even so
it remains powerful. However zealously an Olympian may concern
himself for men and their needs, the son of eternity always returns to the majesty of his heavenly splendor. There, in the
ethereal heights, there is neither pain nor anxiety, neither age
nor death. In the rapture of imperishable youth, beauty, and grandeur they stride through the spaces which shine for them eternally. There they encounter their peers, brothers and sisters,
friends and loved ones, and one god takes joy in another, for the
splendor of perfection rests upon each figure. To be sure, partisanship for men and peoples sometimes leads to a vigorous argument, but dissension never endures for long, and no day ends
without bringing the gods together in festive pleasure for the
common enjoyment of their divine existence. For they know well
that they are all of equal nobility, a single race whose distinguished traits are unmistakably inscribed upon the features of

each. It is with a picture of this blissful unity in heaven that the poet of the *Iliad* significantly concludes his first canto. The rulers have disagreed; the lord of heaven has promised Thetis to bestow honor upon her son and to humble those who affronted him. Thereupon strife begins in heaven; Hera reproaches her husband vigorously, and is sharply rebuked by him. With ill-repressed anger she sits silent, and rebellion moves through the ranks of the gods. Thereupon her son Hephaestus rises to make peace. He calls it intolerable for gods to wrangle for the sake of men and spoil their pleasure of the Olympian banquet; all would be well if only his mother would be reconciled and speak amiably to his father, so that he should not grow angry and make them all feel his superior might. And Hera smiles. Gladly she accepts the goblet which her son hands her. Joy returns to the countenances of the other gods. Laughter rings out, and song, until evening falls, and Zeus goes with his wife, who after all loves him, to their conjugal bed. So the mighty event of the *Iliad* begins with strife among the gods which is quickly dissolved into the harmonious gaiety of the divine world, whereas in the human world struggle and suffering begin in all seriousness.

Occasionally the poet permits us a glimpse, if only in a fleeting flash, of the dwelling places of the gods, their assembly halls and palaces, as the artificer Hephaestus built them on the heights of Olympus and adorned them with gold. But these glimpses present no clear and consistent picture. Nor does it really matter, for though the memory of the Thessalian mountain of the gods never faded and was kept alive by the very name of the "Olympian" gods, men were nevertheless convinced that these gods had their dwelling on no peak, majestically as it might tower heavenward, but on high in the lofty heaven. Even in the sanctuaries which men instituted for their worship they lingered only briefly. They came down to earth from heaven's ether, and thither returned; it was there that the gaze and uplifted hands of the petitioner sought them. Agamemnon prays to "Zeus, most glorious, supreme, that dwellest in heaven and commandest the storm cloud,"[11] and Telemachus speaks of his dwelling in Ether, though he calls him the "Olympian."[12] To direct the fortunes of battle the father of men and gods descends upon the peaks of Ida,[13] and it is from heaven that he sends his daughter Athena to the Trojan fields of battle.[14]

So high are the gods exalted above human existence. And yet their nature is closely kin to the human. To begin with, their outward appearance is the same, though perfection and imperishability remain the privilege of deity. They have incomparably greater knowledge and power than man, but share in human inclinations and passions. Even suffering is not wholly alien to them. The "blessed" often mourn for human favorites. Indeed they themselves can be directly affected by suffering. Apollo had to endure bondage to an earthly master for years; Aphrodite was wounded by the spear of Diomedes, and Dione comforted her with an inventory of gods who had suffered similarly.[15] Once Zeus threatens that his lightning will inflict such wounds on Hera and Athena, if they flout his will, that it would require ten years to heal them;[16] nor did he always stop at mere threats.[17] Finally, the natural kinship between mortals and immortals is put beyond all doubt by marriages between them. Goddesses give birth to children of human fathers, and very many clans boasted that a god had descended to a mortal woman to beget the progenitor of their race. It is this proud and profound belief which is responsible for many of the love stories that early brought the charge of immorality against the Greek world of gods.

The relationship between man and gods, then, is that they are akin to one another, and yet separated by an abyss. Pindar expresses it plainly:

> There is one
> race of men, one race of gods; both have breath
> of life from a single mother. But sundered power
> holds us divided, so that the one is nothing, while for the other the
>   brazen sky is established
> their sure citadel forever. . . .[18]

In the conception of their corporeality, too, this relationship finds a symbolic expression, for with all their similarity the heaven-dwellers are still of much finer clay. They eat no bread and drink no wine, as men do, and therefore it is not blood that flows in their veins but a current of a heavenly and eternal element.[19]

We know that there was a time when the status of the gods was different. The spiritual aspects of that epoch were the subject of our second chapter. Then they dwelt not in heaven but upon earth. Homer preserves distinct memories of the citadel of the gods on Olympus in Thessaly and of Ida as the mountain of Zeus, and elsewhere, too, many indications have survived of the primal awe of "the great mountains, the abode dear to the gods," as Hesiod says.[20] They were still closer to man when they dwelt in clefts of the earth, in caves, in trees, or in rivers. These divine neighbors must have been much more intimate with their worshippers than the dwellers in the region of clouds and remote ether, whose home no son of man could visit and even the eye could only surmise. Their outward appearance seemingly removed them farther from man than did the appearance of the heavenly gods. They preferred to show themselves in the bodies of animals, as is proven by old legends in which Zeus appears as a bull, Poseidon as a horse, and female figures similar to Hera or Artemis as a cow or a she-bear. These animal forms, and surely the monstrosity of hybrid forms, were doubtless assumed in order to arouse dark fears in the heart of the faithful and to set limits to their approach. But in the thoroughly human traits of the divine countenances of Homer there resides a sublimity which enjoins keeping one's distance much more than any animal or fantastic form could possibly do, and they are much more suggestive of the bright faraway than of the homely places of our earthly world. It is a shining illumination that distinguishes the god of the new age from that of the earlier period. The richness of his eternal existence is ennobled by freedom and magnanimity.

A transformation must once have taken place by which a superior race of gods achieved dominion over religious thought. Greek myth has retained distinct traces of the defeat of an old faith. Zeus, so it is related, overthrew his father Cronus and the Titans and shut them up in the darkness of Tartarus.[21] The enormous significance of this drama of the gods was long felt. In

Aeschylus' tragedies the ancient powers still oppose the r
with fearful charges, and can only with difficulty be r
Much here remains enigmatic. But there can be no do
with the victory of Zeus there ascended to the throne of heaven a
nobler race of gods, one destined for world-rule in a higher sense.
The magnificent opening of Pindar's *First Pythian Ode* praises
the blessed harmony of the new world of gods, which hearkens
with rapture to notes of Apollo's lyre and the Muses' choir, while
Zeus's opponents, the savage enemies of the gods upon earth, in
the sea, and in fearful Hades, hear the heavenly song with de-
testation.

But it was only as a ruling community that the old powers were
cast down into the abyss by the new society of gods. That is the
meaning of the statement that Zeus shut the Titans up in Tartarus. His wisdom and strength were far superior to the Titans'
cunning, as Hesiod most significantly makes us realize in the case
of Prometheus. But the Titans too, as later stories told, were
again redeemed. This is surely no independent invention of a
poetic sense of justice, for the conceptions of Cronus as ruler on
the isles of the blessed[22] or as god and king of the golden age[23]
must belong, whatever their first appearances in literature may be,
to the substance of the ancient belief which never perished. Despite their opposition to the Olympians, the existence and the
sacredness of the primal forces continued to be recognized. We
shall see how Homeric poetry mentions much of the ancient belief with respect, though that poetry is a convinced adherent of
the Olympians. From the background of the old beliefs the figure
of the new divinity stands out all the more sharply.

The new belief must have attained dominion in the pre-
Homeric age. The relatively small circle of divine personages who
control destiny in Homer and who continued paramount in the
great age of Greece must have enjoyed general and well-estab-
lished recognition. Whenever the poet places a divinity in a specific relationship to earthy existence, the situation is presented as
simply a matter of course. The sure strokes, often fleeting but
unmistakable nevertheless, by which he characterizes them prove
that each of them possessed clearly defined lineaments, which
were well known to all hearers. Knowledge of the vanquished

gods derives for the most part only from myth; the new lords of heaven, on the other hand, were present to the believing temper every moment. Generally recognized relationships bound them into a close society, whose uncontested chief was Zeus and whose genealogy could be traced back to Oceanus and Tethys, "the primal parents of the gods."[24] The individual treatments above will have shown that the basic character of these Homeric gods was identical with what we know of the gods of the classical period. Post-Homeric centuries may have discovered many a new trait in them but their essence continued the same. Artists vied with one another to conjure them out of marble just as Homer sang of them. The contemporary of Pindar, Phidias, and the great tragic poets could not forget that the figures whose loftiness the Homeric world glorified were the same in which he himself believed. The Greek religion which we know is therefore the creation of the cultural epoch anterior to Homer. Unfortunately we know too little of this age to distinguish between early and late and to recognize a turn to the new at any given point. But there can be no doubt that the age was one of powerful genius, and our admiration can only increase when we penetrate deeper into the meaning of the new concept of the world and simultaneously become aware that with it the spiritual direction of Hellenism was determined.

Among other peoples also, religion received its historical form only as the result of some great transformation. Moses and the prophets preached the doctrine of one holy God to the people of Israel, and from the writings of the Old Testament we know what zeal was required to woo the people from the ancient altars and lead them upon the path of the new fear of God. In Persia, Zarathustra made an uncompromising break with the ancient cult and relegated its gods to hell. The "wise lord" whose shining greatness was manifested through Zarathustra's lips declared war against everything that was not of himself or after his kind. In both cases, among the Israelites and among the Persians, the godhead made a decisive break with the natural and rose to an ideal sphere. Among the Persians, with the geniuses of power, light, purity, truth, and creative abundance it set itself grandly against the realm of the dark, the impure, the mendacious, and the sterile; among the Israelites it stood forth as the sole sanction for judg-

ment and benison to the chosen people. So too the Greek divinity
ascended from the natural to a higher existence. Here too the question must at last be posed with all seriousness: In what direction
did the conception of god move from the natural, and what new
meaning did it acquire? We shall no longer believe that it is less
important to investigate the objects of highest reverence of a
people as spiritually gifted as the Greek than it is to investigate
that of the children of Israel. The polar differences between the
conceptions of god of these two peoples have hitherto greatly
embarrassed religious scholarship and have necessitated various
games of hide-and-go-seek. People spoke of a Greek "religion of
art," and imagined they had removed the problem to a less sensi-
tive area. But no intelligent person would suggest that the great
Greek epics addressed only the aesthetic sensibilities of their listeners. They showed them compelling pictures of all the perfections he aspired to, and glorified no other gods than those to
which the compulsion of all his energies attracted him. We must
not judge so youthful and vigorous a civilization by the gauge of
our own divided state. In our Christian Europe religion walks
alongside material and intellectual life, but they continue alien
to each other, even where they touch. Youthful and unbroken civilizations, on the other hand, know of no religion that is not inextricably interwoven with the totality of human existence. Here
all experience, thought, achievement, find their endlessness and
glory in the idea of god. It is a worthy task indeed to investigate
this idea of god among a people like the Greek, and finally to
pose for Greece too the question which Asiatic religions have long
made familiar to us: Through what new revelation of the divine
did Zeus, Athena, and Apollo become the objects of the highest
vision and the loftiest devotion?

4

The Homeric world knows a large number of divine personages,
but their importance differs widely. There are only a few who are
thought of as present in the contest of life and who enjoy
worship, and among these few the great deities whose sanctity
constitutes religion in the proper sense comprise a very small

group. They alone hold sway over all existence, they alone are always and everywhere near to the pious temper. The others are limited to specific areas, and according to the importance of their areas their activity may be greater or less, but they do not fill life as a whole; or perhaps they lack even such restricted validity, so that they have no share at all in worship but belong only to legend. Among these relegated divinities there are brilliant names, deities who were once powerful, even dominant. Some loom so large in mythic narratives that we might be tempted to judge their esteem in religion accordingly; but we must not be deceived: the numerous specific indications of a living faith yield a quite different picture. For such a faith the divine in the higher sense is limited to the small chosen band. If we wish to understand the spirit of the new revelation we must inquire who these are and how they are distinguished from the others. The others, who must recede, belong to the older faith. Two worlds of religious thought stand opposed to one another, the one brilliantly present, and the other more and more vanishing into the dark. Much out of this old world stepped powerfully forward in the post-Homeric age, and even in Homer it is not extinguished but stands in the background. But it was the new spirit that gave Greek religion its specific and lasting contours. It becomes the more important, then, to measure it against the sanctities of the old, so that by realization of what it is not we may come to know what it is.

5

The realm of the ancient gods is always tangential to the religion of the *dead;* in it, indeed, life is a sibling of death. Nothing is more characteristic of the spirit of the ancient realm, and nothing separates it from the new gods more obviously. The dark house of Hades where the dead dwell is "an abomination to the gods."[25] According to the belief of the classical period, Apollo could not come into contact with the dead. In Euripides that god must leave the house of Admetus, whom he loves, because death awaits Alcestis.[26] The goddess Artemis cannot tarry near her favorite Hippolytus because death is near: "Farewell! For me it is not lawful to look on death or to pollute my eyes with the gasps of the dying. I see that you are now near that sad case."[27] In Homer, at all events, the gods do not scruple to touch a corpse. But the realm of death is alien and repulsive to them, and their devotees have no religious worship to spare for it. The cult of the dead is incompatible with worship of the Olympians. Indeed, belief in the Olympians involved the conviction that the dead had no importance whatever for the world of the living, and that persons whose power had been so deeply felt were now to be considered only as strengthless shadows removed to a distance beyond reach.

It has been argued that the new spirit was devoted to light and life with such ardor that, as if blinded, it could no longer see death. In its admirable clarity, the argument went on, existence was mirrored to the last quiver of life, and even the gruesomeness of annihilation was precious to it as *gestalt*. But beyond this point, it was thought, the brightness of this eye did not reach, and therefore for the new religion the deceased was a cipher and the age-old holiness of the past and of death completely extinguished. Convincing as this sounds, its appearance of truth is deceptive. The Homeric religion does know a realm of death, and the deceased who dwell there are certainly not empty ciphers. Though there can no longer be any connection between them and the living, nevertheless a palpable and quite individual notion of their existence and condition does persist. The new spirit did more than merely delimit. Its idea of death and the past proves, upon careful examination, to be as fresh and bold as it is profound. The dead are not excluded from the new outlook; they have merely received a different place. It must be our first task to recognize this place. For inasmuch as belief in the dead in its earlier sense is one of the most significant traits of the older religion, we may expect that its transvaluation in the new spirit will provide a clear index to the basic direction of this new spirit.

6

In the *Iliad* and the *Odyssey* several passages give the impression that the gods of the nether-world possessed for the Homeric age a large importance similar to that of Zeus and his suite. But the closer we look the quicker this impression vanishes. And when we reflect that the dead no longer have any ties with this world and hence no longer receive honors, and that even in their own world they are only phantoms, we may easily fall into the opinion mentioned above, that the world of the dead and its gods had no serious meaning whatever in the Homeric outlook. But suddenly out of this apparent void a new idea confronts us, and we recognize a spiritual fact of great moment in world history. Hades, the lord of the world of the dead, is often named in Homer. More than once the image of his dark majesty is presented to us with gruesome vividness. He is called "the strong," "the unconquerable," "Zeus of the earth's depths."[28] His "house," of which he is called "the mighty warder," is the eternal dwelling of the dead; thither the victor sends him the spirit of the slain. There his dog keeps watch, a greedy monster with many heads and a horrible threatening voice.[29] When we hear of the steeds with which he drives like the wind, we have before our minds at a single stroke the mighty image of the lord of darkness riding out of the yawning earth and in his golden chariot carrying off Persephone, who was innocently playing in the flowery meadow.[30] Ever since, "noble Persephone" has been enthroned below as queen at his side. These rulers hear the curse when a desperate man smites the earth with his hands and invokes their names.[31] In many myths the god of the dead played an important rôle. The *Iliad* tells us that Zeus's son Heracles once fought with him and wounded him grievously.[32] Once his royal hall is lighted up as in a lightning flash, and a huge spectacle is revealed: above, the earth totters, mountains tremble from foot to peak, and the king of the dead springs from his throne with a cry, "in terror lest the ground crack over his head and lay bare his mouldy mansions."[33] After all this we may well believe that the figure of the royal pair of the nether-world was of vital concern to the religious temper of the Homeric age. But that is not the case. If we discount ancient legends and stereotype locutions, not very much is left, and the god whose grandiose aspect occasionally flashes before the poet is of little concern to the living. Nothing is expected of him, and no honors are paid to him. Only the primal sanctity of the curse and the oath seem to obtain a hearing in the lower world. The dead who dwell in the realm of Hades are themselves completely cut off from the world of the living. No prayer and no sacrifice can reach them, and no road can bring them back. And there below, in the place of their eternal doom, what are they? When the eye of the dying breaks, when his psyche forsakes him, it "hastens from the beauteous earth down to that strong house" where it expects no continuation of life but only a shadowy, dream-sodden, or unconscious existence. The only honor that the living can show the dead is that of memory.

The pre-Homeric age held a different view of the dead. Even in Homer the older belief is still at work, as Erwin Rohde's *Psyche* has shown, at least in certain ceremonial usages. Dead Patroclus is honored by having slaughtered upon his pyre and consumed with him not only sheep and oxen, horses and dogs, but also twelve young Trojans captured for this specific purpose: this is inconsistent with the Homeric view that the spirit of the dead is an impotent shadow which is even without clear awareness. Such usages make it easy to see what respect the dead had at one time enjoyed. He was not wholly departed from the circle of the living, but could hear their prayers and protect them with his mysteriously enlarged power. Hence he must be diligently remembered and sacrifices must be offered at his grave, for his demonic wrath pursued with terror and misfortune the indifferent and the offenders. To this belief belongs the awful loftiness of the god of the nether-world, and to it belong the myths about him which the epic poet knows so well are born of its spirit. And this belief in the continued connection with the departed and in their stature and power, which, as everyone knows, was spread over the whole world, the Homeric age had lost entirely. If Homer were our only source, we should never believe that prayers were ever directed to ancestors and that sacrifices were ever offered to them. Here a different view had long come to prevail. When man has reached the term of his life, he is actually done with in this world. In death he will not grow and surely not become worthy of divine honors. His survivors cannot reach him with any gift, and for the future they have nothing more to hope or fear of him. And in the world below, in the silent realm of the departed, he will be no more than a shadow.

How are we to understand this great transformation in thought?

In its attempt to expound the views and usages of ancient peoples modern science shows a remarkable predilection for the crudest motivations, and hence makes little distinction between different peoples and endowments. The prehistoric religion of the Greeks is presented precisely as that of any primitive society, as if the intellectual conceptions which we all admire had emerged, with no intermediate stage, out of a desert of brutishness and magic. Acccordingly fear is alleged to have been the decisive motive for banishing the dead out of the purview of the living, and the burning of his body was a means of liberating the survivors from him as quickly as possible. Hence the burning of funeral pyres would originally be an act of defense, and the belief in the dead, or better the disbelief, as we find it in Homer, would be a sort of self-redemption from anxiety. Proof of this was found in Homer himself, when he declares expressly that the spirit of the dead could be admitted to the realm of shadows only after burning; that is, only through burning could it be released from this world.[34] Anthropology moreover supplies cases where a dead man whose ghostly vexation had become intolerable was actually ex-humed and burned so that he should no longer be troublesome. But what do such instances prove? If in a desperate case where anxiety and horror is still felt for a dead man a civilization which normally buries its dead takes recourse to burning, this is no proof whatever of the original meaning of ritual incineration. And that incineration was practiced everywhere as an honor to the dead and as pious execution of his own will has been latterly maintained with proper emphasis.[35] But even by itself the notion of explaining incineration as a defense device inspired by fear betrays astonishing frivolity. For one enigma it substitutes an-other and greater. Were not the dead at one time an object of sincere reverence, as they again became in the post-Homeric pe-riod? How could the ancient forebears at whose dark visages reverence had so long gazed with deep devotion suddenly have lost all their noble, amiable, and beneficent qualities and retained only the uncanniness which always attaches to death, so that the only attitude towards them could be one of defense?

And yet Rohde was on the right track when he conjectured a kinship of ideas between the new belief in the dead and the burning of bodies, which is regular and without exception in Homer. By destroying the body, burning separates the spirit of the dead from the area of living instantly. And it takes place, as Homer expressly states, for the sake of the dead himself and to do him honor, for he is mightily impelled to depart, and the bond with his previous environment cannot be loosened quickly enough for him. This was the belief of all peoples who customarily destroyed the body by force rather than leave it to gradual decay or even preserve it by artifice. But if the dead himself wishes to depart and it is a duty to help him do so, then with his whole being he must belong to another world and have become alien to ours. Incineration is proof of a peculiar view of the nature of the dead, a belief not begotten of primitive emotions or scruples but possessing the worth of a genuine idea. The dead is not erased from existence but assigned to a different realm of existence, which can only be imagined in the far, far distance. Nevertheless these same peoples are confident that he can upon occasion reappear here and work good or evil. Belief in the dead is, for obvious reasons, almost never consistent.

But in the spirit of the Homeric age this belief acquired the large and lucid configuration which has never yet been adequately appreciated. Here there emerged the sublime thought of life and death which could never again be lost. The first point is that the dead must consistently remain in the other world. He has become an alien in the regions of the living, his own essence impels him away, and so once he reaches the place destined for him he will never return; every tie with him is severed forever and eternally. What should he do in the realm of the sun and of vitality, this impotent shadow, this mute reflection of what has perished? This then is the second point: even in yonder world the dead is no vigorous being, as he once was, but only a thin mist which possesses the form of his former life but none of its capacities, not even consciousness. This is the ultimate consequence of the view that the dead is essentially alien to all living.

The naïve and emotional belief which subsists to this day sets no absolute distinction between death and life. It assumes that the existence of the deceased whom it remembers persists in palpable reality. Even where deeper insight relegates the departed to a different and distant realm of being, nothing is really changed in this respect, for here too they retain their living reality and the past continues its objective subsistence into the present. But in Homer's picture of the world *being* and *have been* are for the first time opposed to one another as magnitudes of different order. It is not as if the dead were simply equated with zero. The new spirit introduces not merely negation but a positive idea. Life which is concluded, the individual who can have no further history, must no longer appear in person and produce effects, neither here nor there, but must be transfigured into a reality of a special kind.

It is in the nature of genius that its newest revelations often rise out of the depths of primeval conceptions and for the first time make them lucid and mature. That is what happened here. To the clear gaze with which the Greek regarded the world afresh, an age-old thought of humanity was vitalized anew. Such is probably the correct designation for the concept that man does survive death, not, however, as a continuing vital force but by a sort of transposition of bodily existence into something shadowy and misty.[36] This true likeness of the deceased, it was thought, continued to be connected with the body in some mysterious way so long as the body was uncorrupted, and by its appearance could terrify or solace the survivors. But if the body were corrupted or wholly destroyed, the likeness withdrew to the remote place destined for it whither so many departed had already preceded it. In its main outlines this view has survived with astonishing fidelity in modern belief in ghosts, which is again valuable evidence of its age, for in the principal points of the problem of existence the oldest convictions are also habitually at the same time the youngest. Now, primitives have sometimes been quite as positive as Homer in declaring that this spirit of the dead was a dull and strengthless creature which could not properly be said to be alive. This is quite consistent: the cloudy likeness of the deceased lacks all of the energies and humors of life, which the body, which is not destroyed, formerly possessed.[37] But in its more naïve stages belief in the dead is always full of contradictions. That deep shudder which we are too ready to call fear, whereas it may also be the expression of a most solemn and sublime mood, repeatedly draws the dead back into the active present. Remarkably and unerringly associated with the natural conception that the dead is only a phantom is the sense of an obscure will with incalculable forces at its disposal. And even when a new home has received him men still do not cease to imagine him near and to fear or hope for all manner of manifestations of his presence.

But in the Homeric age the primal thought that the dead were impotent and dreamy shadows became central to the entire belief in the dead. All that remains of the deceased is actually no more than a delicate breath in human form without either will or power to act. An infinite chasm separates him from the world where consciousness, will, and act rule, and holds his twilight existence fast in yonder ancient realm of night forever. This is a stark denial of the naïve belief and its favorite fancies. And yet it comprises no mere denial. If the departed may not at least continue the active life, which they once led on earth, in the seclusion of the beyond, as other peoples and the later Greeks themselves believed, what reason is there not to declare them null and void? If we follow Homer's thoughts carefully we suddenly realize that he has given a highly ingenious turn to the primitive conception of the impotence of the dead.

The shade of the dead in Hades below, which can no longer function and does not even possess consciousness, which wanders through the eternal night aimless and inactive, is the form of what belongs to the "has-been." It is no cipher and has substantial existence, but its reality is of a special sort. In it everything is past, everything is static and turned backwards, without present and without future. So for the first time in the world the has-been, the past, has here become an idea. The persistence of the dead is no longer an imitation of life; the essentials of life they have lost once and for all. And yet there they stand, solemnly and turned

inward upon themselves, an eternal image. With this the Greek idea
of death was fixed. Despite strong opposition it remained dominant in Greece, if we may call dominant the belief that representative minds professed. Its fullest expression it found in Attic
art of the fifth century, which was destined to give meaningful
life to so many Homeric revelations. The finished life stands upon
tomb-reliefs in its natural posture as a permanent figure, with
moving charm or grave dignity, and the eye, with nothing to direct it to the future, is absorbed in gazing at the eternity of the
past.

And so the bright mind, of whom it could be said that it was
incapable of looking into the realm of extinction and was blind
to its solemn grandeur, did in truth penetrate far beyond the grave
and there perceived things more important than did the worshippers of death and the past. For him the has-been for the first
time unveiled its ghostly lineaments, and beyond the naïve notions of mankind's belief he alone recognized the meaning of
being past and yet possessing eternal reality. In centuries following, to be sure, the old beliefs again came forward, and pious
groups joined together in the certain prospect of an enhanced life
after death. But the idea formulated by the Homeric spirit was
and continued to be in the proper sense Greek. Tragedy, which
as servant of Dionysus, the lord of the dead, seemed destined to
cause the greatest breach in this idea, was in fact its new victory;
for tragedy does indeed celebrate the noble dead, but it celebrates
them as past magnitudes, not as demonically present ones. Over
the centuries and even among the great Romans the thought
found in its pristine clarity in Homer continues powerful; the
dead can no longer be an active agent, but the figure of the past
is not extinguished. "I have lived, I have finished the course that
Fortune gave; and now in majesty my shade shall pass beneath
the earth." So Vergil makes dying Dido speak.[38] The shade has
full reality. It abides with its peers in "the deepest, the very deepest" earth, whither only an Odysseus counselled by divine wisdom
could find his way, or a Faust, with the help of the magic key
given him by the Devil. It is very significant that Homer's thought
was reborn after a millennium in the spirit of Goethe, when he
sang of Faust going to the Mothers:

> . . . Flee from created things
> Into the realms of forms no lives attend!
> Delight in what have long since not been there. . . .[39]

Only a miracle can lead to the realm where in the infinite there hover

> The forms of life, which move but do not live.
> What once existed in full glow and flame,
> It still moves there, eternity its aim.[40]

Of men too it is this which abides. The Homeric view proves its truth and power to this day. It is the great mastery of the problem of death; it can never be surpassed but only repeated, whether consciously or unconsciously. It is the truly Greek victory over death, for it is at the same time the fullest recognition of death.

9

The celebrated conception whose meaning we have examined seems crystal clear, and yet it has an aspect of mystery. It too is absorbed in the irrational, about it too stirs that obscure shudder which is present at all genuine thoughts of death; and hence it is not wholly free of contradictions. But this very fact proves, if proof is necessary, that it is not the product of logical reasoning but of profound intuition of the depths of being.

The images of past life which dwell in the darkness below are denied all real activity and they appear to be nothing more than their name implies—empty shades. And yet there is in them a mobility, which is given compelling expression in Homer's description of the nether-world.[41] They crowd about the visitor who though alive has found his way to them, and they all wish to drink the blood from the sacrificial pit in order to awaken to full consciousness. Preceding all the rest is Odysseus' mother, news of whose death had not yet reached him; her standing and waiting until she may drink of the blood is poignant—she is uncomprehending and does not recognize her son, and yet she stands before him and waits while with heart woebegone he must fulfill his most important task, must inquire of Tiresias concerning his future. She does not hear what the two say, yet waits nevertheless. Those who were friends in life are together as shades also: next to Achilles is his own Patroclus, and with them is Antilochus, and Ajax, "the best of all the Greeks after Peleus' son."[42]

It is natural enough that the conception of the unawareness of the dead is not sustained with dogmatic rigidity. Later writers, like Pindar, permit the departed below with "spirit dark as the grave" to hear the praises which are sung to them and their descendants in the world above.[43] So Homer's Achilles imagines that Patroclus in Hades has received word of the ransom of the body of Hector, and begs him not to be angry.[44] Of the seer Tiresias it is expressly stated that it was vouchsafed him to retain his mental faculty even in the nether-world.[45] In the second portion of the Descent to Hades[46] the poet barely mentions the preceding draught of blood when one of the dead recognizes Odysseus and speaks to him. Bacchylides[47] has the spirit of dead Meleager speak to Heracles in Hades without having drunk blood.[48] And in the second Descent[49] the denizens of the underworld are given so much awareness that the new arrivals can discuss their fate with their predecessors without further ado.

But the consistent and thoroughly Homeric view is that the spirits of the dead are normally without consciousness[50] and require a special contact with the stream of life momentarily to regain their personality. That such could be the case merits our serious consideration. The shades of the sometime living past can by a draught of fresh blood—but who brings it to them?—be aroused for a moment to life and to the present. To be sure, they remain thin and fleeting like a breath of air; in vain Odysseus seeks to embrace his mother, ever and again she eludes his grasp like a shadow or a dream.[51] But the mute and unaware likeness of past life does for a moment obtain vision, recognizes her son, and speaks to him. After a little it will sink back into its old blindness and be nothing more than a monument of what has been. Does not the mystery itself here speak to us? Only an Odysseus can reach the realm of shades bodily. But is it not our own experience that the form of what-has-been drinks of our blood and suddenly steps out of the past into the present, breathing life—for a fleeting moment? With such profundity has the Homeric spirit transformed the ancient belief that the dead is quickened to life by a draught of blood poured out to him in his subterranean abode.

But the sunken world reveals something more mysterious still. The moment the shade of life awakens to consciousness it raises a plaint for the extinguished light of life. We cannot hear its moving tones without feeling that it too belongs to the realm of the irrational out of which great and powerful thoughts concerning death have emerged in all ages. No doctrine has yet availed to remove their own boding sound from the words "death" and "dead" and to give them a brighter hue; the only solution has been to cast the black shadow backward upon life and to venture the assertion that the beyond is the true existence. Even so, how unavailing has this been in the face of nature, which persists in contrasting the gladness of life's day with the gloom of death's night and permits the eye to roam beyond the grave only through tears! Even the mystic rapture of longing for death is always bound up with a premonition of hallowed and enduring melancholy. If we reflect upon all of this we can hardly be so bold as to explain usages of mourning which have accompanied death from time immemorial as deriving merely from fear or desire, instead of seeking their source in the depths of life's experience. This tone of anguish sounds out of the Homeric poems also. The likeness of the deceased, whose direction is only backwards and which is incapable of action even when it awakens to clear consciousness in contact with the living, in this state becomes conscious of death and mourns for vanished life. Its realization is the more affecting as it limits itself to a cry of pain, without enlarging into a philosophy of life. It is the most brilliant figure of heroism, the crown of the *Iliad,* Achilles himself, from whose shadowy lips the declaration comes: "Speak to me not comfortingly of death, glorious Odysseus. Rather would I be a tiller of the earth, bound to a poor man who himself has little, than lord it over all the dead."[52] These remarkable words are wholly inconsistent with Homer's position; the depths have themselves spoken from the poet's lips. His dead are without consciousness; neither pleasure nor pain can move them; for them the question whether life is unconditionally preferable to death has no meaning. And yet—sorrow hovers over them with

sable wings. If they step into the light of consciousness for only a
moment, sorrow seizes upon them. How could it be otherwise
when the breath of life which is fleetingly wafted through them
brings with it something of the aroma of the sunny world? But
this feeling stands solitary in its gravity. It is not leveled down
into the thought that life must be enjoyed because it is so short
and issues in the sad impoverishment of death. If dead Achilles
prefers the meanest life of a laborer under the sun to his royal
state among the shades, the conclusion to be drawn is by no
means that it is folly to choose eternal glory above length of life.
This lofty spirit is much too proud to linger over his sorrow. The
exclamation is like a sad gesture to turn Odysseus' felicitations
aside. In the brief space of his contact with the living only one
thing is important: news of his father on earth, whether he still
receives his honorable due, and even more, how the son he left
behind is faring. And when he hears of the heroic glory of his
Neoptolemus we see the great shade "striding exultantly over the
meadows of asphodel."

So the mysterious nighness of the dead, age-old and eternal,
which mocks all logic, found recognition in the Homeric idea also.
No rationalist impertinence destroyed it. But it was uplifted to
purest vision. Its bond with the earthly, with the crude weight of
the elemental, with the gravity and sanctity of the maternal
ground, is severed. Its melancholy has lost its primitive mystery
and has become sublime. Only later generations among whom
belief in the palpable and present effect of a departed life had
again become potent had reason to fear contact with the dead
and required rituals to remove the pollution. In the Homeric narrative, though death impinges upon life every moment, there is
no mention of such feelings, and there are only fleeting indications
to remind us that it was once operative—such as Odysseus' cleans-
ing his house with fire and sulphur after the slaying of the suitors,
or the name Phoebus which can only mean that that god of
clarity also liberates men from the uncanniness of demonic pollution. Unlike the Euripidean Apollo (of whom we spoke above)
the Homeric Apollo does not scruple to bestow loving care upon
the corpses of heroes like Sarpedon or Hector.[53]

Its attitude to death is a plain indication of the character of Homer's belief. To him death's mystery is not the most revered, the most beneficent, the most exacting; for death is forever separated from the present in which all life breathes and the gods manifest themselves. And yet its reality has not escaped his perceptive mind and its primeval sanctity still speaks to him, though out of different regions of being.

Upon this pattern we may premise what attitude the new faith would take to other powers of the earth-bound sphere. Of Hades and Persephone, the rulers of the dead, Homer takes virtually no notice. But the others too, whatever name they may bear, are oriented towards the night of death with one side of their nature and, each in his own way, might be called gods of death. If the dead had vanished into another existence, these gods too must forfeit much of their right over life. Their blessing, their wisdom, and their law were after all simultaneously the blessing, wisdom, and law of the dead who were believed vigilant in their deep abyss. All of this holy and mysterious throng which came so near to older generations out of the caverns of night must now shyly recede into the shadows. It was outshone by the brilliance of the new gods—but not condemned and banished, as other peoples treated their ancient divinities when the new had triumphed. This is most eloquent evidence for the character of the new belief; its noble wisdom is remote from jealousy and assertiveness. Its radiant deity possesses sufficient greatness to recognize the dark presence which is not its peer. Thus the ancient and primeval ones remain venerable in the depths, but the crown of true divinity must be yielded to a higher realm.

Homer knows and names virtually all the powers of the deep whom primal piety faithfully served; but they have become withdrawn and subdued, their law no longer rules life, their love is no longer the source of all blessing, and their old dreadfulness has dwindled to a distant cloud. The holy earth which is their home has lost its awesome aspects; the necessity which bound them into a solemn unity was dissolved as with a smile, and several of them, like the Graces, the lovely daughters of the deep, themselves entered the Olympian light and became playfellows of its golden radiance. Others retained their pristine gravity, but the omnipotence of darkness no longer attended their awesomeness.

Night is still holy, "swift Night"—in the south its onset is very sudden. The picture of the silent queen who rushes along with dark visage and drives the terror of death before her has a living presence for the poet. He uses it as a simile for angry Apollo descending to destroy the Greeks,[54] or for Hector impetuously attacking the gate of the naval encampment,[55] or for the shade of dead Heracles who spreads terror even in Hades.[56] Indeed great Nyx is once called "vanquisher of gods and men,"[57] and we hear that Zeus himself once spared the god of sleep who took refuge from his wrath in Night, because he feared to provoke the ill-will of "swift Night." But her name sounds almost legendary. Among the deities who are worshipped she has no place. Now the essence of the divine is to be sought in a quite different sphere.

Furthermore the fearful daughters of Night,[58] the Erinyes, whose connection with deep Earth is also expressed in the revered form of Demeter Erinys, are familiar to the Homeric sphere of thought. They close the mouth of Achilles' horse, whom Hera had suddenly endowed with human voice;[59] as Heraclitus[60] says, they are "the police of Dike" who punish all transgressions, so that for fear of them "even the sun will not transgress its course." Most of all they are concerned with oaths and curses. According to Hesiod they are the nurses of the infant god of oaths "whom Eris bore for the destruction of perjurers."[61] Even "below the earth they exact requital of man, who has sworn a false oath."[62] They are called "spirits of curse" (*Arai*) in their home underground.[63] They hearken when a father curses his son,[64] or a despairing mother.[65] Oedipus they pursued all his life after his unfortunate mother and wife hanged herself with a curse upon her lips.[66] Penelope's curse would have set them upon Telemachus if he had forced his mother out of the house.[67] We can still find it in Homer himself: it is a primeval law they represent, and they prosecute breach of this law with "pitiless heart"—the law of consanguinity. The most powerful example is the fate of the matricide Orestes. Homer, indeed, shows no knowledge of this story; its grim earnestness was recalled only at a later day. But Homeric poetry has preserved such traits of the old law as that the younger must heed the will of the elder because the elder "always has the Erinyes at his side."[68] If we group all such utterances together we can perceive a holy order of high antiquity which is based upon reverence for blood, birth, and death, and which receives its sanction through the divinity of maternal earth in which life and death alike have their home. Of this primeval order we have spoken at length in the second chapter. Things, however, concerning which the Homeric world keeps silence, whatever its knowledge of them may have been, are mentioned directly in Hesiod: the Erinyes are the daimons of the shed blood of parents; the earth-goddess conceived and bore them of the drops of blood streaming down from Uranus, whom his son emasculated,[69] and Rhea expects that through Zeus, to whom she is on the point of giving birth, "the Erinyes of the father" will overtake Cronus.[70] But for Homer these connections and the whole circle of terrestrial weight and gloom to which they belong, no longer possess so high a sanctity. The extreme of gravity no longer resides in the powers of blood, earth, and darkness. They have lost their aspect of the inexorable, for there is liberation in the divine splendor radiating from the eyes of Athena and Apollo, who in Aeschylus justify Orestes in the name of a more spiritual law, even as against the voice of the spilt blood of his mother.

Illuminating evidence for this spirit which does not abolish, much less outlaw, the older and oldest beliefs but rather liberates them from their burdensome weight and brings them into harmony with a brighter world, is offered by the figure of *Themis*. She is one of the most revered manifestations of the maternal earth-goddess[71] and represents her as the spirit and will of justice. Hence it is she who was said to have issued oracles at Delphi before Apollo, as successor to Gaia, as the priestess says at the opening of Aeschylus' *Eumenides*. With profound understanding the myth assigns to her as daughters the three Hours, "Order, Justice, and Peace (Eunomia, Dike, Eirene), who watch over the works of mortal men," and the Moirai, "who decree good and

evil for mortal men."[72] Together with these holy powers Themis
was assumed into the Olympian heaven, and was wed to Zeus.[73]
The twenty-third *Homeric Hymn* shows her enthroned, leaning
upon Zeus, who converses with her thoughtfully. But in the Homeric epics, where Zeus himself is master of all knowledge, Themis
only has the office of summoning the gods to assembly at his
bidding,[74] and also of opening the banquet of the gods.[75] A more
important activity at the side of counselling Zeus is indicated
only by the solemn formula with which Telemachus adjures the
assembly of the Ithacans: "By Zeus the Olympian, and Themis,
who assembles men for counsel and dismisses them again."[76]

Under her transparent name of Gaia the earth-goddess was
worshipped as the holy source of wisdom; it was after all her
words which in earliest times the voice of the Delphian oracle
proclaimed.[77] The memory of her primeval majesty was preserved
not only in the myth of the theogony but also in many expressions
of later date. "Eldest of the gods, eternal, inexhaustible earth,"
the chorus in Sophocles' *Antigone*[78] sings. The praise of this uni-
versal mother whose grace bestows wealth, peace, fair women,
and lovely children we hear in the thirtieth *Homeric Hymn.* Her
sway over burgeoning life is connected with that over death, for
whatever she bears returns to her maternal womb. So her character possesses the dark and stern side which we saw in the
Erinyes. In the conjuration of the dead she is the first to be invoked.[79] In the sanctuary of the inexorable goddesses on the
Areopagus her statue stood next to those of Pluto and Hermes;
there sacrifice was offered by happy men who had been acquitted
by the court for homicides.[80] Thus in the venerable figure of
Gaia converge most profoundly the ideas of birth and death,
blessing, curse, and holy justice. But of all this, in the religious life
of the Homeric world virtually only formulae remain. In the *Iliad,*
the great earth-goddess with her primeval spouse Uranus still appears in the solemn oath of Hera.[81] It is to her and Helios that
the oath sacrifices are offered at the conclusion of the covenant
between the two peoples.[82]

And finally it is particularly noteworthy that even that figure
of the earth-goddess endowed with most regal splendor, the
figure who gives unforgettable expression to motherhood under

the name of *Demeter*, has virtually no standing in the Homeric world, though her dignity goes back to the remotest ages and was maintained till late centuries. In her the unity of life, death, and holy justice found its noblest symbol. But Homer ignores her association with the realm of death. Often enough, indeed, he mentions the queen of the dead, the "illustrious Persephone," but there is no hint of the great myth of her rape and none that she is the favorite child of Demeter, as the *Homeric Hymn* so called first tells the tale. And yet Homer knows the highly revealing and ancient concept of Demeter as it is expressed in the myth which Goethe retells in the twelfth of his *Roman Elegies*:

> Demeter, great Demeter once yielded to a hero willingly,
> When on a time to Jasion, stalwart king of the Cretans,
> She granted the sweet secrets of her immortal body.

In Homer this story is mentioned by Calypso,[83] and when she adds that a thrice-plowed fallow field was the goddess's marriage bed, the most wonderful mystery of the earth-religion is suddenly and vividly present before our eyes. Homer also knows that Zeus once loved Demeter,[84] and once he mentions her sanctuary in blooming Pyrasus.[85] But she herself appears seldom, and her sway is limited to the growth of grain. She is called "the fair-haired." A simile in the *Iliad*[86] pictures "yellow Demeter blowing with the wind to sift the chaff from the grain on the sacred threshing floor"; and the sustenance which the tilth provides is called by her name.[87] This is the sum of her influence and importance for Homeric life.

This exclusion of hallowed and by no means entirely forgotten deities from the society of dominant personages; this acceptance of their dignity and dismissal of the breadth and depth and above all of the awful mystery of their nature, results from definite valuation and intent; this is best demonstrated by the most impressive figure of the entire group, Dionysus. His virility, as J. J. Bachofen has excellently remarked, sweeps the eternal feminine of this domain irresistibly along with him, and yet is completely subject to it. His spirit glows in inebriating drink, which was called the blood of the earth. Primal ecstasy, frenzy, the dissolution of consciousness in the infinite, overcome his devotees like a

storm, and the treasures of the earth are laid open to their rapture. About Dionysus too the dead throng, and they attend his
coming in the Spring, when he brings the flowers. Love and unrestrained frenzy, cold shudders and happiness, join hands in his
rout; in him all primeval traits of the earth-deity are enhanced,
beyond measure and common sense. This irresistible deity is well
known to Homer. He calls the god "the frenzied," and has a clear
picture of his feminine revel-rout brandishing the thyrsus. But the
picture serves him only as simile, as when he compares Andromache rushing out of the house in dark premonition of catastrophe to a maenad,[88] or for an occasional narration of some memorable story.[89] In the living world of Homer there are no maenads,
and we seek in vain for a rôle for Dionysus, even the most modest.
Here the Dionysus "rich in joy"[90] is as alien as the man of sorrow
or the prophet of the beyond. The excess which is appropriate
to him does not tally with the clarity which must here distinguish
all that is truly divine.

From this clarity other figures of the earthly group are also far
removed. They may be clothed with the sweetest enchantment,
they may bear majesty and gravity upon their brows. Knowledge
and sacred law stand by their side. But they are bound up with
the stuff of the earth and partake of its grimness and constraint.
Their favors are that of the maternal element, and their law has
the sternness of all ties of blood. All reach into the night of death,
or more properly: through them death and the past encroach
upon the present and the existence of the living. There is no retiring from the stage, no passing over from objective existence into
a sphere of exaltation, no liberation of daily life and work from
the weight of the past. All that was continues to stand, and always
raises its demand with an exigence from which no asylum offers
refuge. It is only a confirmation of this character when we observe
that the female sex is predominant among the divinities of this
world. In the heavenly group of the Homeric religion, on the other
hand, the female sex recedes in a manner which cannot be accidental. There the gods who are dominant are not only of the
masculine sex, but most decidedly represent the masculine spirit.
Though Athena is associated with Zeus and Apollo in the supreme triad, she expressly denies her feminine aspect and makes
herself a genius of masculinity.

11

So the new gods are sharply differentiated from the old. But we must not be content with marks of difference which, like those enumerated, are mainly negative. The eminently positive aspect of the new conception of deity awaits exposition. But we must tarry with the negative another moment, in order to discover the point where the positive comes into view. Among the three great powers who divided the universe among themselves and represent the divinity of its several spheres, the ruler of the netherworld is pushed into the background. This region has lost virtually all importance for piety; the divine in which piety now believed no longer resided there. Neither does it dwell in the realm of the earth. In whatever memorable forms primeval Mother Earth may have represented herself, they all virtually are eclipsed, for none of them is capable of revealing any part of divinity as it was now conceived in a deeper sense. And if we turn from the nether-world and the realm of earth to the domain of Poseidon's power, here too we shall seek in vain for the aspects that are denied those other spheres.

At first blush this seems incredible. Does not Poseidon as helper of the Greeks in the battles at Troy play as important a rôle as any other deity? We hear too what made him so irreconcilable an enemy of the Trojans: King Laomedon for whom he built the walls of Troy cheated him and withheld his promised pay.[91] His hatred pursued Laomedon's grandson Hector even in death; he is one of those who opposed delivering the body of Hector from Achilles' inhuman fury.[92] In the *Odyssey*, as is well known, it is his anger which pursues the hero over many years and all the seas until he is cast up, naked and alone, on the shore of the Phaeacians; indeed, the prophecy which Tiresias imparts to Odysseus in Hades[93] goes beyond the stories of our *Odyssey*. Even after his return home, after he has overcome the suitors, he must not forget that Poseidon is still angry and must wander unwearyingly until he reaches the place where it is destined for him to be redeemed from Poseidon's enmity. The scenes with Poseidon —his voyaging at the beginning of the thirteenth book of the *Iliad* is a sufficient example—are among the most magnificent and beautiful descriptions in Homeric poetry. It is also a familiar fact that this god was at all times as highly honored by the Greeks as his element the sea, and in the early period he played a part that could hardly be surpassed by any other. But it is just here that we recognize the limits that were drawn by Homeric religion. Poseidon is too closely involved with matter to possess the true majesty of the divine in the sense of Homeric religion. Hence he fared very much as did Demeter, who was in fact very close to him; his sphere, which we know from many witnesses outside of Homer, was limited to the sea exclusively. To be sure, such stereotype epithets as *enosigaios* or *enosichthon* (both meaning "earth-shaker"), *gaieochos*, ("earth-surrounding"), and the name Poseidon itself extend his power over the earth also, whose foundations he shakes, and place him beside the ancient earth-goddess as lord and husband. In the description of the battle of the gods in the *Iliad*,[94] the accompanying earthquake is ascribed to Poseidon: mountain and valley quivered, and in the depths the lord of the dead sprang roaring from his throne, fearing lest earth-shaking Poseidon would rend the earth open and reveal his horrible realm to the light. But the men of the *Iliad* and *Odyssey* think of Poseidon only when they have to do with the sea. For them his power does not operate within the earth, in vegetation, or in animals, or in the abundant water of rivers. If we compare his function with that of a Hermes, not to say an Athena or Apollo, who protect and hallow so many aspects of human life with their divine presence, the difference becomes very significant. The nature of a true Olympian contains, for the Homeric world, a meaning of immeasurable depth and breadth. Poseidon's function, on the other hand, is narrowed down to a strictly circumscribed material domain, and the might of his name echoes something that is past and antiquated. It is unmistakable, as we remarked above, that the poet sometimes gives the presence of Poseidon an air of old-fashioned gruffness and good nature. We need think only of his forthright and circumstantial challenge to Apollo in the battle of the gods,[95] or of the ludicrous contretemps of amorous Ares, at which he alone of all the gods could not laugh, because his sympathy was too great.[96] Thus even the ruler of the sea, who once held Earth in his mighty arms, has no share in the true splendor of divinity as manifested in the Homeric age. He is too much involved in material nature to equal the genuine Olympians in freedom and scope.

For the same reason we understand why a god like Hephaestus could achieve no dignity at all. Should we not expect that as god of fire he would be particularly apt to reveal the grandest and sublimest ideas? And yet in the circle of the Homeric gods he is nothing but a skillful craftsman in metal, and even later he never got much beyond this status. He belongs entirely to the element of fire; indeed he is himself that element, seen with the eye of pious reverence. Homer speaks not only of the "flame of Hephaestus," but simply of "Hephaestus"—to such a degree are the two one. Hence for Homeric religion Hephaestus signifies practically nothing; in the scenes of the gods in both epics he plays not only a very subordinate rôle, but a decidedly undignified and even ridiculous one.

Thus all the figures who, according to Homeric belief, do not possess the crown of complete divinity have this in common: they are constrained by matter and in their persons represent the sanctity of specific elements. Most important among them are the earth-deities, whose motherhood embraces death also and sanctifies it. We have observed their gravity and profundity; even the contemporaries of Aeschylus could be awed by the implications of their once having had to surrender dominion to the new gods. "Alas, ye younger gods, ye have trodden down the ancient laws, have wrested them from my hands!"—so the aroused Eumenides cry out in Aeschylus, before they accept Athena's reconciliation;[97] but then they remain among the citizens of Athens as revered guardians of justice and promise the blessings of the maternal earth to the city of the heavenly and masculine daughter of Zeus.

This reconciliation and recognition is symbolic of the rule of the new spirit and throws a bright light upon its character. If the feminine powers of earth had prevailed they would have sought no compromise. Ineluctably any who disagreed would have succumbed to their blind hatred, for their greatness and fearfulness lay in their undeviating rigidity. Their law is like that of nature and blood, which embraces its own with maternal tenderness, but which, when it is injured or affronted, is unpitying and relentless. The new and heavenly gods, on the other hand, are free enough not to eradicate the old. They acknowledge its truth, and thereby manifest their higher knowledge. It is not their desire, as it is of new gods of other peoples, that all other worship should henceforth be regarded as godlessness, and that everything other than themselves must be forgotten forever. As spirits of the sublime they leave to the darkness of earth the dignity appropriate to it; but it must remain within its limits, for above it there has opened a realm of light to which the loftiest love of the human spirit must henceforward belong. The gods who now rule life as guides and as ideals no longer belong to earth but to ether; and hence of the three realms and their gods with whose distribution we began this section, only one remains as the place of divine perfection, and that is *Zeus's realm of light.*

And yet the dwellers of heaven are not citizens of a beyond, wholly severed from this earthly world. The forms of their existence are the same as on earth—they even have human shape—but for them everything is transfigured and perfect where for us it is imperfect and fleeting. Neither are their effects upon life supernatural, nor do they exert absolute power to force recognition of their law. Their being and doing operate wholly along the paths of nature. The question then arises of their attitude to the realm of matter and nature; they are wholly at one with this realm, and yet their home is high above it, and they belong to two worlds, that of the sublime ether and that of the heavy clod.

Among the gods of growth and the dead there is one whose exclusion from the circle of the great Olympians merits particular attention—Dionysus. As we noticed, Homer is very well aware of him and the behavior of his revel-rout, but in Homeric religion he has not the slightest place. And yet it is Dionysus who lifts man beyond himself in holy ecstasy and who once shook all of Greece with the flaming storm of his spirit. Hence this sort of enthusiasm must have been alien to the spirit of the divine as Homer understood it. There is no doubt that all excess was repellent to him, and most of all where it seemed to achieve its greatest miracle:

the removal of the bounds between the finite and the infinite, between man and god. An important part of Dionysiac religion is belief in the dead, and here too agitated emotion suffers no insurmountable boundary between here and yonder. This emotional faith was completely transformed in the clarity of Homeric thought. The eternal gap between present and past became visible. For the first time the past reveals its specific nature, which, contrary to all desire and fantasy, forever separates it from the present. And yet the mystery retained its sacred right. It retired into its own depth, where no presumption could follow it. Only in conflict against light does the dark attain its profoundest depth. A masculine mind striving towards clarity is fated to have a more overwhelming experience of the night of the eternal abyss than a dreamy feminine disposition fascinated by anything mysterious. This experience, which may be had at all times, is confirmed in the Homeric belief in the dead.

This disposes of any doubt that the Homeric conception of the gods belongs to the realm of *spirit*. It is the spirit that gave the primeval belief in the dead its new and ever memorable form; it is the spirit that rejected the enthusiasm of Dionysiac religion. This significant word has often been used thoughtlessly or capriciously. It serves as a favorite designation for the boundless and incorporeal, for what is beyond all form or description. But where spirit is, there clarity and form hold sway. Its element is so far from being supernatural and supersensory that an indissoluble bond connects it with nature. Nature and spirit live in and for one another. The first great manifestation of spirit is the Homeric religion, which is simultaneously the first great manifestation of nature. In later Greece the spirit continued to emerge in manifold aspects, but never in so original a form as in this religion of the living spirit. With it Hellenism uttered its eternal word concerning the world.

The spirituality of the new gods is bound up with the closest fidelity to nature; and it is this fidelity that first enables us to understand their spirituality completely. How it can draw the most profound spirit to nature at its quickest, is best expressed by Hölderlin in his lines on Socrates and Alcibiades:

> Holy Socrates, why, knowing much greater things,
>   Do you honor this youth, offer him homage still?
>   Why so lovingly, raptly
>   As on gods, do you gaze on him?
>
> Who most deeply has thought loves what is most alive,
>   Who has looked at the world values high virtue most;
>   Often finally wise men
>   To the beautiful bow their heads.[98]

These verses may well stand as a motto for what follows.

12

Primeval worship of the elements and natural phenomena is plainly perceptible in Homer, and was never wholly lost to Hellenism generally. A peculiarly broad and large devotion speaks to us when we hear night, day, and evening called "holy" or "divine" in the Homeric poems, or when sea and streams, countries and cities, grain, olives, and wine, even noble humanity are crowned with divine glory by such words. This profound majesty of the world was not denied by the new gods. Else they would have been forced into stark opposition to the old geniuses, and what would then become of the wholeness and harmony of the Homeric world? The sanctity of nature was assumed in the essence of the bright divinities and now appears in them as enlarged meaning and spiritual grandeur. What this means we can learn from each of the great divine personages. They are loosed from the earthy and yet present in all of its forms. *How* they are loosed and *how* present merits reflection.

The new deity does not act as a power that sets the world in motion from without; its place is rather within the world itself. Yet it is not a single, specific thing. The sanctity of fire might well merit worship as the genius of a specific element, but it can never merit the rank of the divine in the larger sense. Even the majesty of the sea could not reach up to this sphere. Always divinity is a totality, a whole world in its perfection. This applies also to the supreme gods, Zeus, Athena, and Apollo, the bearers of the highest ideals. None of them represents a single virtue, none is to be encountered in only one direction of teeming life; each desires to fill, shape, and illumine the whole compass of human existence with his peculiar spirit. For mankind as such, divinity never denotes a single duty or aspiration but always the totality of life; and in the world at large, which embraces all elements and forms of life, including man, it manifests itself even more completely and diversely. To be sure, it is never an all-pervading world-soul, a mysterious ground for the life of all earthly beings, but always a defined entity; yet its special character is always the signature of a world complete in itself.

This is to be seen at its most beautiful precisely where we should expect a strictly circumscribed and one-sided sphere of action. Aphrodite arouses the desires of love and vouchsafes their fulfillment. Considered from this aspect alone she appears to be a genius of a single natural force. But she is infinitely more; she shapes a whole world and inspires it with her spirit. From her comes not so much the ecstasy of desire as the charm which kindles and propels it. She is the enchantment that radiates from things and beings and enraptures the senses with its smile. Not only men and beasts but plants, inanimate images and appearances, even thoughts and words, derive their winning, moving, overwhelming sweetness from her. And so her enchantment brings into being a world where loveliness moves toward delight, and all that is separated desires blissful fusion into oneness. In it all possibilities and desires are included, from dark animal impulse to yearning for the stars. We find the same thing in all the great deities of the new order. They constitute and manifest a creation which is always complete in itself. Whenever the world displays one of its large aspects, it is their spirit that shines out of it.

A wholly different, but again a whole world is that which is reflected in the virgin goddess Artemis. Here there is nothing of the rapture which impels to embrace, to the bliss of becoming one. Here everything is mobile and withdrawn and pure. The lucidity of the goddess hovers over meadows and lakes; her bright spirit is wafted in the solitude of forests, in the lonely lights of mountains; she causes the mysterious magic of solitude in nature and its breathless tremor, its playful tenderness and the sternness into which it can suddenly transform itself. To her belong the beasts of field and forest, which she protects maternally in their need, and harries to death as game with reckless pleasure. But man too belongs to her realm. Her manifestation is the tart sweetness of the young body and the young soul, the loveliness that shrinks from being conquered, the tenderness that takes fright at the fervor of the lover and turns cruel if he approach too near. Inspirited by her is lightness of foot, which can only run or dance; hers is the morning freshness with its shimmer and clarity, in which, as in a dewdrop, the colorful fire of the heavenly rays glint and gleam. Thus Artemis too is the meaning and spirit of a reality which encompasses man, beast, and nature and which has received the eternal form of its essence from the goddess.

Very different is that aspect of the world which bears the divine name of Hermes. This is its nocturnal visage, which may show itself even in sunlight when things happen mysteriously and wonderfully, when despite bright daylight there is insight into the dark. Not in the peace of night, not in its majesty, does the spirit of Hermes make itself known, but in its menace and favor, its sudden windfall and loss, its uneasiness and sweet pleasure; in its eeriness, its phantasms, and its melancholy, from which all magic has sprung.—And so in the case of each deity we find anew that it is most intimately bound up with the things of this earth, and yet it never denotes one single facet but is an eternal form of existence in the whole compass of creation.

Even the late-born is awed and reverent when these powers manifest their essence and therewith the realms of the world; with astonishment he comprehends the breadth and depth of view which has measured these realms, even unto the sacred darkness of mystery, even to the limits of the irrational, where beauty and dread are one. A wonderful insight, which we may also call experience, has perceived in large spheres of existence the lofty spirit which carries their essence and reveals it to the illuminated gaze. Suddenly the deities stood over the realms of life, living manifestations of the eternal meaning which pervades each of them and which is as present in the splendor of the sublime as in the earthy breath of valleys and hills, in the burgeoning of plants and in the beating pulse of animal life. These powers are not of

such sort that belief in them could have gradually expanded from
modest conceptions of individual functions and then become
spiritualized in the degree that thought advanced and standards
rose. The new entity and the multiplicity brilliantly radiating
from a central point were present at a single stroke, as the form
of a realm of existence which in them had unlocked its eternal
content. So the primeval sanctity of nature reappeared, transfigured in a higher reality. In the birth hour of its true religion
the Greek spirit bestowed upon this higher reality its first and
greatest reverence. The Greek saw and knew: everything individual is imperfect and transitory, but the form abides. In it reposes
the meaning of all being and happening. It is the true reality, it is
the divine. Everywhere present, it is one with all phenomena of
the sphere of life which it rules. But as highest essence and permanent being it stands by itself and high above the earthly in the
splendor of the ether.

Modern man tends to confuse the general validity of such
conceptions with abstract modes of thought. Even at this date
the student of religion is seldom capable of perceiving behind
the divine personages of ancient faith anything beyond either
natural objects and physical forces or disembodied general concepts. But these interpretations wavering between coarse sensuality and rationalism will always be put to shame by the plastic
vitality of the Greek gods. They give proof of a higher insight,
in which seeing and understanding are one and the same thing.
This insight always discovers totalities, and in them seizes upon
precisely those traits for which the intellect has no gauge—loftiness and majesty, solemnity, magnificence, kindliness, aloofness,
strangeness, craftiness, grace, fascination, and many other significant and at the same time obvious values which rational thought
must pass over. This insight does not even need to name what
it perceives, for it conceives the forms in shapes constantly born
anew of the spark carried from spirit to spirit. Its proper language
is the plastic creativity of poet and artist; but this should not prevent us from recognizing its eminently religious significance. For
what would be religious if not man's emotion when he glances
into the depths of being? And here the depths speak to the il-
lumined spirit. A moment may suffice for the blazing forth of

figures worthy of veneration to whom no temple has ever been built. So in his fifth *Isthmian Ode* Pindar prays to a being who appears there and nowhere else, though he gives her the name of Theia, mother of Helios;[99] this being is the mighty enchantment which glows in gold, the magnificence which shines over racing craft in the sea and horses in the race course, the glory on the garlanded head of the victor in the games—it is the brilliance, the actual radiance, "the divine One" (Theia), of whose splendor the sun bears witness and also the soul of man when it flares up in the blissfulness of the perfect moment.

This remarkable example, for which many parallels could be cited, plainly shows us the religious orientation of the Greek mind after it had discovered itself. Its self-discovery is the great event of the pre-Homeric epoch. It was then that a race of gods emerged from the outlines of the perishable world with such convincing clarity that it needs must capture and retain the highest reverence. For an understanding of the persons of these new gods, the significance their cult may have had in primitive times is a matter of indifference. The birth hour of the specifically Greek conception of the gods was the great moment when through its essence the deity revealed the meaning inherent in a special sphere of existence, and bestowed upon it permanence, unity, and nobility.

13

It is worthy of the most ingenious and creative of humankind that in the period of their greatest religious inspiration they resolved to recognize and worship the divine not in absolute power, wisdom, or will, but in the primal forms of reality; thus their religion exhibits the same evidence for the unity of nature and spirit as does their plastic art.

Out of this unity too proceeds the pure *human form* in which divinity was vividly present to the Greeks from the Homeric age onward. If the Homeric poetry occasionally still betrays a slight reminiscence of the ancient animal forms, the fact need not trouble us here. Occasional exaggeration of a divine image into colossal proportions, as when Hera in taking an oath lays her hands on lands and sea,[100] or when fallen Ares' body covers nine acres,[101] do not in any case controvert resemblance to humankind; not to mention the fact that such images are rare and never consistently maintained. All that we need to understand is the significance of the human form of representation and its predominance over all other forms. By itself the human form is no novelty, for it had doubtless long been familiar in the early period along with the animal form. But now it had become sole and exclusive, and this marks the decisive break of the new belief from the old.

Manifestation in animal form is proof of an unspiritual divinity bound to the elemental and material, and of the tremendous and overwhelming emotions which were aroused by confrontation with it. Human form, on the other hand, proclaims a divine nature whose perfection is spiritual. This spirituality makes the new view an apparent approximation to our own, but its sanctification of the natural form puts it at the farthest possible remove from our vision. The clear definiteness of the natural form was accepted as a genuine manifestation of the divine, and hence deity itself must be presented in the noblest of all natural forms—the human.

Such views of the divine the modern philosophers of religion refuse to recognize. Brought up in a religion wholly oriented to the supersensual, directed by inner anguish and the prototype of oriental religion towards a source of salvation, they expect valid information about what is holy only from emotional upheavals and ecstatic raptures. If any outward signs of its awful mystery are required, they may admit the use of symbols, but never of a human image. They must even prefer the monstrous images which we encounter in the religions of many peoples because by bursting the bounds of natural forms and limits they suggest the unexampled, ineffable, incomprehensible, and overwhelming, and thus by use of earthly means give expression to what the sole content of religious experience is expected to be.

To the approach of these thinkers the spirit to which the divine human form was manifested stands diametrically opposed. In joyous clarity, so palpable to the senses, they can see only superficiality and frivolity. But the free and spacious Greek conception of the divine, whose witnesses have been not prophets and hermits but great creative artists—and not in antiquity alone—cannot be lost to mankind. It is as if it protested in the name of nature and spirit against the concepts of anguish, restless yearning, and desire of death; indeed, it is as if it threw the charge back at the opposition—declaring that in attacking their predilection for the supernatural, it was opposing an all-too-human frailty, inasmuch as the greatest human failing is the overweening pride which rejects the guidance of nature and presumptuously thinks and aspires beyond nature's limits. Here, then, the perfect human figure takes the place of an image of monstrosity which confounds the senses, or of a symbol for the absolute. For if all the forms and phenomena of this world point to the godhead, then the most excellent of them must be its image. Godhead here implies the full significance of a whole realm of existence, the clothing of each of its forms with splendor and nobility, and the manifestation at nature's highest point of its greatest glory and true visage. In that the god himself bears human traits, he exhibits in its most spiritual aspect the realm all of whose forms, from the inanimate to the animal and the human, are reflected in him. Thus his image consistently remains in the line of nature, but it stands at the highest point of that line.

Deity is the configuration that recurs in all forms, the meaning that holds them all together; and it reveals its spirituality in the human form, which is the most sublime.

V

BEING AND HAPPENING

THE MANIFESTATIONS OF THE GODS

1

Wᴵᵀᴴ ᴛʜᴇ ɪᴅᴇᴀ of the being of the gods, that of the mode and manner of their effects upon human life is closely related. This too was never formulated dogmatically, but it is clearly perceptible in all the accounts of gods who manifested themselves through men. It is the basic idea which Greek religion could never lose. Since the period of the Enlightenment certain of its manifestations may have appeared strange and objectionable, but its central meaning could never be affected by criticism. Even today its truth is confirmed; for, innocent of conceptualism, it honors only the lively awareness of the presence of the divine in this world, without being oblivious to human freedom or to the regularity and calculability of events. Imbued with this idea, the Greek faith is the most magnificent example of a wholly undogmatic religion, which contradicts no human experience and yet penetrates and encompasses all existence. Its greatest and purest witness is the world of which the Homeric poems apprise us. There it is still so much alive that it nowhere requires justification.

There is no worse mistake than to think that an awakening criticism implies growth in seriousness and a deepening of religious consciousness. It is only when belief begins to waver that the intellect can assert its demands; this wavering is a phenomenon which can never be explained, but only be indicated, by the image of a receding of the divine presence. But Homer's world is still completely under the spell of the divine presence.

The importance that divine activity had for this world, which was anything but mean-spirited and small-minded, is wholly without parallel. Every state, every capacity, every mood, every thought, every act and experience was mirrored in the deity. Whatever the poet may be describing, it cannot seem important to him without his uttering the name of a god or the divine in general. This constant remembrance of the divine, this permanent sensitivity to heavenly presence, must leave a deep impression even upon one to whom Homeric religion is alien. Even though in numerous instances reference to the gods had become a mere formula, it nevertheless proves an alert emotion; and it remains true that there is no other conception of the world in which earthly and human existence is so filled with the presence of the divine, no society (unless it be a religious body) which took thought of the divine with such loyalty and reverence every moment of its existence.

And our astonishment at this piety that penetrates all experience grows in the degree in which we come to understand its character. The deeper our understanding penetrates, the more despondent must our criticism become. So it goes with all complex configurations which are born of the fullness of experience and carry their justification only in themselves. The living meaningfulness of their structure itself rejects an alien gauge. Whether this meaning is familiar to us or strange, we must leave it as it is. And indeed in men of our time it can seldom find echo and response. For in religion we seek another and mysterious world, whereas it is basic to the character of the Greek that it associates reverent recognition with acute observation of reality. Its divine is neither a justifying explanation of the natural course of the world nor an interruption and abolition of it: it is itself the natural course of the world.

2

The gods whose spirit is perceptible in every happening operate partly individually and independently of one another and partly in combination as a unity. Both modes are of equally great significance. Their willfulness, indeed, sometimes causes division in earthly affairs; but this only reflects the multiplicity and contradiction of existence, which to the active man must seem the more unappeasable the livelier and richer his experience is. Ruthless assertion of personal claims might have made this divine disunity intolerable. But the personal factor was not sufficiently important to Greek thought to make it conceive of differences and contradictions in human affairs as jealous conflicts for power and prestige. Contradictions among the gods are basically analogous to the tensions which subsist among the elements of the world, and their personalities were not disposed to accentuate these tensions. The mythic conception of a family under the leadership of a royal father permits the tensions to persist and yet at the same time provides a symbolic image of harmony. Harmony becomes unity in the person of Zeus, who not only stands above the gods as supreme power and directs great destinies according to his will, but also appears as exponent of divine sway in general, so that it is he who is effective in all and to whom all prayers rise. We shall yet encounter this greatness of Zeus, which waxes towards the infinite and issues in the inconceivable; here we must take thought of another and no less significant general conception of the divine, in which the divine, as a majestic essence, is wholly and unexceptionably contrasted to man.

In many cases Homer (and of course later Hellenism) attributes the instigation of important events to "gods" in general (*theoi*) or to "god" (*theos*). The latter expression does not at all imply a definite personality, in the monotheistic sense, but rather bears the same meaning as the first—the unity of the divine world as it communicates itself, despite its diverse manifestations, to living sensibilities. When Diomedes sharply rebukes Agamemnon for his counsel to desist from war, and for himself and Sthenelus offers the solemn assurance that they would in any case fight to the end, forasmuch as "it was with god (*theos*) that we made our way hither,"[1] he speaks in the trust in the higher world which stands above man. This is what the poet of the *Odyssey* means when he says that a thing came about "not without god (*theos*)."[2] Because "the god" is with him Hector has the upper hand, and Menelaus may avoid him without shame.[3] When none of the Greek heroes answers Hector's challenge, Menelaus declares that he will essay to fight, "but victorious outcome is in the hands of the immortal gods."[4] Hector is aware that he is not Achilles' peer, "but," he says, "this lies upon the knees of the gods, whether, lesser though I be, I may deprive thee of life by the cast of my spear."[5] And after his defeat we hear from the victor's mouth that the "gods had granted him to vanquish this man."[6] When Hector becomes aware of Athena's deception, he himself feels that "the gods summon him to death."[7] To repentant Helen Priam affectionately says: "Thee I blame not; the gods do I blame, who fixed upon us this Achaeans' war of many tears."[8] For Agamemnon too the fall of Priam's city depends on whether "the gods grant it,"[9] just as at the beginning of the *Iliad* Chryses expresses the wish, "May the gods who dwell on Olympus grant you Greeks to destroy the city of Priam and to return home in safety."[10]

In the *Odyssey* invocation of "god" (*theos*) is frequent. With pious awe Telemachus banishes the thought of sending his mother from the house: "May the god never bring such a thing about!"[11] Of the faithful servant who loves his master, Eumaeus says that he works diligently "and god blesses his work."[12] At the sacrificial meal Eumaeus says with pious devotion, "God will give or deny as his will is; for he can do all things."[13] Not to all men, says Odysseus to Euryalus, do "the gods" give tall stature and keenness of spirit; one man may be unattractive to sight, but "god" lends charm to his words.[14] "Always the god brings like unto like," Melanthius mocks, when he sees Odysseus in beggar's guise accompanied by the swineherd.[15] Very characteristic is Odysseus' complaint to Athena: So long as the war against Troy endured he was always aware of her nearness; but from the moment that "god" scattered the Achaeans he no longer received any sign from the goddess.[16] When Euryclea recognizes Odysseus by his old scar, he commands her with a threat to say nothing of the discovery which "god" had given her; else she must not count on mercy when "god" would destroy the suitors through his hand. And when the thought of that longed-for moment arouses the old woman's desire for vengeance, he restrains her, again enjoins silence, and bids her leave the rest to "the gods."[17] Trouble and sorrow are inflicted upon man by "the will of the gods."[18] They give and they deny: "the gods" gave Helen no more children after her return.[19] "Easily can the gods who hold wide heaven now make mortal man glorious and now debase him."[20]

The unity of the heavenly power becomes quite obvious when, as often in the *Odyssey*, "the gods" operate as a power of fate and their operation is expressed by a word that properly denotes the spinning of the thread of destiny (*epiklotho*). Of this we shall speak later. Of Odysseus it is said that "the gods" determined the year in which he should return home;[21] it is "the gods" who doom men to destruction[22] and apportion all manner of suffering to their lot.[23] It is the gods too who have fixed the simple laws of nature. Penelope is very willing to hear more from the stranger she has not yet recognized as her husband, "but it is not given man to continue sleepless always, for the immortals have set a portion in each thing for mortals on life-giving earth."[24]

Individual gods retain their particularity and the tensions between them persist. They are the world, and the world is manifold. And yet man knows of the oneness of the divine. He knows of it, but he can no longer grasp it by way of representation. It is no longer form. But for the very reason that it is beyond representation moral ideas could be attached to it.

3

Where and how do the gods impinge upon earthly existence? This question always implies another: What can or does man effect out of himself? Every idea of the function of deity is, insofar as it concerns man, the obverse of a specific psychology, and a people's thoughts about its gods cannot be understood without understanding what it thought about man. It is not as if human self-knowledge came first and knowledge of deity followed. No view could be more perverse. But it is also wrong to place consciousness of deity first, ahead of self-consciousness. Neither is without the other. In devout experience both are present simultaneously and are one and the same.

Man has always been aware that he could not be held wholly accountable for his resolves and his deeds, whether good or bad. Events in the outer world obviously determine his aims and actions and often force him to deeds he would willingly forgo. And within himself too a great deal happens, beneficial or ominous, to his own surprise, for he was never conscious of the requisite will or strength.

The Greek's sensation of life was of such a sort that in all these points he sensed a divine presence. But this statement is not explicit enough. It might seem as if the divine occurred to him only where we too might be surprised and awed by something miraculous—sudden, incomprehensible events or strange thoughts or passions which, as it were, assail us. The Greek also senses that what he chooses and does in full consciousness is something given to him, and his awareness touches on the divine even where we think of nothing more than the familiar regularity of events or of our own shrewdness and ability. And yet man is no mere tool of the gods, his existence is not merely a field for their sport. He himself is something, and his own action is demanded of him. Man's active mobility meets with the wonder of the enchanted world, which enchants him also. The fullness of the world and the fullness of man are present simultaneously. No answer can be given to the question where the human ceases and the divine begins, because belief is rooted in the experience that one is encompassed by the other and both coincide. In place of conceptual formulation there stand the images of happenings, which we shall come to know in what follows.

The Greek image of divine-human operation contrasts remarkably with the view familiar to ourselves. The Greek deity does not operate from the beyond upon the inwardness of man, upon his soul, which is connected with it in some mysterious way. The deity is one with the world and approaches man out of the things of the world *if he is upon the way* and participates in the world's manifold life. It is not through turning inward that man experiences deity but by proceeding outward, seizing, acting. To the man who is active and enterprising the deity presents itself with immediacy, whether it facilitates or hinders, enlightens or confuses. Deity looks upon the kindled lover out of the eyes of beauty with their searing glow, and the missteps into which he is swept are as much the deity's work as his. Indeed, the deity's in greater measure. And so along with man's self-assurance in great achievements, his self-condemnation in questionable ones is disposed of. To us the serenity with which the deity is here made responsible for some great injustice is incomprehensible. Helen, who deserted husband and child with her paramour and brought indescribable woe upon two peoples, does indeed reproach herself bitterly, but the real blame is accounted Aphrodite's, and Helen remains the great woman she was.

In this expression of Greek belief one who is remote from

it sees a desecration of deity and at the same time a serious danger to morality. What an inducement to sin if responsibility can be shifted to the gods! But we must consider that it was only later, when this belief had begun to waver, that there was occasion to complain of frivolity and immorality. If we take a sharper focus on the question of responsibility we recognize a viewpoint which differs from ours considerably, to be sure, but not because it is less serious. There is no suggestion that man need not bear the consequences of his bad actions. On the contrary; they overtake him with a ruthlessness which terrifies us. Tragedy, which drew its subject matter from ancient epic, is full of these awful consequences. That is just what tragedy means: there is no escape, and good intentions do not come into question. What has happened must work its course out. No repentance, no humbling oneself before god, can obviate its course. But in return, remorse has lost its poisoned barb. Whether the deed was good or evil, whether man may praise or blame himself for it, in no case can he believe that he brought it about himself, that he himself embodies a sovereign will whose goodness or evil is alone responsible for his acts and his derelictions. Transgression is no more condoned than its consequences are abrogated. But the feeling of wretchedness does not enter. The perpetrator does not have the sort of humility that assumes the entire burden of guilt, but rather the sort that refuses to see himself as the sole author of what had happened. Hence he can remain large and proud, even in his fall. Whatever has happened, even if it must destroy him ultimately, belongs, like all else in the world, to a higher providence; even the passion which was its source has its wonderful and eternal visage among the gods, and to this he may look up even when he is crushed.

As long as these views retained their full seriousness, that is, as long as they were associated with a firm belief in the divine nature of the world, they could not endanger morality. In that early age man could see the world and his own existence in the mirror of genuine myth. Only when thought, which had become self-determining, protested that impulses other than moral and beneficial must not issue from higher powers; only when the questing eye turned to man's inwardness in its search for the

cause of wrong-doing, could Helen be rebuked as Hecuba rebuked her: "Your own heart transformed itself into Cypris at
sight of my son."[25]

Condemnation of the human heart is much older than Euripides' tragedy. It belongs to theosophic mysticism, which set a
different myth in place of the large and genuine one. We do
not know for certain where it arose. In the post-Homeric centuries
its importance was considerable. But we must not forget that it
is wholly alien to the spirit expressed in the lofty creations of the
Greeks. Its doctrine was that human nature is fundamentally corrupt. This sad condition pointed backward to a primeval curse on
the whole race. There was a divine world to which man belonged
in some mysterious fashion and out of which he had sunk into this
night of error and evil. But the divine realm desired to help him
return, and revealed a holy path to him for his ascent. The transformation of belief which is here sketched took place among
several peoples in various forms. For most historians of religion
it goes without saying that this implies a decided advance, a purification and a deepening of religious, as of moral, thought. The
conception of deity appears to have become larger and purer,
that of man himself more serious. And yet the very pathos which
is the overtone of this sphere should indicate that something has
been broken and torn and could only be restored to a whole by
effort and struggle. As long as the original whole subsisted, man
himself had no need to fathom his own inwardness because he
found outside himself the great myth, embracing one and all, in
which he too was subsumed. How this security, which is like that
of a child sheltered in its mother's arms, could or had to be lost,
is not our question. But the security itself and its hold on life
must stand firmly before us.

In the midst of this world filled with divine figures stands man,
not as an alien but directed to it with all his faculties, attached to
it, receiving and expecting from it knowledge and decision, success and failure, pleasure and pain. To be sure, he is as fully
aware of the capacities of his spirit and temper as he is of those
of his body. He knows that he possesses inwardly something we
call soul; he calls it *thymos*. This inward man he distinguishes
plainly from the outward. In moments of need he even speaks to

it, as a man speaks to his brother or comrade.[26] Once Odysseus
spoke to his heart when, in the night before his battle with the
suitors, aroused by the impertinent laughter of the maids, he
"bayed" like a hound on the point of attacking an intruder to protect her young: "Endure, O my heart; you have endured worse."[27]
But this inwardness itself has no language; it becomes aroused,
but it never addresses a man. It has no world of its own, it
somehow lacks the dimension of depth. Its world is the great
realm of life without. Hence there is no myth of the soul, and
there can be none, for the soul faces only outward, as it were,
towards the world of forms, not inward, towards an invisible
realm accessible only to itself. It is difficult for one who belongs
to a later civilization to free himself of the prejudice that this
condition must derive from want of depth and insight. He calls
it primitive or childish, and regards the conceptions that emerged
in later ages as the result of development and improvement. But
the want lies not in the earlier mode of thought but in our own
understanding. Nothing is lacking in that ancient conception of
existence; it is round and complete in itself. The aspects which we,
under the compulsion of quite different outlooks, desiderate would
have corrupted it. Their addition would not, as we so readily imagine, have constituted enrichment and deepening; only after
it disintegrated could they infuse it, as essential elements of a
new conception of the world, with a new center and new criteria.
If in the old conception of existence inward man had no myth to
himself, this means that he was entirely integrated, in a single
and complete configuration, with the warp and woof of the myth
of the world. His experiences are no property of his soul, anchored
in deep solitude or in a formless beyond kindred to the soul, but
a portion of the world which has its place and its meaning in the
great myth of the world. Hence there is no lack of depth, as we
may like to think. For here the sensitivity with which we scrutinize
the soul's depths is directed to the world and its configurations, and
in its image is able to recognize aspects of experience so faithfully
that even we, who are accustomed to a quite different mode of
thought, are swept away by the truth of the vision. And here we
notice with astonishment that it was once possible to explain from
the world about us, apprehended with largeness and depth, what

we seek to understand by steeping ourselves in our inwardness; and we notice with admiration that nothing of its content is lost in the process but that it is rather enhanced to magnificence— whereas we with our knowledge of psychology are always in danger of losing ourselves in the petty and the trivial.

That age had no doubt that man, when he was not subject to external coercion, was determined by inclinations and convictions. But these impulses do not point inward to some emotional center or basic will, but outward towards the largeness of the world. What we in a moment of decision experience as motivations are here, for the enlightened, the gods. With them, and not in the human heart, resides the depth and the fundament of everything significant that transpires in man. This means that he knows he is surrounded by a great being and its living forms. Who these forms are is the most important question. If he knows them he knows himself; for contact with them is that decisive event, which he experiences now in one direction, now in another. Far from limiting himself to the subjective, therefore, and persisting in this groove, becoming at once insecure and obstinate, he expands towards the objective and substantial, towards the being of the world and hence towards the divine. This applies equally to fortune and misfortune, to good and evil. Even when an objectionable and fateful sphere attracts him, it is the realm and form of a god, and if its fascination has seduced him from orderliness and duty he may, in his sorrow for what has happened, refer to its power of compulsion and think of its greatness. However bitterly he may lament his action, his conscience need not torment him, for the decision was no defeat of submerged good intentions in a struggle with evil inclination.

What is right, proper, and benevolent, all that is required of a man in the name of good, also has its objective reality beyond man and is therefore less a matter of conviction, temperament, and choice than of insight. And insight is darkened when man succumbs to a bewitchment which is hallowed in the realm of gods but which must injure his life and honor.

It has often been a matter of wonder that the Greek is inclined to seek motivation for moral decisions not in will but in cognition. Today such a conception is considered an error. This is extraordinary: as if this conception could be taken as an isolated factor without regard to the totality of a world-view in whose context alone it has meaningful validity. One who understands the objectivity of the ancient Greek view of the world, one who is capable of following its orientation outward instead of inward, towards the myth of the world instead of the myth of the soul, can only find consistency in the emphasis upon cognition rather than upon will or emotion. In the world of objective forms justice and honor, prudence and moderation, tenderness and charm, are not in the first instance subjective modes and personal attitudes but *realities*, permanent forms of being which at any significant moment may confront man with divine substantiveness. To the Greek, therefore, it is not so essential that this or that is *felt* as it is that it is *known* and *understood*. The man who behaves benevolently, nobly, or justly *"has knowledge of"* the benevolent, the noble, and the just. For him they are things of which he possesses cognition, whereas others do not. It is possible that he too did not always possess it, that it once "came to him," as we say, through instruction or experience. Our own language reminds us that the conception is not wholly alien to us, that we unwittingly adhere to it in many respects, and may be able to penetrate further into it. In the Greek language, on the other hand, even in Homer, this conception is paramount. Here moral attitudes are based less upon notions of sensibility or inclinations than on those of knowledge and understanding. Where we say of a man that he "thinks" fairly, Homer has "he knows fairness." The same mode of expression is applied to everything which we are accustomed to include under the notion of disposition. A man of friendly disposition is one who "knows friendliness." In expression, therefore, it makes no difference whether a man possesses a desirable disposition or whether he "knows" good counsel.

It need hardly be said that this does not mean knowledge derived from conceptual reasoning. There must be another mode, that "other kind of cognition" (*allo genos gnoseos*) which according to Aristotle is inextricably bound up with virtue[28]—a comprehension which is not rational and yet sharply differentiated from emotion and desire, and which belongs to the realm of enlight-

enment, insight, knowledge. The fact that Hellenism bestowed
its most distinguished attention upon this aspect of the moral
problem definitely indicates that it was not preoccupied with
the rational: here we have beautiful testimony to the objectivity
of its perception and thought. It does not even possess a specific
word for the will; the expression which properly denotes insight
(*gnome*) is here applied equally to resolution.

It was this "knowledge" which was darkened or altogether
absent when a man let himself be carried away into an improper
or fateful course. The Homeric Greek does not think of evil or
sinful inclinations. To him the impulse to pleasure and power is
neither good nor evil but natural. Even the noblest possess it,
and it may grow into a passion that threatens to overrun everything. But he has a higher knowledge of noble and meaningful
forms of the world process, a cognition that belongs not to calculating understanding but to the perceiving spirit, a consciousness of stately and eternal realities—or gods!—which as soon as
it is distinctly grasped converts into will and sets limits to the desires of the heart. But there come moments when this consciousness is darkened or entirely extinguished. Then man becomes involved in guilt and doom. But his blinding, like everything decisive, is a work of the deity.

The mode of thought here characterized as having an outward
orientation is none other than the mythic. Both man and his world
of experience take on objective form. Primal forms are imaged
forth in his joys and sorrows, his appetites and insights. But the
will, good and evil, remains insubstantial. The divine is the pure
form of the world, its explanation, its myth. Here the thought
cannot conceivably turn away from the world, towards the divine. The existence of the world is not submerged in the deity.
Man, in whom the deity manifests itself, is no mere point of
transition to a higher world. It is not as if some other spoke and
acted through him, visited him with an emotion, will and knowledge which are not his own. This would have destroyed the mystery of the contact of the divine and human. We recognize the
wonderfully lucid spirit of the Greek in his myth, the myth of
specifically this world and *specifically this* man. Its images of
events which give proof of gods and their deeds carry irresistible

conviction even for us, and their truthfulness abides whether or not we believe in these gods and their power. In other religions reference to the deity all too often denotes a falsification of experience; here we see the marvel of full agreement between knowledge and faith. The truest image of actuality is at the same time the liveliest testimony for the existence of the gods.

4

For the religious interpretation of natural happenings which we have discussed above, the following examples may be offered from Homer.

Odysseus was sad and anxious when he looked upon the host of the Greeks rushing wildly to their ships.[29] Only to test them Agamemnon had counselled them to give up their senseless enterprise and to return to their dear homes. To characterize Odysseus the poet uses an expression which sets his shrewdness and resourcefulness beside Zeus's.[30] But now these qualities seem to have left him in the lurch—nay, at this very moment they were to assert themselves brilliantly. And this comes about when the man whose cleverness has been compared to Zeus's finds at his side the clever daughter of Zeus, whom that "lord of counsel" (*metieta*) had borne out of his head and who of all the gods is "most excellent in acuteness and shrewdness."[31] She makes him realize the disgrace of cowardly retreat—but it was just this that had made his heart heavy; and she enjoins him to go among the men instantly and without hesitation, to address them one by one and with winning speech to restrain them from their purpose. He does so, as we are told in the lines following, with great skill and success. Thus we have confirmation of Odysseus' proverbial cleverness, whose boast was that it supplied the right thought for every difficult moment. But what might be described as invention is in truth the inspiration of the clever man by his heavenly escort, the goddess with the sharp and clear eyes. He hears her voice and immediately turns to action. Of her approach and departure we hear nothing.

In the same manner Athena has another of her favorites,

Diomedes, come to the right decision.[32] Together with Odysseus
he had invaded the camp of Rhesus at night. While Diomedes
was slaying the sleeping warriors, Odysseus detached the king's
horses from their chariot and led them out. Now it was time to
make for safety, and Odysseus gave his comrade a sign. But
Diomedes hesitated whether to drag the king's chariot away or
continue slaying the Thracians. While he was thus pondering,
Athena appeared to him suddenly and admonished him to decamp
at once: at any moment the Trojans might be at his throat. Him
too the goddess accosts in a moment of doubt and supplies the decisive thought, the saving resolution. Without delay—nothing
more is said of the goddess—Diomedes breaks away with Odysseus. It was high time. A Thracian chief had awakened out of his
sleep and his wails were summoning the Trojans.

Similar, and in part in the same words, is the story of Athena
addressing the raging Achilles with the voice of reason,[33] but
here the illumination is enhanced to the proportions of a vision.
The provoked lion feels himself touched from behind, turns
about, and sees the flaming light of the divine eyes. Immediately
he recognizes Athena and shows her his heart burning for vengeance. But she counsels wiser and worthier self-mastery. And
the mighty hero heeds. All this is the matter of a moment. No
one else could see the goddess, no one noticed the conversation.
Before she began, Achilles loosened the sword from its sheath;
when she finished, he thrust it back again and she was gone.
She had made him choose the sensible course. But this time too
she came at a moment of indecision, and one of his alternatives
was just what the divine word urged and made convincing. So
her intervention tipped the scale of sensibility and thought.

Of special interest is the manner in which the goddess of good
counsel arouses in Telemachus the thought that it is high time
to leave Sparta and return home.[34] For a noticeably long period
he had remained the guest of Menelaus, whom he visited to inquire for his vanished father. In the meantime the suitors had
persisted in their insolence in Ithaca, and there was no knowing
whether things had gone to irremediable lengths. Thereupon
Athena entered the youth's chamber suddenly by night and reproached him for staying away from home so long and taking no

thought for the critical situation in his ancestral halls. He must hasten if he still wished to find his mother at home, because her kinsmen were insistently urging her marriage. It might very well be that she might take some of the family property with her, against his interest; he well knew how unreliable the mind of a woman is when she has turned to another husband. After this discourse the goddess gives Telemachus detailed instructions for the voyage home, and then she disappears. Immediately the startled youth arouses his travelling companion. He does not wish a moment's delay but is determined to depart the same night, without saying his farewells.

Fault has been found with this narrative. It is inconceivable, it has been said, that Athena could suspect Penelope in this fashion, and inconceivable that Telemachus should be so senseless as to wish to depart in the middle of the night, like a thief and a rogue. And yet the whole thing is marvellously true as soon as we transport ourselves to the soul of the young man and regard the events from that vantage point. First of all it is important that here too the goddess does not appear without preparation, but supplies words for a thought which had already been on the way. It is night; Telemachus' friend is sound asleep at his side but he himself cannot sleep because his head is full of thoughts of his father whom he misses sorely and for whom he has undertaken this voyage—so much is expressly told by the narrator. Then he is suddenly oppressed by the thought of the length of his absence and of the condition in which he left matters at home. The night magnifies everything to enormous proportions and turns anxieties into huge specters. Is it any wonder the sleepless youth should become frantic and that he should go so far as to imagine his mother behaving in a way which would seem to him incredible and ridiculous in sober daylight? Is it any wonder that he finally loses his head entirely and wishes to depart at once without waiting for daylight and a courteous farewell to his hosts? Here, it seems to me, the poet has created an excellent picture of the soul. And towards the end[35] he characterizes his hero's state of mind admirably with a touch which has been regarded from antiquity onward as a spurious addition because it recurs verbatim in the *Iliad*[36] and is alleged to be appropriate only there.

After the goddess's speech Telemachus awakens his friend with
a kick. It is objected that he is lying at his side and could touch
him with his hand; in the case of Nestor in the *Iliad* it is understandable that the old man cannot bend down to Diomedes and
so arouses him with his foot. Doubtless; but Telemachus is frantic,
and that is why he kicks his bedfellow instead of politely using
his hand. There could be no plainer way of indicating his mood.
And Athena? What did she do to intensify Telemachus' will to return to such a degree? She gave his thoughts of home compelling
force. Her divine voice and the articulation of this thought are
basically one and the same. The modern reader must transpose
what happens here to the man to his psychological frame of reference in order properly to recognize its truth.

Actually, as we see here, there can be no alternative between
the independent action of a human and the influence or injunction
of a deity. What a man wills and does is himself and is the deity.
Both are true, and in the last analysis the same. Here it is impossible to object to Helen, as is done in the *Trojan Women*,
"Your own heart transformed itself into Cypris at sight of my son,
for we call all folly Aphrodite."[37] When Medon says to Penelope in
the *Odyssey*[38] that he does not know whether a god instigated
Telemachus to his journey or his own mind impelled him, he has
in mind the possibility of some divine injunction without wishing
to deny that what he calls Telemachus' own mind may have received its decisive impulse from the deity.[39] The thought that even
what proceeds out of a man "himself" has its origin with the gods
is very beautifully expressed by the bard in the *Odyssey*: "No
teacher have I had; it is god who implanted the riches of song in
my heart."[40] In this sense he calls himself self-taught. Sometimes
the divine impulse is mentioned along with man's will. Diomedes
says of Achilles that he will enter into battle "when the heart in
his body urges him to and the god drives him."[41] "Do not have
such a thought in your mind," the aged Phoenix admonishes
Achilles, "let not god turn you that way."[42] This two-fold motivation does not imply that under certain circumstances man relies
wholly on himself. That is not the intention even in the admonition with which Peleus sent his son forth: "My child, for the matter of strength, Hera and Athena will give it if it be their will.

But be it yours to master the anger of your proud heart"[43]—for in other passages self-mastery is ascribed to the sudden intervention of a god. Mention of divine impulsion gives special emphasis to the moment of decision without thereby implying that the antecedent inclination to the act was purely human as distinguished from divine operation.

"Zeus inspired Hector, who was eager enough already, to assail the ships,"[44] is to be understood in this sense. When the attempted reconciliation fails, Ajax says that it is time to go, for "Achilles is savage and remorseless; he is cruel and cares nothing for the love of his comrades." But then turning to Achilles himself he says: "The gods have put a wicked unforgiving spirit in your heart, and this all about a girl."[45] The second statement of the situation is merely more solemn and serious than the first, but in no way contradicts it; Achilles' hardness of heart is no less effected by deity if he hardens it himself.

It is evident that this conception, closely as it binds man to deity, does not signify that he actually lacks freedom. The impression of constraint is all the more ruled out as man's action is predominantly related to the state of his insight. No external will or desire took possession of him when he chose the worse course, nor was it that his nobler feeling proved powerless in the face of his cruder inclinations. It is only that his clear perception of the beautiful, the just, and the reasonable—three great realities—was confounded. So a noble woman like Helen could fall; Aphrodite's girdle has a magic power that robs even the prudent of their sense.[46] The mysterious darkening of the spiritual eye is the means through which the deity leads to his ruin a man destined to fall. This thought is given unforgettable expression by the chorus in Sophocles' *Antigone*:[47] "For with wisdom hath some one given forth the famous saying that evil seems good, soon or late, to him whose mind the god draws to mischief." On this passage the scholia cite the proverb, "For whom god wishes to bring mischief he first confounds the mind."

A famous case is Agamemnon's affront to Achilles, which brought indescribable misfortune upon the Greeks. At the solemn reconciliation after the death of Patroclus—the loss of his best beloved was the penalty Achilles himself had to pay for his irrec-

oncilability—Agamemnon declares to the assembled Greeks that
he had often enough heard their reproaches for his former conduct, "but," he continues, "it was not I that did it: Zeus and Moira
and Erinys that walks in darkness struck me mad when we were
assembled on the day I took from Achilles the meed that had been
awarded to him. What could I do? All things are in the hands of
heaven, and Ate ('blindness'), eldest of Zeus's daughters, shuts
men's eyes to their destruction."[48] He goes on to recount how
Zeus himself was deceived by her and forced to look on at the
consequences of her gruesome sport. "Even so did I grieve when
mighty Hector was killing the Argives at their ships, and all
the time I kept thinking of Ate who had done me such mischief.
I was blind, and Zeus robbed me of my reason; I will now make
atonement, and will add much treasure by way of amends." And
Achilles himself corroborates this explanation. "Father Zeus," he
cries, in accepting the atonement, "of a truth you blind men's
eyes and do them mischief. The son of Atreus had not else stirred
me to so fierce an anger, nor so stubbornly taken Briseis from me
against my will. Surely Zeus must have counselled the destruction
of many an Argive."[49]

It is incomprehensible to Helen how she could have deserted
home, husband, and child to follow the handsome foreigner into
a strange country. Only a deity could have so confounded her
sense: Aphrodite, whose enchantment coerces hearts; and behind this power stood the will of the gods who had resolved upon
the war. In the *Odyssey* she remembers the days in Troy when
she yearned for her home: "I was unhappy about the blindness
that Aphrodite inflicted upon me, taking me over there, away
from my country, my little girl, and my lawful wedded husband,
who is indeed by no means deficient either in person or understanding."[50] And in the justly admired scene of the *Iliad* where
the Trojan elders, in sight of the blood-drenched battlefield, admire the beauty of that fateful woman, aged Priam addresses her:
"Come, my child, take your seat in front of me that you may
see your former husband, your kinsmen, and your friends. I lay
no blame upon you, it is the gods, not you, who are to blame. It
is they that have brought about this terrible war with the
Achaeans."[51] In the *Iliad* Helen herself applies the bitterest re-

proaches to herself and her deed, but she too finds the true source of the evil in the gods.[52] Similar judgment is passed on Clytemnestra's unfaithfulness also. The seductive arts of Aegisthus could never have moved her, for she possessed a prudent mind, until finally "the will of the gods mastered her."[53]

Similarly, if a man resolves upon a right course, it is again the deity which has enlightened him. Aged Phoenix, who speaks to Achilles in the *Iliad*, had once experienced this divine intervention very plainly in his youth. He suffered from his father's curse and was prepared to kill him, "but some god stayed my rashness and bade me think on men's evil tongues and how I should be branded as the murderer of my father."[54] Anger would have driven him to the deed blindly, but thought of the horror of the actual deed interposed and prevailed over passion. This thought, which invaded his soul with such power, was produced by the deity.

In spheres other than moral also the deity stands behind all man's important decisions, whether they bring him fortune or misfortune. We have already noticed a number of examples. Odysseus tells his son that he would pass him the signal for removing the weapons on the decisive day by a nod of the head; that would happen when "Athena shall put it into my mind."[55] The *Iliad* tells us that Hector would have succeeded in burning the ships of the Greeks "had not Hera put it into Agamemnon's mind" to kindle the resistance of the Achaeans in his own person.[56] Shipwrecked Odysseus, who swam safe to Scheria, would have perished miserably by the breakers on the rocky shore "if the goddess Athena had not shown him what to do" to withstand their rush; and then he would certainly have perished in the waves "if Athena had not helped him keep his wits about him" in order to find his way to safety.[57]

But very often man makes a perverse choice at a moment of decision and so forces himself and others to destruction. This too is the work of the deity. Just as the god gives power to the good, so also does he to the bad and fateful thoughts and wishes in the heart of man. Achilles had instructed Patroclus to content himself with liberating the camp of the Greeks and not to pursue the Trojans into the plain because there he would be exposed to dangers

to which he was not equal. Intoxicated with victory, however,
Patroclus forgets this good counsel and impetuously pursues the
Trojans. "The infatuate! Had he but obeyed the bidding of the
son of Peleus he would have escaped death and have been scathe-
less; but the counsels of Zeus pass man's understanding; he will
put even a brave man to flight and snatch victory from his grasp,
or again he will set him on to fight, as he now did when he put a
high spirit into the heart of Patroclus"—which carried him to his
doom.[58] After the fall of Patroclus, when Achilles roused himself
like a roaring lion, Polydamas imparted to the Trojan assembly
the sensible advice of retiring from the field and withdrawing behind the walls of the city. But Hector, whom victory had made
confident, brusquely rejected the suggestion, "and the Trojans,
fools that they were, shouted in applause, for Pallas Athena had
robbed them of their understanding, so that they gave ear to Hector with his evil counsel, but the wise words of Polydamas no man
would heed."[59]

The Homeric conception does not construe human resolution
as constraint. It remains the thing that a man experiences in himself and that one who understands the soul can describe. But even
as such it derives from god. It is man himself who decides, and
yet it is not he. In this sense, devout and at the same time large
and free, Homer faces the eternal problem of free will and responsibility without casuistry or litigiousness. The man who goes
wrong must blame himself and must also bear the consequences
of his acts. But he does not need to torment himself with remorse, for despite responsibility and requital his deed rests in
the lap of the gods.

If a man's will and thought is so articulated into the divine
configuration of the world, such is surely the case with his capacities. We too say that all success is with God, and everyone
knows how much the legends and stories of peoples are motivated
by higher powers. But the consciousness of god on the part of a
race of heroes which is set forth in Homer is without parallel in
all the world.

The fact that each of the famous heroes has his own tutelary
deity at his side upon whose counsel and assistance he can trust
in all his undertakings is not unique. Other peoples have the same

thing; and there is also a common consent concerning the conviction that the self-assured man who thinks he can succeed without the deity is doomed to fall. Of this Sophocles' *Ajax* gives us an example from ancient legend.[60] When the young hero first went forth to war, his father advised him: " 'My son, seek victory in arms, but seek it ever with the help of heaven.' Then haughtily and foolishly he answered: 'Father, with the help of gods even a man of naught might win the mastery; but I even without their aid trust to bring that glory within my grasp.' Then once again, in answer to divine Athena—when she was urging him onward and bidding him turn a deadly hand upon his foes—in that hour he uttered a speech too dread for mortal lips: 'Queen, stand thou beside the other Greeks; where Ajax stands, battle will never break our line.' By such words it was that he brought on him the appalling anger of the goddess, since his thoughts were too great for man." The tragedy shows us the fearful consequences of Ajax's attitude. But, as has been remarked, this thought is familiar to other religions also.

The thing that distinguishes the Greek is the ever lively awareness of the nearness of the divine, which fails him neither in any rational activity nor in the passionate excitement of heroism. These proud and free warriors never forget that no cast and no thrust can succeed without the gods, and they utter this thought in places where, to our way of thinking, it is hardly consistent with the hero's posture. Here is an example. Achilles stands face to face with Hector, who has slain his dearest friend. He is deaf to the proposal that the victor should spare the corpse of the vanquished; there can no more be an understanding between him and Hector than between wolves and sheep. Achilles' contemptuous words reveal a savage lust for vengeance which has finally caught up with its victim, who is a prey of whom his superiority can make him quite certain. And yet in such a mood he can bid his opponent to gather all his strength, for now there can be no escape: "Pallas Athena will forthwith vanquish you by my spear."[61] Hector succeeds in avoiding the cast. "You have missed," he taunts Achilles, "Zeus has not yet revealed my doom to you, as you declare. You were a false-tongued liar, to make me forget my valor and quail before you. You shall not drive your spear into the back of a runaway; drive it into me as I make straight towards you, if god has granted you to do so." And now Hector makes his cast, but his spear rebounds from Achilles' shield and Hector has no other. He calls to his comrade-in-arms to retrieve the spear, and suddenly realizes that he is alone: it was Athena who had deceived him by taking the guise of his friend. Now he knows. "Alas, the gods have lured me on to my destruction . . . so Zeus and his son Apollo the far-darter have willed it, though heretofore they have been ever ready to protect me. My doom has come upon me; let me not then die ingloriously and without a struggle, but let me first do some great thing that shall be told among men hereafter."

So the valiant warrior, whose fame remote posterity will sing, thinks of his deeds. In the twenty-first book of the *Iliad* Achilles drives the Trojans before him with superhuman and awful grandeur, and the city seems hopelessly lost. There Agenor resolves to withstand the mighty man who is without peer: "His flesh too, I take it, can be pierced by pointed bronze; he has but one life, and men say he is mortal. It is Zeus son of Cronus who gives him glory."[62] Wherever energy and skill are in request, eyes look to the gods, who can give success or deny it. For this the athletic contests which Achilles institutes in honor of fallen Patroclus offer one example after another. Every success and failure is here attributed to the participation of the gods.

But this is not enough. These fame-loving people ascribe to the gods not only the good fortune which they require but also the strength and prowess of which they are proud. The moment of exaltation when a wonderful quickness gives wings to every motion they call god-given; but god-given too is the capacity to act manfully and intelligently, as are also the emotions through which men can demonstrate their noble character. Thus it turns out that even what we regard as the expression of personal quality flows directly from the hands of the gods. It is only through action that this quality can, at each occasion, assert itself, and in the act, not in some fixed inward being, it has its reality for the ancient Greek view of the world. But every act depends on the world forces manifested in the event, eternal forms of which are the gods.

To Bellerophon the gods granted "surpassing comeliness and beauty."[63] Here is Polydamas' reproof to Hector: "Because god has so richly endowed you with the arts of war you think that you must therefore excel others in counsel; but you cannot thus claim pre-eminence in all things. God has made one man an excellent soldier . . . in another Zeus has implanted a wise understanding of which men reap fruit to the saving of many."[64] Athena bestowed upon Penelope "a prudent spirit, talent in handicraft, and acute intelligence."[65] "I did not care about farm work, nor the frugal home life of those who would bring up children," Odysseus says to Eumaeus, representing himself as of noble Cretan descent, "my delight was in ships, fighting, javelins, and arrows—things that most men shudder to think of, but the gods implanted a liking for them in my heart. One man likes one thing and another another."[66] In the *Iliad* Strophius son of Scamandrius is called "a mighty huntsman and keen lover of the chase whom Artemis had taught to kill every kind of wild creature that is bred in mountain forests."[67] Phereclus "was skilled in all manner of cunning workmanship, for Pallas Athena had dearly loved him."[68] The metal worker who could cast delightful objects must surely have been "taught his versatile art by Hephaestus and Pallas Athena."

5

When Odysseus naked and uncouth stepped out of his thicket, Nausicaa's startled maidens scampered off in all directions; "only the princess stood her ground, for Athena took all fear away."[69] "Strength Athena and Hera will give you, if it be their will," says Peleus to his son Achilles, when he is to join Agamemnon's campaign against Troy.[70] When Diomedes is wounded by Pandarus' arrow he prays to Athena, "and she fills his heart with the stalwart courage of his father Tydeus," who was once her favorite.[71] On another occasion she gives him timely strength to overtake a flying enemy;[72] and when at the night raid on Rhesus's camp Odysseus admonishes him to demonstrate his gallantry, "Athena inspired him with courage."[73] Because Zeus had determined to grant Hector one more glorious moment before his end, "the war god entered him, so that his inward body was packed full of force and fighting strength."[74]

Boldness and fear, the one as well as the other, come from the gods at moments of decision. The hostile heroes contend over the body of Sarpedon, who has fallen by Patroclus's spear. Zeus determines to give Patroclus one more victory and drive the Trojans to flight. "In Hector first of all he put a temper that was without strength. He climbed to his chariot and turned to flight and called to the other Trojans to flee, for he knew the turning of the scales of Zeus."[75] Thus the corpse of the Lycian prince, which Glaucus had so tearfully urged must be saved, lay unprotected. Later Glaucus reproaches Hector bitterly when he retreats from Ajax in the battle for the corpse of Patroclus, and refers also to the desertion of Sarpedon's body. Hector replies: "I despise your wisdom when you say that I dare not meet the mighty Ajax. No terror have I of battle or din of chariots, but the intent of aegis-bearing Zeus is ever strongest, and even a brave man he overaweth and lightly snatcheth from him victory, and yet anon himself arouseth him to fight."[76]

Rightly, then, the warrior may not even boast of his courage and steadfastness, any more than of his justice and good will. Man, whatever he is or can do, that is, whatever takes shape in him or proceeds from him, belongs to the great spectacle of being which has received its explanation in the divine myth.

This myth maintains its character as genuine explanation of happenings in the world by the fact that it only rarely introduces anything which, externally considered, must be described as a miracle. Marvellous as things may appear to our inward view, to our senses they are natural; and, in reverse, whatever we see and understand as natural *is the divine*. This applies even in those special cases—which will later be dealt with separately—where a god confronts his protégé in corporeal appearance and speaks to him as friend to friend.

The encounter of Odysseus with Athena after his arrival at Ithaca[77] is among the most perceptive and charming pictures of a present and helpful deity, and calls to mind many works of painting or sculpture which show the goddess offering sympathy and encouragement at the side of the hero. Odysseus had been deposited by the Phaeacians on his country's soil in his sleep. When he awoke he found himself alone in an unknown land, for the goddess had made the air about him misty, so that he did not recognize the homeland he had so long yearned for. He complained aloud of the cruel trick the Phaeacians had played on him, and lamented for his lost home. While he was wandering along the seashore in his sadness, Athena suddenly confronted him in the guise of a noble youth tending his father's herds. Odysseus rejoiced at encountering a native and inquired the name of the place. The stranger seemed astonished at such ignorance. Proudly he described the excellence of his country, famous far and wide, and finally pronounced the name of Ithaca. But the soretried man must restrain his joy. Prudently he tells the stranger an invented story of his Cretan origin and how an unhappy accident had brought him where he was. Thereupon Athena smiles and strokes him lovingly. Suddenly she assumes her true shape and scolds him for not recognizing his divine friend for all his great cleverness. Now Odysseus adjures her by her heavenly father to tell him the truth, for he fears that she only wishes to mislead him with the assurance that he has finally arrived at Ithaca. The goddess is not annoyed but rather pleased with the clever prudence of her friend, and she confesses that it is just this quality which attaches her to him in misfortune. Thereupon she disperses the mist, and with joy overflowing Odysseus recognizes the dear old landmarks of his home, one after another. Then the two sit down under an olive tree and Athena enjoins her hero to reflect how he must deal with the ruthless suitors who had been lording it in his house for years while his wife was sighing for his return and checking their importunate demands with deceitful hopes. Odysseus realizes with horror what must have befallen him if the goddess had not apprised him of these conditions. He wishes Athena would herself devise some plan of vengeance and always stand at his side to give him strength. She promises loyal support, but for the present she wishes to transform his appearance to that of an aged beggar so that no one should recognize him. Then he must go to the swineherd Eumaeus, who has remained faithful to him, and let Eumaeus tell him all. She herself would go to Sparta in the meanwhile, to summon Telemachus, who had journeyed forth to get news of his father. Odysseus is displeased, and asks why she, who knew all, did not herself inform Telemachus instead of exposing him to the danger of a distant voyage while his property was being devoured by others. But Athena calms him: she herself had conducted Telemachus, and her purpose had been that he should acquire noble fame. He was faring well in Sparta, and would escape all danger on the homeward voyage. After these words she touches Odysseus with her wand and transforms him into the figure of a beggar. Then she disappears.

Considered externally, this narrative is full of miracles. But if we look closer the miraculous recedes into the background and the natural enters convincingly into the foreground to take its place. Moving indeed is the awakening of Odysseus. After years of straying he has again slept on his own soil for the first time, and yet does not know that he has come home. He looks about him. The region seems strange. How often had his fair hopes been cruelly disappointed! Then the scales suddenly fall from his eyes, as it were, and he recognizes spot after spot with happy certainty. In the deeper conception which the poet gives us, all of this happens through the goddess, who made the place unrecognizable at first because she herself wished to inform Odysseus about everything.[78] Then he is met by a native who describes the island to him and names it Ithaca. But his eyes do not yet convince him. That happens only after the goddess steps forth bodily in the shape of the young man. Solitary, overheard by no one, the man who has been tossed about for a decade experiences the presence of his goddess in the wonderful hour of his return. The friendly stranger was she. What her own lips now tell him the stranger as a real man might well have said. But the goddess gives greater weight to everything. The essential gain which conversation with her brings to Odysseus is the assurance that she would help him when it came to battle. For the dangerous undertaking against the superior force of the suitors she gives him no directions. She only lets him feel how necessary it is to devise some stroke, and when he requests that she herself contrive the plan of vengeance and stand at his side, her only reply is the promise of her presence. Thus what is natural here seems miraculous, and the miraculous natural. Only at the end does something incomprehensible take place. The goddess knows that in order for Odysseus to learn the true state of affairs in his house and choose the right moment for his deed he must be unrecognizable. Her transformation of him is the only miracle in the passage. Athena does this immediately before she vanishes. Odysseus stays behind as a miserable old man, and need not fear that anyone in his own house could recognize him as its master. But this too comes very near simple naturalness: decades of war, wandering, and suffering had gone by since his departure.

Such accounts can give us some notion of what the operation of the gods meant in this world-view. We are often tempted to substitute the word fortune—but in the deep and broad significance intended by Schiller in his poem of that name—in place of the names of the gods. "How merit and fortune are interrelated" —that is the theme which the many descriptions offer to our thought in ever new aspects. Here merit is paramount. It is for the sake of his cleverness that Athena loves Odysseus and is always near him; she tells him so herself.[79] Certain as it may be that such advantages are themselves due to the gods, something must nevertheless proceed out of man to enable the god to enter and attach himself to him. He is not inside the heart of man, but outside upon the way, and man has to start out if he is to encounter the god. The most beautiful stories of palpable divine assistance make this evident and hence ring so true. The unbeliever may call a thing that seems to happen miraculously a lucky accident. Logic cannot fix the boundary where human activity ends and divine begins. But upon the elect and enlightened the divine comes at one point of his path and with overwhelming certainty, and in special cases it raises him to a direct view of the deity.

6

Most enlightened of all is the poet. He sees events through and through even when the participants see only the surface. And often when the participants sense only that a divine hand is touching them the poet is able to name the god concerned and knows the secret of his purpose. This distinction between his own deeper understanding and the awareness of his hero is one of the neatest proofs of the living truth of his religion. There is much more of the miraculous in what he reveals to his listeners than in the experience of the figures of his tale. They do sense something superhuman, or they find everything quite simple and natural. So can anyone else who wishes to do so come to terms with the story; he will not be wrong, for that too is true.

We shall now cite a few examples to show how the inspired poet (and only he) sees the divine background of events.

In the *Iliad*, after the great assembly of the host, the companies of the Greeks arranged themselves for battle. Only a little while before, the invitation to return home, by which Agamemnon had only meant to test them, had been received with jubilation, and it required all of Odysseus' eloquence to win them back for war. But now war was their only thought. This, the poet is able to say, was the work of Athena, who unseen swept through the ranks of the Achaeans with her aegis and kindled each man's heart. "Thus war became sweeter in their eyes even than returning home in their ships."[80]

On the eve of the day of decision Penelope unexpectedly appears in the men's hall, where Odysseus too was present, unknown to all save Telemachus. The suitors were charmed at sight of her; never before had she seemed so beautiful, and each man's heart burned with desire. It is at this moment that Odysseus sees her again for the first time, and he looks at her with pride and pleasure. He hears her speak cajolingly to the suitors, but he knows that her heart is minded otherwise. Thus stands the woman for whom the following day will see a battle unto death, a marvellous prize before the eyes of the unruly suitors and of her own husband, and she enchants both. Such was Athena's intention. The poet is able to tell us[81] how she put the thought into Penelope's mind to show herself to the suitors. Suddenly she laughed peculiarly and told her maidservant that now she desired to come before the suitors, much as she detested them; she wished also to advise her son to have no more to do with the suitors. The maid advised her to wash her tears away first and anoint herself.

Penelope disdains this advice and requests only that two maid-servants be sent to accompany her. Thus she is alone for a few minutes. Athena sends a sweet slumber over her. She sinks back in her chair, and her limbs are relaxed in sleep. And while she is at rest Athena anoints her face with the precious ointment which Aphrodite uses when she goes dancing with the Graces. "She made her taller and of a more commanding figure, while as for her complexion, it was whiter than sawn ivory." The maids come to the door talking loudly, and Penelope awakens. She passes her hands over her face and is surprised at having fallen asleep. No one knows what happened in the short space of time. But the royal lady is radiantly beautiful when she steps through the door of the men's hall between her attendants. Was the thing that happened a miracle or the most natural thing in the world? The sudden wish, at which Penelope herself wondered, came out of the deep wisdom of her woman's nature, and it was the way of divine providence also. And is not sleep always something both natural and wonderful, in its essence as in its effects? When after his endless suffering and toil Odysseus lay hidden on the Phaeacian shore, a god sent him off, as he himself says, into a very deep sleep.[82] But the poet himself speaks of the event as follows: "Athena shed a sweet sleep upon his eyes, closed his eyelids, and made him lose all memory of his sorrows."[83]

Another picture. In raging battle great terror may sometimes assail even the mightiest hero. So it befell the gigantic Ajax.[84] He stood dazed, threw his shield over his shoulders, and crouched backwards step by step. He retreated slowly, and from time to time turned back to fight, but he retreated nevertheless. In the language of the poet, "Zeus struck fear into the heart of Ajax." Ajax succeeded in gaining safety, but Patroclus fell defenseless into the hands of the enemy.[85] In the midst of his furious assault he was suddenly opposed by Apollo. He did not see the god, but only felt the mighty hand that smote his shoulders from behind, so that he was stunned and his eyes grew dizzy. Apollo beat his helmet to the dust, the spear broke in his hands, his shield fell from his shoulders to the ground, and the god also undid the fastenings of his corselet. With his mind clouded and his limbs failing he stood dazed, and Euphorbus's spear struck him in the middle of the back. He could still make one final attempt to save himself, but now Hector sprang to the fore and ran his spear through his body. This was the end of his brilliant course of victory. There is something appalling about the fate of Patroclus, and it is so gripping because it is so true. No opponent could have overcome him if he had not already been crushed by a demonic shock. His eyes grow dizzy, his helmet tumbles in the dust, his spear breaks in pieces, his armor comes undone. What we call demonic—the fearful coincidence of inward and outward failure—is here the work of the deity. The man whom fate demands it places as an unresisting victim before the weapon of the enemy. And the spot struck by the weapon is precisely where the god's hand smote so hard that the unconquerable hero reeled in his senses.[86] He did not see his executioner, but as he dies he knows and can say to exulting Hector that it was Zeus and Apollo who stripped his armor from him.[87]

Even Achilles, as is shown by his famous encounter with Aeneas,[88] was unable to perceive the dominating rôle of the divine. Only the astonishing result led him to conclude that a divine factor was involved. In the midst of his duel with Aeneas, at whose shield he had just hurled his spear, he was suddenly unable to see clearly. When his vision cleared, his opponent had vanished, and the spear, which had penetrated the shield, lay at his feet on the ground. He was astonished and had to acknowledge that "Aeneas too must have the friendship of the immortal gods." But as to what had actually happened, he remained baffled. The poet, however, can tell us. Poseidon had suddenly come up, clouded Achilles' eyes, and laid the spear that was sticking in his adversary's shield at his feet. Aeneas he removed to the edge of the battlefield in a trice, and there appeared to him to inform him what folly it was to fight with Achilles, who was so far his superior. Then, unseen, he dispersed the cloud before Achilles' eyes. This story provides much food for thought. Remarkable things happen when warriors clash, and the emotions of a passionately aroused temper are remarkable. Where is the line of demarcation between the natural and the miraculous?

The same question may be asked at the very similar account of the duel between Achilles and Hector,[89] which ends, however, with Achilles' knowing the identity of the god who deceived him of his victory. With a fearful cry he springs upon Hector, bent on killing him—but his adversary has disappeared. Thrice he springs forward, and thrice he wastes his blow upon the air. Now he knows that Hector has been carried to safety by his protector Apollo. The poet tells us that the god had made him invisible in a thick cloud at the moment of Achilles' assault and had removed him from the scene of battle. This account is similar to, and in part verbally identical with, another[90] where Diomedes, whom Athena had enabled to see the gods, thrice assails Aeneas, who is protected by Apollo and swathed in a cloud,[91] and is thrice thrown back by the god, until at the fourth attempt the god terrifies him with thundering words. In the former passage the poet says nothing of Achilles' seeing the god at work. The victim of whom he felt sure quite unexpectedly eludes him; at each new assault he smites the air, and then he knows who has deceived him. Even in the last encounter between the two heroes, Apollo was Hector's helper, but when Hector was doomed to die Apollo had to leave him.[92] At each occasion Athena was at Achilles' side.

Especially thrilling is the scene[93] where Achilles again loses his opponent at the very moment of attacking him, and is enticed farther and farther away in the delusion that he is close upon his tracks. Here the miraculous comes forward out of the background all at once without disguise. In the lonely distance Achilles suddenly looks into the eyes of the god whose trick lured him there. The poet's account proceeds as follows: In order to restrain the terrible hero, Apollo encourages Agenor to venture opposition to Achilles. The first onset would naturally have finished him. But Apollo, unseen, suddenly spirited him away, and himself assuming Agenor's form ran before pursuing Achilles, who expected to overtake him every moment, until he had led him far from the city and out into the plain. In the meantime the straitened Trojans could reach safety behind their walls. But far out on the plain the god suddenly turned and mocked his pursuer: "Why, son of Peleus, do you, who are but a man, give chase to me, who am immortal? Have you not yet found out that it is a god whom you pursue so furiously? You did not harass the

Trojans whom you had routed, and now they are within their
walls, while you have been decoyed hither away from them."[94]
This episode involves only Achilles and the god. It is a familiar
enough phenomenon in the life of storm and battle that a man
should long pursue a phantom. But here it happens that the deception suddenly and in solitude shows the man gone astray an
eternal visage and gives him to understand that his furious determination was only the vehicle of a higher power. That is so
great and so true that we are prepared to believe in the miracle.

7

The meaningful combination of the natural and the miraculous,
which leaves the rights of each unimpaired, has found classic
expression in the famous stories of the gods who appear upon the
earthly scene in *human form*. Apparently this comes about quite
naturally. In a situation of whose gravity the participants may
not be aware, suddenly some good friend or acquaintance intervenes and says or does something momentous. Only the poet
knows that beneath the unremarkable exterior there is hidden
a god who has assumed the form of the man. Upon those involved
the intervention always produces a great effect. They become
attentive to something and immediately realize its significance,
and if energetic action is required they are at once infused with
a fiery spirit of fortitude and strength.

When Aeneas was put out of action by Diomedes,[95] Ares in
the form of the Thracian chieftain Acamas mingled with the Trojans to give them courage. With a shout he asked the Trojans
whether they meant to wait until the Greeks stood before the
gates of their city: mighty Aeneas lay prone, and it was now their
task to rescue him. No one answers the speaker, and in what
follows nothing more is said of his person. We may say that he is
wholly *effect*, for immediately after his speech the situation
changed. All are passionately aroused. What the god in human
form had said, Sarpedon says to Hector as if on his own impulse,
and the words sting Hector to the heart. Straightway he leaps
from his chariot and fires the Trojans to fresh resistance. Ares

shields the soldiery and in human form[96] fights at Hector's side until the Greeks finally begin to waver. Then Hera and Athena, with Zeus's consent, resolve to support the Greeks against Ares. Hera approaches them in the form of Stentor, who had the mightiest voice of all,[97] and shouts into the throng that their failure to resist the Trojans, after Achilles' withdrawal, is a shameful thing. This kindles their spirit, and at once their hearts beat high again. To Diomedes alone it is vouchsafed to see his goddess. Suddenly she stands before him and addresses him. She even mounts his chariot and drives his horses directly against Ares.[98]

The description of Apollo's intervention on another occasion[99] is very instructive. It is the hour when Patroclus's doom is to be fulfilled. He had forgotten his friend's warning. Intoxicated with victory he storms forward towards Troy, spreading death and terror on all sides. "The gods have summoned him to death,"[100] but before its extinction his star is shining its brightest. He had all but climbed the walls of the city, but now Apollo intervened. It was only Patroclus himself whom his divine majesty confronted. First this happened at the city wall, where the thundering voice of the god threw him back in astonishment, and then it was out in the battlefield. In the meanwhile Apollo dispatched the man who would deliver the death-blow. This was Hector. To Hector he appeared in human form, as an elder kinsman, his mother's brother, Asius by name, and said to him: "Hector, why have you left off fighting? It is ill done of you. If I were as much better a man than you as I am worse, you should soon rue your slackness. Drive straight towards Patroclus, if so be that Apollo may grant you a triumph over him and you may kill him."[101] It was a kinsman, then, a quite unremarkable figure, that called Hector's attention to Apollo's favor, and out of this man Apollo himself had spoken. Without a word of answer Hector goes into battle, making directly for Patroclus. What the god announces through human lips must prove true. To be sure, Patroclus must still reach the pinnacle of his glory. A stone which he hurls kills Hector's charioteer, and about his body there ensues a fearful melee which ends with the victory of the Greeks. And now Patroclus hurls himself upon the enemy afresh—and is smitten by the fearful blow of Apollo which delivers him to his enemies defenseless and permits Hector effortlessly to win the glory which Apollo in the form of Asius had foretold.

After the fall of Patroclus, Hector pursues his war chariot with its divine horses, which are speeding away with Automedon driving. Meanwhile Euphorbus has begun to fight with Menelaus for the body of Patroclus.[102] Euphorbus falls, and Menelaus is on the point of stripping off his armor. At this moment Hector suddenly sees Mentes, chief of the Ciconians, before him. "Hector," he calls, "your pursuit of the horses of the wise son of Aeacus is hopeless. They are hard for mortal men to master and to drive, for any other than Achilles, whom an immortal mother bore. Meanwhile, Menelaus, Atreus' warlike son, bestriding Patroclus, has slain the bravest of the Trojans, Panthous's son Euphorbus, and has ended his furious valor." When Hector hears this, dreadful grief seizes his heart. He looks about him, and sees his friend lying in his blood and Menelaus in the act of stripping off his armor. Hector advances with a shout, and Menelaus shrinks back. So narrated, there is nothing miraculous in the episode. It was lucky for the Trojans that a comrade informed Hector of the fall of Euphorbus at the right moment, so that he returned to the critical conflict. But the comrade who spoke the word was actually, as the poet knows, Phoebus Apollo, who had assumed the guise of Mentes for the purpose. So the gods are not merely the producers of decisive factors: they are themselves decisive factors. As such they accost man upon his way, and the familiar figure who crosses his way at a significant moment is only the covering of a god. In the story recounted above, the divine-human intervention is nothing else than *effect*. Hector makes no reply; he only feels the sting in his heart and turns about. But the speaker vanishes.

Again the battle rages about the body of Patroclus.[103] Zeus determines to encourage the Greeks and sends them Athena. Veiled in a luminous cloud she descends from heaven and moves unseen through the ranks. Desire for battle is aroused in all hearts. The first man she encounters is Menelaus. It is not the goddess that he sees, however, but the familiar graybeard Phoenix, who points out the disgrace of allowing the man whom great Achilles loved

best to be thrown to Trojan dogs. Upon Phoenix's appeal to hold
steadfast and urge on all the host, Menelaus replies: "Would
that Athena would give me the strength and ward off the rain
of missiles; then I should be willing to stand by and guard
Patroclus, for his death greatly grieved my heart. But Hector has
the dreadful might of fire and never leaves off slaying with
bronze, for Zeus gives him the glory." Athena rejoices at the hero's
thinking of her before the other gods, and she fills him with
strength and makes his heart steadfast so that nothing can terrify
or confuse him any more. So he strides to attack, and slays a warrior especially dear to Hector. He is even able to drag the body
without difficulty from the range of the Trojan weapons to his own
people. Even Hector did not hinder him.[104] Had he not noticed
what had happened? Shortly before he had shrunk back from the
two Ajaxes.[105] Now, at least, he is made to realize the situation.
His friend Phaenops stands before him and reproaches him to his
face: " 'Hector, who else among the Achaeans could fear you
any longer when you have fled thus from Menelaus, who was
before now a soft spearman? Now he has alone snatched a corpse
and gone with it from the Trojans' midst and slain your faithful
comrade, a brave man among the foremost ranks, Podes, Eëtion's
son.' At these words a black cloud of grief enveloped Hector, and
he went through the front ranks armed in gleaming bronze."

These two pictures give us a very clear understanding of divine
intervention and its effects. We find nothing strange here; but
everything is experienced and regarded in true Greek fashion.
Hector sees Menelaus dragging the corpse of his dear friend
away. He is struck by indescribable sorrow and also by deep
shame. This grief and this self-accusation are the voice of Apollo,
who, unrecognized, speaks to him. The thoughts immediately become act. Nothing more is said of the man through whose lips the
deity spoke. Menelaus too is tormented by a piercing sense of his
fecklessness. But what can he, the lesser hero, do against mighty
Hector and his fortune? So he answers the admonishing voice,
which in truth is Athena's, with a prayer to that same goddess.
Straightway his limbs are all infused with the spirit of the hero-
goddess. It is not actually the petition that brings divine help:
its utterance is rather a sign that the deity itself is present.

We recognize the same factors in the story of Aeneas's encounter with Achilles.[106] Even though his previous experience had
given Aeneas good cause to avoid Achilles, he here confronts
him with stalwart courage and scornfully disdains his mighty adversary's reminder that the contest between them is unequal. This
boldness was the work of Apollo, who had suddenly stepped into
his path without his being aware of him. For Aeneas it was one of
his kinsmen, Lycaon, son of Priam. Lycaon asked him mockingly,
"Where are the boasts you made among the wine-cups to the lead-
ers of the Trojans that you would fight with Peleus' son Achilles
hand to hand?" Aeneas answered that Lycaon must know that
engaging Achilles was out of the question; always there was a
god at his side to protect him. He himself had discovered this
when only flight with a god's help had delivered him from those
terrible hands. If heaven would only make the odds equal,
Achilles would have his man. The supposititious Lycaon then
answers significantly: "'Warrior, you too may boast of the immortal gods; they say you are a son of Zeus's daughter Aphrodite,
whereas Achilles sprang from a lower goddess, for Aphrodite is of
Zeus, and Thetis of the old man of the sea. Carry the stubborn
bronze straight against him and let him not turn you aside at all
by shameful words and threats.' So saying he inspired great might
in the shepherd of the people and he went through the front
ranks armed in gleaming bronze." So the poet tells the tale. To the
last words Aeneas made no reply, nor is anything more said of the
friend who spoke to him. There is only a wonderful *effect* here:
Aeneas, who was still timorous, is suddenly filled with courage.
This the presence of the god brought about. We are not even
told that Aeneas followed the advice to pray to the gods. Here too
it is the divine presence which produces the thought and at the
same time the exaltation in which prayer and fulfillment are one.

Several passages in the *Odyssey* show special subtlety in so
presenting the personal intervention of a deity that the miraculous
seems natural and the natural miraculous.

Odysseus has arrived at the shore of Phaeacia helpless and
naked. Nausicaa clothed and fed him and escorted him part of the
way. But at the grove of Athena she had to leave him to his
luck[107] and could only advise him to inquire for the palace, walk

quickly through its hall, and supplicate her mother who was enthroned at the hearth. Following her wish Odysseus waits for a
time before proceeding to the city. He reaches it without being
addressed or molested by anyone. The royal residence is pointed
out to him, and after a few moments of contemplation he passes
the threshold. In the hall the men are assembled for their evening potations, but no one pays attention to him. Thus he arrives
at the hearth without interference, and it is only then that the
stranger is noticed crouching at the feet of the queen. His tearful
petition for safe conduct to his home produces an extraordinary effect. The king raises him with his hand and escorts him to a seat of
honor. The defenseless man is safe and his fate decided. Here a
deity was at work. His path to the city and the palace might
have brought the unprivileged alien many annoying and even
dangerous encounters. Indeed we hear that the Phaeacians were
not very amiably disposed to foreigners.[108] It is true that the sun
had already set[109] and darkness might obviate attention; but luck
too was required. And the stranger must depend on luck if his
inquiry on the way to the palace was not to be addressed to exactly the wrong person. This luck—so the poet tells us—was the
work of goddess Athena. Indeed she is herself luck, and we have
here actual confirmation of the saying that the gods are the
facilitating factor which a man encounters in his undertakings.
Before he leaves the grove of Athena Odysseus prays to the
goddess, "Give me to find love and pity among the Phaeacians."[110]
As he moves towards the city she makes the darkness about him
—it is already night—so thick that no passer-by could notice and
detain him. At the entrance to the city, however, where he needs a
guide, he suddenly meets a young girl, going for water with a
pitcher. The girl is very willing to show him the way. Before he
enters the palace she encourages him and gives him certain valuable directions: He would find the nobles within at table; first
he must apply to the queen; if the queen is friendly he might hope
to regain his homeland. Odysseus does as bidden. In the hall no
one notices him until he embraces the knees of the queen. This
is due to the impenetrable mist with which Athena has veiled
him and which she now disperses, so that the sight of the kneeling
stranger evokes speechless astonishment. But Athena was also the

friendly girl who had given him such good directions and advice. He himself is not aware of this, and we too, if the poet had not suggested it, would have found nothing incredible in the story and would have felt nothing more than that its hero was attended by "luck." This "luck" remains true to him on the following day also, at the Phaeacian council and at their games; here too the goddess Athena is herself involved in every propitious occurrence.[111] In the morning the king's herald goes through the city summoning the councillors to the assembly where Alcinous awaited them to present a visitor: the stranger was worth meeting; his very air suggested the immortals, and he had had many experiences in distant seas. Thus the interest of the Phaeacians has been engaged for Odysseus in advance. But when they see him in person they are filled with admiration, for the goddess had endowed him with commanding beauty and force. All therefore agree with the king's proposal to equip a ship for his homeward journey. Then a festive reception takes place in the king's house, and after the banquet games are arranged. Here, by Athena's plan, the stranger whose beauty, wit, and presence had won all hearts would impress all present by his peerless strength. His initial refusal to participate is interpreted by a brash young man as a confession of incompetence. Thereupon Odysseus seizes the heaviest discus and hurls it far beyond the mark reached by the best of his predecessors. The whistle of the mighty heave produced a general stir, but when the stone came to earth there was a man there who set a mark and shouted out: "Stranger, even a blind man's dim groping hand would pick out the dint of your stone; it does not lie confused among the crowd of marks, but is alone, far in front of all. Be confident, for this event at least. No Phaeacian will reach your throw, much less exceed it." Odysseus rejoices at having found a friend in the meet; he had reason to be grateful to him, for it was through him that his achievement received proper notice. But this man was in reality Athena.[112] She was also the herald who summoned the elders to the assembly and advertised Odysseus' merits. Here too, then, the divine miracles of the background consist of quite unremarkable but yet decisive incidents. It remains for the poet, who is enlightened by the deity, to recognize this background while the participants can notice only a natural flow.

8

But at a special moment and for a special person the deity itself steps forward out of this background and shows itself to the elect individual in its true form. So it happened to Odysseus when he was brought home from Phaeacia in his sleep and on awakening failed to recognize Ithaca. As he walked back and forth on the seashore lamenting there came to him a young man of gentle mien who told him where he was.[113] But suddenly, as he was making every effort to deceive the stranger concerning his own identity and origin, he felt the touch of a loving hand, and there before him instead of the young man stood a smiling woman—Athena! Of her remarks to him and the significance of her appearance we have spoken at large above.

Such corporeal manifestations of divine beings are recounted in a number of passages in the Homeric poems. But before we deal with the circumstances and forms of their appearance we must become better acquainted with another mode of divine manifestation, whose peculiarity is that the human does indeed notice and sense the proximity of the deity, but only after it has departed, and without being clear about its identity.

In the fearful crisis of the battle at the ships, just as Hector is leading his companies to the attack with savage cries, Poseidon in the form of Calchas suddenly appears to the most proven heroes of the Greeks, the two Ajaxes, upon whose valor everything now depends.[114] They do not lack desire to fight, but the god disguised as a friend must bring the seriousness of the present danger home to them and at the same time appeal to their self-confidence. He does this with great subtlety, by referring them to deity: "May some god put it into your hearts to make a firm stand here, and to incite others to do the like. Then you will drive Hector from the ships." Then he struck both of them with his staff "and filled their hearts with daring; he made their legs light and active, as also their hands and their feet." The next moment he was gone "winging his way like a soaring falcon."[115] "Ajax son of Oileus was the first to know who it was that had been speaking to them, and said to Ajax son of Telamon, 'Ajax, this is one of the gods that dwell on Olympus, who in the likeness of the prophet is bidding us fight hard by our ships. It was not Calchas the seer and diviner of omens; I knew him at once by his feet and knees as he turned away, for the gods are soon recognized. Moreover, I feel the lust of battle burn more fiercely within me, while my hands and my feet under me are more eager for the fray.' And Ajax son of Telamon answered, 'I too feel my hands grasp my spear more firmly; my strength is greater and my feet more nimble; I long, moreover, to meet furious Hector, son of Priam, even in single combat.' " So great is the immediate effectiveness of the divine presence. But only one of the two plainly recognized the miraculous element behind the covering of naturalness, and even he knew only that it was "a god" that had spoken. Only the poet can say that it was Poseidon. He tells us also that Athena shed oblivious sleep over Odysseus' eyelids when he had come safe to the Phaeacian shore,[116] whereas Odysseus himself knows only that "the god" shed deep sleep upon him.[117] We meet with these significant distinctions in Homer quite often. In the course of the narrative which begins with the experience of the two Ajaxes, Trojan heroes are several times incited by Poseidon, sometimes in the form of Calchas and sometimes in another,[118] but no one notices that the speaker whose words are so effective is anything more than a man.

In the story of Telemachus[119] too the deity present in human shape is recognized at the moment of vanishing. Old Mentor, who visited Nestor as Telemachus' escort, was in reality Athena. Evening darkness had fallen[120] and the sacrificial banquet at which the visitors had been entertained was breaking up. Nestor invites them to lodge at his house. Mentor refuses for himself and suggests that Telemachus accept the invitation; he himself was minded to sleep with the crew and to continue his journey at dawn. He recommends Telemachus to Nestor—and suddenly vanishes. The departure was like the flight of a great sea-bird,[121] and all present were astonished and amazed. Old Nestor is the first to find words: it was a god who had accompanied Telemachus, and none other than the majestic daughter of Zeus, the protectress of his noble father. He concludes with a prayer to the goddess. It was at the departure that the miracle revealed itself,

this time before a cloud of witnesses. But it was the hour of marvels, late dusk, which all at once makes things nearby vague and
then causes them to vanish. The poet surely does not mean to say
that Athena suddenly exchanged the shape of Mentor for that of
a sea-eagle. His image serves only to vivify her fading away,
which was astonishing but quite in keeping with the marvels of
dusk.

At his first encounter with Athena[122] Telemachus had no such
interpreter as Nestor at his side. And yet from the peculiar stride
of departing Mentes, in whose shape she had appeared, he recognized that it was a god who had spoken to him though he did not
know which.[123] Sunk in thought he was sitting among his mother's
gay and bibulous suitors; the image of his father hovered before
him, and he thought how fine it would be if his father should suddenly come and chase the presumptuous intruders from his possessions.[124] Then he saw a guest enter. With knightly courtesy
he conducted him to the place of honor and sat down at his side.
His intention was to inquire after his absent father.[125] The stranger, who identified himself as Mentes, chief of the Taphians, and
an old friend of the family,[126] promptly began to speak of Odysseus and assured Telemachus that he was alive and would shortly
return: so had the immortals put it into his heart to speak. He
listened to Telemachus' account of the behavior of the suitors,
and expressed the wish that Odysseus might suddenly enter and
make short work of them.[127] Thus his thoughts and images coincide with those which had preoccupied Telemachus at the moment of his arrival. Then he earnestly exhorts him to show himself
a man. He must seek to rid himself of the suitors and then journey
to Nestor and Menelaus for news of his father. He was now old
and strong enough to act independently. He must know how
famous Orestes was throughout the world for having slain his
father's murderer.[128] After these words the guest takes leave. Telemachus' pleas do not avail to detain him—and suddenly he vanishes, while Telemachus's breast swells with strength and courage,
and the image of his father is more vivid than ever to his eyes.
Amazed, Telemachus senses the miracle and surmises that he had
spoken with a god. The poet compares the extraordinary disappearance of the goddess with the soaring of a bird.[129] But it was

only Telemachus who sensed the miracle. The suitors were preoccupied with listening to the bard, as the poet expressly remarks
at the beginning and end of the god's visit.[130] Thus they took no
notice of the stranger. Only Eurymachus later asks Telemachus
who it was;[131] he had been struck by the fact that the stranger had
suddenly sprung up and was gone before inquiry could be made
concerning his origin. But he thought of no miracle; that was reserved for Telemachus, who was the only one it concerned. Indeed it so grew out of the naturalness of the situation that we
must see it as part of that naturalness.

Here too, as in many cases we have already examined, the
miraculous is no alien impingement upon nature but a momentary
emergence from its background which may suddenly shock the
soul of the elect and arouse in it a premonition, in some cases
even a clear recognition, of the divine. What did Athena in the
shape of Mentes say to Telemachus that, according to our conception, his own heart might not have said to him? He sat in the
midst of the detested suitors, and the image of his royal father
rose before him: would that he might come and put a sudden stop
to their insolent evildoing! And when Athena departed, his heart
was fuller than ever of thoughts of his father. She had quickened
the hope that he would return; she had aroused his manly determination, and had made him think of inquiring in Pylos and
Sparta for the father he yearned to see. To our way of thinking
his own reflections and dreams brought him to this point of themselves and lifted him to a higher mood. But for the Greeks such
decisive thoughts and attitudes are always effected by the presence of a god; and in the present instance what transpires in the
man is so significant that he senses the presence of a god. He sees
the guest who had just spoken to him departing and in the next
instant, even before he has reached the door, disappearing like a
bird which suddenly soars aloft and is gone. What he has heard
has made his heart beat high. There can be no doubt: it must
have been a god. The description of Athena's departure has been
found inappropriate. But the image which the poet uses is as de-
liberate and apt here as it is in the scenes discussed above, where
the divine personage is recognized as such by the marvellous
manner of its disappearance. With Nestor, it is true, the marvel

happens after dusk has fallen, whereas here it is still daylight. But Telemachus, who was the object of the visit, is also the only one who saw the miracle. The suitors noticed nothing.

Contact with the deity is always followed immediately by the decisive deed. Telemachus at once mingles with the suitors in order to act.[132] He informs them of the name and character of the guest who is no longer present, though he himself knew well that he was more than man.[133] On the following day he speaks in public to the Ithacans with manly courage, and when he is perturbed by the lack of good will that meets him he goes to the seashore to pray: "Hear me, you god who visited me yesterday and bade me sail the seas in search of my father who has so long been missing. I would obey you, but the Achaeans and more particularly the wicked suitors, are hindering me that I cannot do so."[134] Hardly had he spoken when Mentor, who had interceded vigorously for him in the assembly,[135] was before him. It was he whom Odysseus had exhorted to care for his house when he went off to war. With energetic words he strengthens the youth's self-assurance and he promises to provide a ship and himself to accompany him on the journey. That this time too a deity was concealed in the form of his friend was noticed by Telemachus only later in Pylos, at his departure, where Nestor's remark led him to the realization that it was Athena who had accompanied him. For though the poet had mentioned her name previously,[136] he had no intention of suggesting that Telemachus was aware of it.

At a highly critical moment in the battle between Odysseus and the suitors Athena again appears in the guise of Mentor.[137] Many readers have found fault with this scene, but it is essential, for in truly Homeric fashion it emphasizes one of the great turning points in the story by the intervention of a deity. Its seeming shortcomings, moreover, disappear if we follow the poet attentively and without prejudice. Odysseus has spent all his arrows. Armed for the last and deciding battle, he stands upon the threshold, with Telemachus and the two herdsmen at his side. How tiny is their band compared to the company of suitors! Soon the spears would fly. At this moment Athena in the guise of Mentor suddenly stands at Odysseus' side. Gladdened by the unexpected appearance of his friend, Odysseus invites his assistance: "'Men-

tor, lend me your help, and forget not your old comrade, nor
the many good turns he has done you. Besides, you are my age-
mate.' But all the time he felt sure it was Athena."[138] To the
threats of the suitors Mentor pays no heed. He reminds Odysseus
of his heroism at Troy, where his sword had laid many a warrior
low and the city of Priam had fallen through his clever counsel.
All this he had done, moreover, for Helen's sake; "how comes it
that you are so lamentably less valiant now that you are on your
own ground, face to face with the suitors in your own house?
Come on, my good fellow, stand by my side and see how Mentor,
son of Alcimus, shall fight your foes and requite your kindnesses
conferred upon him."[139] Now we expect some action, but nothing
happens; the speaker suddenly disappears. At first this may seem
strange, but after short reflection we realize that the incident is
consistent. Odysseus must look to the final decision with sanguine
courage. The points that Athena makes—the much harder tasks
at Troy, and the, to him, incomparably greater importance of the
present issue—a modern story teller would have pass through the
mind of Odysseus himself at this fateful moment. In Homer
thoughts so pregnant proceed out of the deity, and so they are
suggested to Odysseus by Mentor, who is in truth Athena. This
Mentor will also show him how energetically a friend would act
in such a situation out of mere friendship.[140] The mood which the
moment demands is thus achieved; there is no need for the supposititious Mentor. Odysseus had even sensed who it was that
spoke in Mentor's guise. Now he had suddenly vanished. This
makes the opposition overconfident, which was Athena's second
purpose. A regular battle was to begin, and "she wished to prove
Odysseus' own prowess and that of his son."[141] "Mentor has gone
away after having done nothing but brag," the same suitor who
had previously threatened Mentor now cries in triumph.[142] But
the poet tells us that "she flew up to one of the rafters in the roof
of the smoky hall and sat upon it in the form of a swallow."[143]
Her disappearance, then, is after the same fashion as that after
her first encounter with Telemachus.[144] The poet surely had no
intention of saying that Athena (or Mentor) transformed herself
into a swallow; as in the passages previously discussed, the simile
is intended to make the manner of her disappearance vivid. In-

visibly she sits aloft in the rafters, and invisibly (like Apollo in the *Iliad*[145]) she there raises the fearful aegis, whereupon the catastrophe begins.[146] The suitor who later recounts the event to Agamemnon in the underworld knows only that "some one of the gods was helping them."[147]

9

Odysseus recognized Athena in the guise of Mentor, but he behaved exactly as if it were in fact Mentor. None of the others noticed anything supernatural; nor should they have, for in Homer the epiphany of a divine being is conceivable only as the experience of a chosen individual. Such incidents are not infrequent in the two epics. But if we expect that here the miracle will be contrasted with natural ways we are greatly mistaken. Here too the miraculous grows out of the natural situation and shows the man experiencing it—who remains the sole witness—its eternal and divine visage. The introduction of a deity is never required to make an event intelligible in our sense. The stories could all be told without the slightest reference to deity, and they would undergo no substantial change. But the spirit of the Homeric world makes these references necessary, for it must link every decisive factor to the divine, however intelligible it may be to us on natural grounds. For this too, finally, we subjoin a number of characteristic examples.

Athena's appearance at Achilles' quarrel with Agamemnon[148] has been discussed in another context.[149] Achilles starts up in his anger. He reflects for an instant whether he should strike Agamemnon down or master his rage, and already he is loosening the sword in its scabbard. At this moment he feels himself touched from behind, turns about, and finds himself looking into the flaming eyes of the goddess. She advises him to master his passion, and he thrusts the sword back into its scabbard. Achilles alone saw[150] and heard the goddess, and this immediately before the decision, while reason and passion were still struggling in his breast and the die had not yet been cast—the intervention of the goddess was in itself the decision, according to the truly Greek mode of thought. All that others saw was Achilles starting up, struggling with himself, and his sudden composure.

Just as the manifestation of the deity here gives human will its turn towards reason and dignity, so at critical moments it makes the forces of life triumph over infirmity and weariness. Hector collapsed unconscious when he was struck by the boulder Ajax hurled. The dazed man was happily brought to safety, and at a distance from the enemy his faithful friends tried to revive him.[151] The Greeks were sure that he was killed, and were jubilant. But suddenly their hearts sank; the man they believed dead appeared again in the enemy ranks, vigorous and bold, as if nothing had happened to him.[152] "I take it he will kill many of us Danaans," one of them says, "for the hand of Zeus must be with him."[153] What actually happened only Hector himself and the poet know. And the poet tells it in such a way that we see the miracle in complete accord with nature. Apollo suddenly approached Hector and inspired him with fresh strength and lust for battle. But he did not approach him when he was unconscious and half dead. He did not out of the fullness of his divine power say to a man whose life was despaired of "Live!" Hector had already recovered consciousness. He was no longer prone but was sitting upright and recognized the faithful friends who surrounded him. The will of Zeus, says the poet,[154] revived him. At this moment he saw a god standing before him and heard him say, "Hector, son of Priam, why are you so faint, and why are you here away from the others? Has any mishap befallen you?" Hector did not know who the god was, and wondered at his question. In a weak voice he told how Ajax had struck him with the boulder and how he believed his last hour had come. Apollo then reveals his identity; he tells Hector to take courage and boldly lead the Trojan chariots against the ships of the Greeks. He himself would go before to smooth the way. Then he infuses strength into Hector,[155] and suddenly all weariness has vanished. The man who has just awakened from a swoon storms forward like a full-fed battle steed who has broken loose and again leads his charging men. The wonderful restoration of vitality, his animation upon recovery, the kindling of his heroic spirit—that was the god. And the convalescent saw him with his eyes and heard his voice. But only he. We hear

nothing of any effect upon his friends, who were standing close
by the while. And even for Hector himself the manifestation is
re-absorbed into events, just as it had suddenly emerged out
of them: as soon as Apollo had filled him with strength and valor
he flung himself into battle, and nothing more is said of the god.
Later, when Apollo was going before the Trojans as he had promised to do, he was invisible.[156]

Another time Apollo exhorts Hector to reason, as Athena had
exhorted Achilles.[157] Hector had resolved to oppose Achilles
boldly, and was summoning his men to attack. The battle-cry had
already sounded—when Apollo stood beside him and warned
him: "Hector, on no account must you challenge Achilles to
single combat; keep a lookout for him while you are under cover
of the others and away from the thick of fight, otherwise he will
either hit you with a spear or cut you down at close quarters."
Hector was alarmed and withdrew into the crowd[158]—and instantly terrible Achilles sprang up and slew noble Iphition. Here
the warrior became aware of his terrible danger at the last moment. This sudden flash of awareness was the manifestation of
Apollo. But he was seen only by the man to whom his warning
was directed. And that man immediately does as the god suggests;
of the god nothing more is said.

As convincing as it is effective is the story of how Odysseus,
lying sleepless, was comforted by a divine manifestation,[159] when
what the manifestation communicated to him was in fact only
the conclusion of his own reflections. Confidence in the deity of
whose support he is certain puts an end to his anxious restless-
ness, and he sinks into relaxed slumber. But this confidence is itself the effect of divine presence. It is the night before the battle
with the suitors. Odysseus tosses about restlessly, for anxiety for
the morrow makes him sleepless. Suddenly Athena stands before
him in the guise of a mortal woman, and he recognizes her at
once. "My poor unhappy man," she says, "why do you lie awake
in this way? This is your house: your wife is safe inside it, and so
is your son who is just such a young man as any father may be
proud of." Odysseus speaks of his anxieties and doubts, but she
reproves his foolish lack of faith: "For shame! Anyone else would
trust a worse ally than myself, even though that ally were only a

mortal and less wise than I am. Am I not a goddess, and have I
not protected you throughout in all your troubles? I tell you
plainly that even though there were fifty bands of men surround-
ing us and eager to kill us, you should take all their sheep and
cattle and drive them away with you. But go to sleep; it is a very
bad thing to lie awake all night, and you shall be out of your
troubles before long." With these words she shed sleep over him
and disappeared.[160]

Shortly before, Athena had appeared to Odysseus at the moment he was to make himself known to his son.[161] Odysseus was
sitting, dressed as a beggar, in the house of the swineherd. Eumaeus had gone away, and father and son were together alone.
Odysseus saw Athena standing outside and motioning to him.
She had the form of a tall and beautiful woman. Telemachus did
not notice her presence, "for the gods do not let themselves be
seen by everybody."[162] Besides Odysseus only the dogs were
aware of the goddess. They did not bark, but drew back whim-
pering. At a nod of the goddess Odysseus stepped out. "It is now
time for you to tell your son," she said. "Do not keep him in the
dark any longer, but lay your plans for the destruction of the
suitors, and then make for the town. I will not be long in joining
you, for I too am eager for the fray." As she spoke she touched him
with her golden wand. The beggarliness and hoariness disappeared, and infused with the magic of youth and dressed in fine
garments Odysseus returned to the house, where Telemachus
looked at him in utter astonishment. "I am your father," he said,
but the son could not believe. He feared that some god was making sport of him, for only a god could perform the miraculous
transformations he saw before him.[163] Then Odysseus explained
that this was the work of Athena, who had the power to show him
now as beggar and now as a well-dressed and youthful man: "It
is an easy matter for the gods who live in heaven to make any man
look either rich or poor."[164] Then Telemachus fell sobbing upon
his neck. When Eumaeus returned, Athena again approached
Odysseus, who was preparing supper with Telemachus. With a
stroke of the wand she again made him hoary and dressed him
in beggar's rags, for the swineherd must not yet recognize him.[165]
Here too, despite the magic wand and the transformation motif,

there is nothing essentially unnatural in these wonderful events. We recognize the true lineaments of nature in a higher illumination which makes them into plastic phenomena. The important moment had come. Odysseus, who had hitherto played the hoary beggar in order not to be recognized, found himself alone with his son. Now the father must make himself known. This great moment, the sudden realization that it was time, the overwhelming experience of return in the true sense—all of this was divine, was deity itself, was Athena. Something of the same sort is expressed by Euripides' Helen when she suddenly recognizes her husband again in a foreign country: "Ye gods, to recognize one's friends is god."[166] The whole scene stands under the sign of the divine. Odysseus feels that his son must now recognize his father. He withdraws for a moment and returns with a youthful and royal appearance, and the young man is speechless with astonishment. This means that Athena had enlightened his heart with the thought and had transformed him. That she uses magic is not essential for the effect of her action. In the Homeric understanding the miracle to be revered lies not in overcoming nature but in the infinite exaltation of the significant hour.

With this scene we must compare the happy encounter of Odysseus with Hermes, which has been discussed above.[167] In the solitude of an unknown region, near the house of Circe where his companions had disappeared, a youth suddenly accosts Odysseus and asks about his intentions with obvious solicitude. He explains that the woman of the house is a wicked sorceress who has transformed his friends and would do the same to him if he did not use prudence in dealing with her and protect himself against her enchantments with a magic herb. The magic herb grows at his very feet, and the youth, whom Odysseus recognizes at once as Hermes, digs it up. Here too the corporeal manifestations of the divine is nothing else than the illuminating moment itself in its highest and eternal essence. Odysseus had gone forth alone to find his companions. He knew only of the house of a woman who sang at her loom and whose invitation his companions had accepted and then failed to return.[168] Despite the tearful pleas of the messenger who shuddered at the thought of returning to that house, the hero threw himself into the adventure alone. He was now in sight of the house—and there, in dangerous proximity to it, his eyes were suddenly opened and he knew all: a witch lived there; she had bewitched his envoys, and threatened to ruin him also. And the kindly moment not only enabled him to comprehend the true facts concerning the uncanny woman at a single stroke, but also showed him the magic herb that grew out of the earth close by him. All of this, which we can understand so well and so easily express in our language, was the divine person, and the voice of awareness was its living word. What we experience amorphously appeared to the open senses of the Greek as an encounter on his way. Here it is Hermes, the lofty spirit of the favorable moment and its sudden wisdom, who manifests himself to the solitary way-farer. How he encountered the aged King Priam on his dangerous night journey has been told in detail in the proper context. There too he came as a young man; but at his departure he made himself known to his protégé. Before Achilles could see him he had vanished, for "an immortal god must not befriend a mortal man thus openly."[169]

A man fighting for his life also can see an embodied deity before him if in his greatest need he suddenly senses marvellous assurance and strength. In despair Achilles wrestles with the waves of the Scamander and complains to the gods for letting him die so miserable a death. Suddenly Poseidon and Athena are at his side, grasp his hand, and assure him that Zeus is protecting him and that the stream is powerless against him. But Achilles, whose courage had previously sunk so low, strides intrepidly forward, with the steadfastness and strength which the deity had given him.[170] He had seen Poseidon and Athena face to face, they themselves had spoken their names. But the miracle which came about through them is nothing else than the common experience of a hopeless man who in the midst of a torrent of destruction suddenly breathes the air of life again and senses strength and triumph. Achilles answers his divine friends not a syllable, nor do they expect it, but vanish as directly as they had come. What remains is the *effect* in his spirit and limbs. He is not lifted above toil and struggle, but he now fights with the high spirit of the conqueror.

Surely the much debated appearance of Athena to assist Achilles in his fight with Hector[171] is of the same character. The instant that the scales of Zeus show the fall of Hector Apollo forsakes him.[172] A moment before, he had infused Hector with such vitality that Achilles could not overtake him.[173] Now, however, he must leave him forever. But at the same instant Athena joins Achilles. Luck flies from the one and supports the other—so say we, dimly conscious of a power whose essence and effects scorn our cleverness. For the spacious mind of the Greek these are gods who at the peak of an event can present themselves to their sole elect, even visibly, and whose activity is yet nothing else than the natural course of things and the mysterious consequences which must ensue under good omens or evil. Achilles sees the goddess— he alone—and hears from her with delight that *now* the moment of his triumph has come. He need no longer weary himself with running, for Hector will now stand up to him. And just that happens; it is the first act of doom. Hector believes that he sees a comrade nearby who will confront the terrible enemy at his side. But the deception which lulls him is his fate, is the goddess—the fortune of Achilles which proves his misfortune. With noble gallantry he proceeds to the duel; and in the first passage at arms he can even exult in glad confidence, for Achilles' spear flies over him and buries itself in the ground. It was vain boasting, then, when Achilles had claimed divine fortune for himself and had prophesied, "You have no escape left; Pallas Athena will forthwith vanquish you by my spear."[174] But the mischief had long been coming. Even what seems an advantage is in truth a disadvantage, while everything miraculously turns to the advantage of his adversary. Athena returns Achilles' spent spear to him.[175] How this comes about we are not told, and Hector has not noticed it. In any case, Achilles again has spear in hand. Now Hector hurls his weapon and hits—but it rebounds off the shield of Peleus' son.[176] To him it is lost. Loudly as he may call, the brother in arms whom he trusted has completely vanished.[177] Now he knows all: the gods have summoned him to death. The semblance of his brother was a trick of the goddess Athena.[178] Now all that is left is a heroic and glorious death.[179] He wrests his sword from its scabbard and springs upon his adversary—straight onto his spear, for his armor left a vulnerable area near the neck unprotected, and there the bronze penetrates. The story is as true as it is grand. We can think the divine figures away without its course being altered. But then it would only be true to nature. By the introduction of the divine, however, the element of accident disappears. The details of the event and their totality are mirrored in the eternal, and yet none of the blood and breath of the living present is lost.

Nowhere in the *Iliad* does a deity intervene in the course of events so personally and consistently as Athena does in favor of Diomedes in the fifth book. She wishes to cover him with glory,[180] and therefore fills him with strength and boldness. She makes his weapons shine like blazing fire, and throws him into the thickest fray.[181] The first cast of his spear lays a noble Trojan low. Then like a winter torrent he rushes through the battlefield and routs the phalanxes of the Trojans.[182] He is struck by the arrow of the archer Pandarus.[183] Pandarus exults, in the belief that he has dealt Diomedes the mortal blow.[184] But Diomedes asks Sthenelus to draw the arrow out of his shoulder and prays to Athena: "Hear me, daughter of aegis-bearing Zeus, Atrytone! If ever you loved my father well and stood by him in the thick of a fight, do the like now by me; grant me to come within a spear's throw of that man and kill him. He has been too quick for me and has wounded me; and now he is boasting that I shall not see the light of the sun much longer."[185] And Athena hearkened to him. She made his limbs wonderfully supple.[186] Moreover, she herself appears before him and tells him that she has placed his father's strong spirit in his heart; he must enter into battle without trepidation; he need not be fearful of gods in mortal shape, for she has drawn the veil from his eyes to know gods and men apart; he must avoid the immortals, with the exception of Aphrodite: if she should appear on the battle scene he must strike her with the edge of the bronze.[187] Athena's words immediately become deed; she herself vanished when she uttered them, and Diomedes springs upon the enemy. If he had been eager enough for battle before, now he was three times fiercer, like a lion who had broken into a sheep-yard.[188] Wherever he turns, some Trojan is crushed under his stroke. Aeneas does not recognize him. He watches him with horror, and urges Pandarus to aim his bow at him;[189] but straightway he fears it may be a god concealed in the form of a

bloodthirsty mortal. Pandarus thinks he recognizes Diomedes—
but then, as he thinks, he had wounded him fatally with his arrow
a little while before. If it is really he, some god must be accompanying him unseen and protecting him from all harm. And
Pandarus curses his bow, which could bring him only the illusion
of success. But Aeneas persuades him that they two together can
confront the man. He has Pandarus mount his chariot, himself
takes the reins in hand, and the two drive against Diomedes.[190]
Diomedes is informed of the danger by his charioteer Sthenelus,
but he is only angered by Sthenelus' advice to draw back. He will
not even mount the chariot, but will encounter the two just as
he is: "Pallas Athena bids me be afraid of no man!"[191] He declares that at least one of the two will meet his doom; but if
Athena should grant him the great glory of slaying both,[192] then
Sthenelus is to drive the horses of Aeneas from the battlefield as
booty. The battle begins. Athena guides the spear of Diomedes,
and Pandarus falls, wounded to death.[193] Aeneas leaps from the
chariot to protect the body of his friend,[194] and is struck by a stone
hurled by Diomedes. He sinks to his knees, darkness covers his
eyes, and only the speedy arrival of Aphrodite saves him from
destruction. She gathers her son in her arms, covers him with her
robe, and carries him away.[195] But Diomedes, mindful of Athena's
instructions, pursues the goddess and strikes her hand with his
spear. Aphrodite cries out, lets her son fall,[196] and goes wailing to
Olympus. Apollo takes defenseless Aeneas up, and wraps him in
a dark cloud. But though Diomedes recognized the god[197] he
would not desist, until Apollo terrified him with an awful shout:
"Take heed, son of Tydeus, and draw off: think not to match
yourself against gods, for men that walk the earth cannot hold
their own with the immortals."[198] Diomedes draws back, and the
god carries his unconscious burden to his Trojan sanctuary, where
Leto and Artemis nurse him. But the Trojans and Greeks he
causes to fight over a wraith of wounded Aeneas.[199] Then Apollo
draws Ares' attention to Diomedes; he urges him to turn his might
against the man who ventured to attack even gods and to draw
him out of the battle.[200] The god of war needs no urging; he assumes the form of the Trojan Acamas,[201] and cheers the Trojans
on to show themselves true men: "Aeneas the son of Anchises has

fallen, him whom we held in as high honor as Hector himself.
Help me, then, to rescue our brave comrade from the stress of the
fight."[202] Ares' words took immediate effect, and grim fighting
flared up. Marvellous to relate, Aeneas, the wounded man over
whose unconscious body men still thought they were fighting,
suddenly reappeared among his comrades. Apollo had sent him
back from his sanctuary and had filled his heart with valor.[203]
But this no one knew. "They were overjoyed at seeing him alive,
sound, and of good courage; but they could not ask him how it
had all happened, for they were too busy with the turmoil." Led
by Ares and Enyo[204] the Trojans drive forward. Diomedes, who
alone is able to recognize the god in furious Acamas,[205] is in fear,
and advises his side to draw back fighting. Then much carnage
is wrought as Hector and Ares lay about them,[206] until finally
Hera and Athena, with the consent of Zeus,[207] come in person to
help the distressed Greeks. This they do in the familiar manner:
the crowd is aware of no divine presence, and only one chosen
individual may experience it at the moment of highest significance. Hera appears among the Greeks in the form of Stentor,[208]
and her huge voice cries shame upon them for having proved so
cowardly when Achilles was no longer among them. But Athena
approaches Diomedes, who stands at his chariot, weary and cool-
ing his wounds. "The goddess laid her hand on the yoke of his
horses and said, 'The son of Tydeus is not such another as his
father. . . . I stand by you and protect you, and I bid you be
instant in fighting the Trojans; but either you are tired out,
or you are afraid and out of heart, and in that case I say that
you are no true son of Tydeus the son of Oeneus.' Diomedes
answered: 'I know you, goddess, daughter of aegis-bearing
Zeus, and will hide nothing from you. I am not afraid nor
out of heart, nor is there any slackness in me. I am only following your own instructions; you told me not to fight any of the
blessed gods; but if Zeus's daughter Aphrodite came into battle
I was to wound her with my spear. Therefore I am retreating,
and bidding the other Argives gather in this place, for I know
that Ares is now lording it in the field.'" Now Athena is more
kindly. "Man after my own heart," she says, "fear neither Ares
nor any other of the immortals, for I will befriend you."[209] And

now the episode takes on enormous proportions. The goddess removes the charioteer from Diomedes' chariot and herself mounts
at the side of her hero.[210] The axle groaned aloud, for the chariot
was bearing the mighty goddess and the great hero. Athena
seized the reins to drive straight against the terrible adversary,
who was stripping a slain man of his armor; she donned the helmet of Hades in order not to be seen by him. When Ares caught
sight of Diomedes he left the corpse and strode towards him.
Murderously he hurled his spear at him, but Athena caught it in
her hand, unseen, and let it fly over the chariot. But when Diomedes thrust his spear, Athena drove it into the pit of Ares' stom-
ach. When his flesh was torn, Ares roared so loudly that Achaeans
and Trojans were panic-stricken. Then Diomedes saw Ares ascend
to heaven in a dark cloud.[211]

The Diomedes sequence in the *Iliad* is full of extraordinary
happenings, and to a reader who bears in mind the sacred books
of mankind with their thousand miracles it may communicate the
impression of being a record of miracles. But this is a superficial
and biassed view. If we read the story attentively we can only
be astonished at the unerring ascription of exceptional experiences to the intense feeling of a single individual, here as
elsewhere, whereas outside his range these experiences are resolved into purely natural and familiar processes. From the
religious point of view it is significant that here man's mightiest
achievements are explicitly regarded as deeds actually brought
about by the agency of a god. The hero driving on irresistibly
seems so huge to the enemy that he can regard him as a deity in
human shape.[212] But if his spear wounds his opponent fatally, it
is because Athena directed the weapon with true aim.[213] And in
the boldest venture of all we see the goddess herself standing at
the warrior's side and herself driving the spear, which his
hand thrusts, against the body of Ares, so that he is painfully
wounded.[214]

The belief which prevails throughout the epic that every success—be it only the blow that strikes home or the arrow that finds
its mark—indicates the immediate intervention of divine powers,
has here reached its highest expression: the embodied goddess
stands by her hero, she puts her own hand to the task, and he

sees her and speaks with her. But if we distinguish what the il-
lumined poet can report from what Diomedes himself experiences,
we see that there are only two instances when he actually sees and
hears the god. And we observe not only that these are moments of
intense excitement, but also that they are in fact only moments,
for their miraculous element vanishes at once or dissolves into the
invisible. The story begins with the unseen influence of the
goddess: she inspires Diomedes to battle, makes his armor shine
like fire, and sends him into the midst of the thickest turmoil.
Only in his need, when the bleeding hero sees the lucky archer
gloat and with the greatest intensity of feeling prays to the goddess who had once loved his father to put his enemy in his power,
does she not only revive him but stand visibly before him[215] and
address him. And what does she say to him? In his great straits
he had suddenly remembered his father who had achieved mighty
deeds with Athena's help. "Fear not," says she, "I have set in your
heart the spirit of your knightly father Tydeus." He need not fear
even the superhuman, for Athena had made his eyes discerning,
so that he could recognize and avoid gods if they took part in the
fighting. What are the goddess's words and visible appearance
but the exuberant, nay, even the ecstatic, certainty that his prayer
has been answered? Diomedes does not reply. He cannot reply:
his divine interlocutor has vanished, the heavenly visions have
immediately passed into great happenings, into deeds. He fights,
his passion is tripled, he is like a lion. He sees gods at work
where others recognize only mortals—Aphrodite, Apollo, and
finally Ares. From Ares he draws back, and he advises the Greeks
to seek safety. Then he sees the goddess for the second time. This
time he does not pray. And yet it is plain that the divine appearance is in answer to his heart's need. Her speech, indeed, is like
an utterance of his anguish and at the same time its glorious solution. One recalls Odysseus' experience after the assembly of the
host in the second book of the *Iliad*. All were rushing to the ships
to sail home at once; all the toil and hopes of many years were to
prove vain; Troy would triumph, and the Greeks sailing ingloriously home would be pursued by the taunting laughter of the
Trojans—could such things actually be? Tormented and confused
by these thoughts, Odysseus looked at what was going on. Sud-

denly Athena stands before him, and what she says are these very
thoughts, but also a solution: he must intervene, talk to one man
and another, and convince them of the folly of their course. So too
in the present case. Diomedes sees himself forced to stand cowardly
aside while the mischief grows apace. In his earlier distress he
had thought of his great father, and so now Athena reproaches
him as being unworthy to be called the son of the ever intrepid
Tydeus. That is the very thought which is gnawing at his heart.
But he knows too that his inglorious withdrawal is only the bidding of Athena, who had enjoined him not to confront a god fighting in human form. And yonder Acamas fighting in front of the
Trojans is Ares. This he says. And now the torment of doubt is resolved into wonderful certainty: the huge venture is not too great
for him, for Athena herself will fight at his side. And he sees her
leap onto the war-chariot, at his side; the charioteer Sthenelus
disappears and the goddess herself takes the reins and storms
against Ares, who is hit by the hero's spear and vanishes in a dark
cloud. At this moment the curtain falls upon earthly matters. We
hear no more of Diomedes. Even earlier a veil had been spread
over the experience of the hero. The poet knows that Athena was
standing at his side and tells us what she did. But she herself became invisible for Ares, and more certainly for Diomedes. He feels
the divine presence, but he acts quite as if he were alone. With
such superior knowledge and perfect tact the poet makes us witnesses of a miracle only. Diomedes experiences this miracle. And
now we can see how he experiences it. For everyone else the thing
that Diomedes experiences as a miracle is a natural event; and we
cannot sufficiently admire the truth to nature and the consistency
with which the poet brings this too before our eyes. With a cast
of a stone Diomedes wounded Aeneas so seriously that he sank to
the ground and darkness covered his eyes. But when he sets himself to slay Aeneas, he sees him safely ensconced in Aphrodite's
arms, eluding his attack. But he does not give up, he follows the
goddess and drives her off. But again his victim evades him: he
sees Aeneas under the protection of Apollo, who carries him off
wrapped in a mist. Despite this he determines to attack, but the
god drives him back with his awful voice and disappears with his
protégé. Of all of this the other warriors know nothing. For them

Aeneas lies unconscious on the ground, and friend and foe fight bitterly over him. The poet alone can tell us that this was not Aeneas himself but only a wraith resembling him. Nor does anyone see Athena with Diomedes. The grandiose scene where she stands at his side, drives the horses against Ares, and thrusts the hero's spear into the god's body, is played before the hostile armies as a normal single combat. For they do not detect Ares, as Diomedes does, but see only the Thracian chieftain Acamas; and Athena's presence is wholly hidden from them. The end of the fight in which a god is defeated is a tremendous event for the hosts, with things natural and marvellous intermingled. The wounded god cries out—men believed they heard the roar of a myriad, and a shudder passed up and down the embattled ranks.

10

It is in the most astonishing images of divine manifestations, then, that we can most plainly see how alien to the spirit of true Greek piety is miracle in the commonly accepted sense, which other religions seek out and sanctify. That piety is the more significant in that the same spirit accomplishes all things, from the greatest to the least, through the gods, indeed conceives of them as being accomplished by the gods themselves; and it is so completely alive to this relationship that it never forgets to emphasize the rôle of the divine even when the prowess of the most admired heroes is to be celebrated. The deity that is here the object of faith is not an absolute master over nature who exhibits his sovereignty at its loftiest when he compels nature to act contrary to itself. It is the sanctity of the natural itself and one with its sway, present with its spirit in all that can be experienced and received with reverence by the pious soul. It is demonstrated as well in what is very simple and perfectly regular as in astonishing and awesome experiences of which only a great heart is capable. In the epic, to be sure, where mighty men do and suffer, it is the extraordinary that is repeatedly brought before our eyes. But everywhere it presents itself in the same sense: not as the miracle of a god triumphing over nature, but rather as the experience of a great heart to whom

—and to whom alone—at the height of his being and doing the deity presented itself out of the ordinary lines of nature.

In the face of this not much should be made of the circumstance that once in the *Iliad* the sun—that is, the sun-god—is made to set prematurely.[216] The occasion is important enough. After a desperate struggle the Greeks finally succeeded in securing the corpse of Patroclus from the enemy. "They laid him on a litter, his comrades stood mourning around him, and among them fleet Achilles wept bitterly as he saw his true comrade lying dead upon his bier." Then, constrained by Hera, the sun set, "loth though he was," and all was quiet on the battlefield.—On a no less important occasion in the *Odyssey* Athena restrains the goddess Dawn and makes the night last longer.[217] It was the night on which Penelope recognized her returned husband, and could not sate her eyes with gazing at him or loose her arms from around his neck. Now his wanderings and her lonely tears were ended. But these are isolated ventures of the poet, and in them everyone feels the natural truth which is the basis for their enduring effectiveness. They show an hour of life in its fateful grandeur, and it is that which grips us, not the absolute power of a god.

Once the *Iliad* tells of a miraculous deed of Apollo.[218] But the intensity of passion, which is given a lofty background in this picture, is unmistakable. The Trojan masses were streaming into the naval encampment. Dike, moat, or wall could not stop the furious chariots. It is Apollo who goes before them. The brandishing of his aegis threw the Greeks into such terror that they fled in panic.[219] At the attack on the trench and wall "Apollo went before and kicked down the banks of the deep trench into its middle so as to make a great broad bridge. . . . He kicked down the wall of the Achaeans as easily as a child playing on the seashore kicks down the house of sand which he has built."[220] At the beginning of this description it is expressly stated that the god was invisible.[221]

As against the overwhelming impression of an abundance of evidence a few petty divergences signify little. The epic makes its conception of divine rule perfectly plain. The images which we have to learn from are indeed creations of the poet, but it would be myopic to see in them only the thoughts of an individual or small group. In contrast to what must have been the views of the earlier period, they give expression to a revolution in thought whose importance cannot be rated too high and which must necessarily have been consummated before poetry of the Homeric sort could be possible. For the more astonishing the specific character of Homeric faith must appear to us upon close examination, the more noteworthy is the fact that it presents itself with no pathos and no criticism or justification, as something natural and self-evident. Here there speaks a new race, grown perfectly sure of its conception of the world, calmly able to permit ancient and antiquated elements—and Homer knows a great many that were once important—to come forward out of the background as fairy-tales, without troubling about the alien spirit of these stories, which is perceptible even to us. And if any proof is still called for to show that what we have here are not merely the poet's fancies but Greek thoughts upon the world, the attitude of the Greek spirit in the post-Homeric age must carry conviction. For what is this attitude other than the acknowledgement of a nature which is not opposed to the divine and eternal but one with it? The extraordinary influence of Homeric epic upon Greek thought and creativity has often enough been stressed. It could not have become a guide to the future if it were not the expression of the true Greek spirit. Emerging victorious out of primeval visions, it here created its first and eternal monument.

VI

GOD AND MAN

MAN, GENESIS proudly asserts, was created in the image of God. The same notion is presented in the Greek account of the creation: "The earth, newly fashioned and but lately drawn away from lofty ether, still retained seeds of its kindred heaven; these Prometheus tempered with fresh running water and moulded after the image of the gods who govern all—

finxit in effigiem moderantum cuncta deorum.[1]

The perfection which divinity possesses, that is to say, is reflected in humanity.

What, in the mirror of the Greek spirit, is the purest manifestation of humanity, its noblest transfiguration, in which the image of divinity is revealed? What ideal of humanity, large and momentous, confronts us in the reflected visage of the divine? The characteristics which are the fundamental and essential determinants can never be apprehended from direct statements. Verbal assertions concerning the character of a divinity, numerous though they may be, can almost never give us more than a distorted and exaggerated conception. Even in religions where doctrine is paramount we owe our profoundest conceptions to prophets endowed with plastic vision, who make our perception of deity vivid. The picture is most compelling when there is no intention to improve or reproach or comfort the world but only to testify to the greatest, most majestic, and most worshipful vision and faith of which the spirit is capable. Among the Greeks creative men of genius are not, as they are among other peoples, merely secondary and irresponsible witnesses of divine truth: in this natural and undogmatic religion it is precisely they who are the dedicated prophets.

To the poet the gods reveal themselves in deed and word; the plastic artist presents them to our very eyes. The masterpieces of plastic art regularly produce a profound impression upon the spectator. But he hardly ever analyzes this impression; otherwise he would be forewarned to judge the ancient Greek conception of their gods by the attractive and frivolous tales recounted in later poetry. The statues breathe a nobility and majesty which can only arouse reverence; they find a parallel only in ancient hymns or in the shattering or jubilant invocations of tragedy. If we are able to comprehend the meaning of this nobility and majesty, we shall have discovered how the ancient Greek spirit conceived the perfection of man and at the same time the image of the divine.

The gods and their dominions, whose significance we have examined in some detail, testify to the thoroughly vital and open spirit with which the Greeks were able to recognize the divine in the manifold shapes of existence, serious or gay, powerful or amiable, manifest or enigmatic. Never is it the flight of man's dreams and aspirations, always and everywhere it is the power of reality, the breath and bouquet and glitter of the life which billowed about him, that steeped him in the purple brilliance of the divine. If he encountered his deities in the likeness of man, if he discovered his own nobility and grandeur in their image, we cannot look for any attempt on his part to transcend nature or free himself from it; rather did he regard nature itself with such honest, unerring, and pure truth as only a god could or might possess.

We moderns cannot find it easy to follow the path of the Greeks. The religious tradition in which we were brought up recognizes in nature only the field for the exercise of pious virtues whose spiritual home is found in a region beyond that of their budding, growth, and maturity. Out of the organic and teeming world our mechanical and technical mode of thought has made a mechanism of unintelligible forces. All being is resolved into a swirl of functions and strivings; man is only a being who wills or desires, endowed with greater or lesser capacities. The Greek at every turn of life saw the visage of a god and even in death rested among the symbols of his self-sufficient life which decorated his tomb with simple truth; for us all of life is a pursuit after ever receding goals, and the worth of man is comprised in his energy. Man's highest values must be at the farthest remove from the simplicity and directness of present existence, for which we use the pejorative expression "merely natural." Internal difficulties, contradictions with the external world, the insolubility of causal nexus and motives, the long travail of search and collision—these are what engage our interest. Compared to this ideal the Greek images, readily as we acknowledge their beauty, seem to us much too childlike, too uncomplicated, too empty of problems. Only what is born of strife do we recognize as significant or profound. We may find delight in the bloom of the Greek phenomenon, but we save our respect for struggle, for titanic will and demand, for all that is absolute, that pushes forward into the limitless and the superhuman, for all that is incalculable and labyrinthine in humanity. Such a conception of life can naturally find but little nurture in the Greek figures. It is indeed shut off from the large configurations which had so much to say to the ancient Greek spirit. Whereas we tend to the utmost in subjectivity—whether it be will to good and evil in its most powerful manifestations, or constraint seeking a way out and asserting itself in torment and affliction—it was the character of the Greek genius to see the realities of human existence in the eternal forms of growth and maturation, of laughter and tears, of play and earnest. His attention was directed not to forces but to pure being, and the forms of human being presented themselves with such truth that he could only revere them as gods.

2

Among the treasures of the Terme Museum there is a head of a sleeping woman. She has been variously and falsely labelled, sometimes as Medusa, sometimes as a Fury. She must be Ariadne, or a dancer strayed from the rout of Dionysus. The majestic creature is asleep. There is holiness in the placid smoothness of the brow, holiness in the tightly shut eyes, holiness in the unconscious mouth through whose half-opened lips there flows in gentle alternation the breath of life. But this holiness we can call neither innocence nor salvation nor profundity of soul. These relaxed features speak of neither gaiety nor affliction, neither kindliness nor spite, but only of the divine abyss of sleep.

Its timeless grandeur has been so compellingly embodied and
the force of its being so manifestly represented that any thought
of symbolism or sublimation becomes a desecration. We gaze
into the bared depths of being and experience an encounter with
the infinite and divine. Only ancient poetry finds words that are
comparable. This is how Propertius saw his slumbering love:
"Like Ariadne lay swooning on the desert strand . . . or like a
Thracian maenad foredone by the unending dance, lies sunk in
slumber on the grassy banks of Apidanus."[2] He stood transfixed
by the loftiness of perfect nature and sensed a deity too great for
benevolent praise, such as Goethe felt constrained to bestow upon
his beloved in a poem inspired by Propertius:

> Upon her lips dwelt calm fidelity,
> Upon her cheeks sweet loveliness held sway,
> And the innocence of a kindly heart
> Stirred in her gently heaving bosom.

So the stature of the divine is imperceptibly transmuted into the
sentimental. The vision of the Roman poet is almost terrifying,
for it suddenly sweeps us from bourgeois sensibility up to the
heights where the Greek divinities abide. When our eyes become
accustomed to this level, when the depths and height of living
nature lie exposed before us, we no longer desiderate deep-felt
emotions, no longer miss the otherworldly expression of holiness
which is regarded as the genuine mark of the divine.

The natural grandeur of man's primal image is at the same time
an image of divinity. To consider this a depreciation of the divine
implies want of understanding, for it is precisely the questionable
traits of humanity that are eliminated. The image is not only free
of the faults which may degrade an individual human but it is
also free—and this is far more significant—of any jealous constraint and straitness, of all, that is to say, which is in truth all
too human and is yet so often esteemed as god-like perfection.
Its countenance confronts us with a clarity that knows no fanaticism; its pride displays no solemnity of self-assertion. We feel
that it demands respect, but also that it has no wish for con-
tinual praise and is not minded to allot favor by the measure of
devotion. Whenever we attempt to penetrate its individuality it

7. Sleeping Maenad

withdraws into its elemental being. However diverse the disparate traits of individual gods may be, the aspect which confronts us is one of magnificent tranquillity. No visage is dominated by a single thought or mood. None desires to proclaim a specific virtue or truth, or virtue and truth in general. Nowhere is the salient point of an event or a decision given expression in the glance of the eyes or the play of the lips. Whatever stories myth may tell about the gods, neither joy or sorrow, victory or humiliation, nor any other issue affects their existence. Marked traits of personality would only disturb the expression that mirrors the essence of life with elemental power. These figures have no history because they *are*. Even where they are most anthropomorphic, the primacy and eternity of their *being* are superhuman.

The divine visage shows no determination. Violence and passion are alien to it. Upon its brow is limned not terror but a serenity before which all reminiscences of barbaric monstrosities disperse and vanish. There is no flicker of the capricious in the glance, no mystic or baffling enigma plays about the lips, no intensity distorts the majestic cast to make it whimsical. The divine manifestation never shatters ordinary limitations to achieve the colossal; unlike the Asiatic mode, it does not represent gigantic potency by grotesque forms and multiplication of members. All such monstrous dynamism the pure grandeur of nature disposes of with a smile.

With a being of such a nature it is inconceivable that our intercourse should employ terms of intimacy as with a friend or lover. Before it we should feel petty, even shamed and humbled, were it not that the existential power of the grand visage extinguished any feeling of self and recalled buried life to bright light. A moment of absorption in this visage is like a bath of rebirth in eternal waters which wash away all human dross. Be it only for the dream of a moment, in that dream there vanishes the ungodlike man, who has been degraded not by sin and greed but by pusillanimous zeal and the constraint of the bonds he has himself imposed. He is the slave of his own prudence, at once narrow-hearted and timorous, whether his anxiety is for the commonplaces of life or for virtue and salvation. But where straitness is transcended by the extraordinary, where even striving for

holiness appears only as a relic of earthiness, then is god reflected in man and man in god.

Oneness of god and man in elemental being—that is the Greek
view. Here we see revealed the whole significance of the human
form in which the divine was manifested to the Greek. For other
peoples too the idea of the essential in man is one and the same
with the recognition of godhead. But whereas these others sought
the divine in the perfection of human capacities, as absolute
power, wisdom, justice, or love, it offered itself to the Greek in
the figure of natural man. We know that it was left for the Greek
alone to look upon and comprehend man as man and that he alone
could set himself the task of educating man to no other goal than
to be himself. This is not an invention of philosophy: it belongs
to the spirit that conceived the image of the Olympian gods and
thus determined the direction of Greek thought. To this spirit
man became, like trees and animals, a creature of eternal form
whose pure lines are those of divinity. Instead of raising his
powers and virtues to heaven by pious fantasy he perceived the
outlines of divinity in the delineations of his own nature. All
objections to Greek religion on the ground of anthropomorphism
are therefore idle gossip. It did not make divinity human but regarded the essence of humanity as divine. "The purpose and goal
of the Greeks," wrote Goethe, "is to deify man, not to humanize
deity. This is not anthropomorphism but theomorphism."[3] The
most significant achievement of this theomorphism is the discovery of the primal image of man; this is the sublimest revelation of nature, and at the same time the most genuine manifestation of the divine.

3

The image of divinity directs man away from the personal and
towards the essentiality of nature. None of its traits calls attention to itself; none tells of an ego with peculiar will, peculiar
sensibility and destiny. A definite being does indeed take shape in
the image, yet this being is not of single occurrence or unique,
but rather a permanent component of the living world. Hence it

must always disappoint souls hungry for love who desire an intimate bond with it. Their tender longing must be chilled when, instead of an ego ready to love or hate, they encounter a timeless being, which can attribute no absolute worth to their ephemeral existence. Only a man who is touched by this reality in its loftiest and holiest sense can be drawn up to the gods in reverence and love.

For this reason a true monotheism could never develop in Greece. Even in later times when the notion that all being and all happening must ultimately derive from a single source had become familiar, it was not considered important to bear this unity constantly in mind; the Greeks could not understand the scruples of Jews and Christians who regarded it as an outrageous affront to the One if honor was shown not to himself but to the numerous manifestations of his creation. Emphasis upon self which cannot tolerate another on the same level is alien to the Greek god. He never introduces himself to the world in such selfconscious terms as "I am so-and-so," which is so characteristic a tone for oriental deities.[4] Even hymns of praise, which are so apt to exalt their subject to limitless heights in other respects, are mindful that he knows other gods besides himself and recognizes their high merits.

The best example is the god who long exerted the greatest influence upon the religious life of Greece and yet never wished to exploit his authority for the suppression of other gods—Apollo. For centuries Greeks from all parts sought counsel of his oracle at Delphi in matters religious or secular, public or private; his prestige extended far beyond Greek borders to East and West, in countries of different nationality, language, culture, and religion. Many of the sayings vouchsafed in his name to inquirers from far and wide are known to us, and even today his wisdom speaks to us through the mouth of a Pindar. But how different is Apolline prophecy from that of Yahweh of the Old Testament! On the one hand we have the passionate proclamation of the god and his thrice-holy name; on the other, the courteous withdrawal of the god's personality. Zeus, who gives oracles through Apollo, reveals the right but never himself. Neither does Apollo speak of

himself or his greatness. He requires nothing more than the respect obviously due his godhood and the gratitude due to his
revelation of the truth. Frequently as he was consulted in matters
of religion and morality, he never directed the inquirer to himself as the highest object of reverence; neither Greeks nor foreigners were advised other than that they should remain faithful
to their ancestral deities. The larger they were the remoter were
Greek gods from jealousy for their own person. Elsewhere with
the deepening of religion the personality of the divine being increases in gravity and sanctity: here it is dissolved in loftiest
worship. As Socrates solemnly acknowledged before his death,[5]
Apollo directed him to a sacred breadth of vision—not his own,
however, but reason's. What he meant was neither faith nor
visions but a lucid perception of essentials.

A similar superiority of the essential over the personal is evident in the case of Athena. Hymns and statues show her at the
side of the best warriors. Heracles, Tydeus, Achilles, Odysseus,
and many other mighty heroes rely upon her. At moments of
crisis they feel her divine breath, and often, in the enthusiasm
of high venture, she stands bodily before their eyes. She glances
at her hero; she points to the goal, she lends him her divine
arm, and the incredible transpires; a smile from the goddess hails
the intrepid warrior as victor. Where prudence is required, where
the clever warrior takes counsel, she stands behind him alert and
furnishes correct inspiration. Inevitably we think of the heroes
of other peoples and ages who have also been associated with a
divine woman and achieved their deeds in her sight and with her
assistance. But the difference is astonishing. In the latter instances
the knight strives for the honor of the heavenly Lady and seeks
to win her favor by his strength and boldness. But Athena is never
the divine lady of her paladin, and his prowess is not directed to
win her love and honor. Like any other deity she does indeed demand that her strength and wisdom be acknowledged and that
no one presume to dispense with her assistance. But she does not
make it a condition of her favor that the warrior dedicate himself
to her service fervently or even exclusively. Wherever a great
heart throbs and rages, wherever a liberating thought flares up,

there Athena is present, summoned rather by heroic readiness
than by humble supplication. From her own lips we hear that
she is attracted by prowess, not by good will or devotion to her
person. The men who can most surely rely upon her offer her no
unusual reverence, and it is unthinkable that her assistance should
ever be motivated by the exemplary obedience of her protégés.
In the famous conversation with Odysseus[6] in which she reveals
herself as a goddess and informs the sorrowing hero that she
would never forget him, she expressly declares that it is his
superior spirit that pleases her and binds her to him; the bright-
eyed goddess would always stand by the shrewd and inventive
hero. And when the sorely tried Odysseus disbelieves the goddess's assertion that he has indeed arrived at Ithaca, it does not
occur to her to consider her holiness offended; she is not angry at
the doubter but rejoices at the fresh proof of his vigilance, and
because of his shrewdness assures him that she will never forsake
him.

It is a mistake to consider stories of the vengeance of a neg-
lected or even a scorned deity as proof of jealous personality.
Do not we too regard complacency as a provocation and do we not
fear that we may bring misfortune upon us if we speak of our
prosperity too loudly? This fear is ineradicable—which shows how
deeply rooted it is in nature. So with man's presumption, when
he measures himself against gods; many myths warn against this
offense. In her pride Niobe, the mother of twelve handsome
children, ridiculed the goddess Leto, who bore only two.[7] In
requital she lost them all at a single stroke and became an everlasting monument of sorrowing desolation. Other myths show the
terrifying fall of a man who had forgot one of the heavenly powers
or had boasted that he could dispense with their assistance. The
man who is blind towards the higher powers they destroy. It is
obvious that these typical stories are true to life. It is particularly
significant that one deity will exact vengeance for having been
slighted for the sake of another. Hera and Athena were passed
over in the judgment of Paris and became deadly foes of Troy.
Possible earlier versions of the story of the goddesses' contest in
beauty need not trouble us; for the Homeric spirit the story has
a serious meaning. In scorning Hera and Athena, Paris decided

in favor of wantonness[8] and against propriety and heroism. The
spirits which he rejected could only turn against him. Surely our
own thinking follows the Homeric view when we say "it was his
fate that he had to make a choice." Every power in life is jealous,
not when another is recognized along with it, but when it is
rejected and scorned for the sake of another. Paris rejected the
geniuses of dignity and action. Hippolytus, according to Euripides' story, took the opposite course. Here the myth does not
represent fate as approaching man from the outside, as imposing
the choice upon him; his own character is responsible for the
decision that sets the tragedy in motion. With the whole zeal of
his pure heart the young prince reveres Artemis, the goddess of
dewy freshness whose brightness is reflected in the flower-
spangled meadows. Just as the chaste virgin contemns the lan-
guors and caresses of love, so Hippolytus' innocence is offended
by the mere thought of the goddess of sweet nights.[9] But he is not
merely offended; he turns back on the goddess in disdain. His willfulness knows no respect for the divine power that hurls all that
lives into the arms of its kind. Proud and inexorable, he passes
judgment upon the unhappy woman who is kindled by his
flame. His virtue is untouched by the sublimest grace of Aphrodite,
the spirit which understands and remains lovable even in denial.[10]
Hence she becomes his doom. The favorite of a goddess is
crushed, and she is unable to save him, because of his arrogant
and inhuman contempt for another. This example demonstrates
the interval between the human and the divine, however "human"
the divine may appear. In the heavenly sphere the forms that
confront one another are pure and grand. There the chaste
Artemis can look upon Aphrodite's tenderness with dispassionate
detachment. But for man it is dangerous to attempt to stand upon
a lonely peak and be as unaffected as only gods can be. They do
not require such restraint of him; they desire him to comport
himself with moderation in the sphere appropriate to him, where
all divinities work their effects and none will brook disdain.

Differentiation between divine and human is the burden of the
doctrine and admonition emanating from the gods. They do not
speak to man of mysterious origins and ordinances, they show
him no path from the natural form of his being to a superhuman

condition of perfection and bliss. On the contrary, they warn him
against overweening thoughts and aspirations and sharpen his
perception of the order of nature. Dionysiac and Orphic sects did
believe that revelation had vouchsafed them a higher knowledge
and that they knew the sacred path that would lead to perfection,
but they stand apart from the piety of the great centuries. The
Olympians, who informed the character of religion from Homer
to Socrates and who speak to us still on the lips of an Aeschylus or
Pindar, had no thought of initiating man into supernatural mysteries or of revealing to him the secret character of their divinity.
It is not heaven but himself that man must study, and this does not
imply examination of conscience or confession of sin. The admonition "Know thyself," which goes back, if not in the identical
words, to the Homeric Apollo, means this: Observe the sacred
form of nature, consider the limitations of humanity, realize what
man is and how great an interval separates him from the majesty
of the eternal gods!

4

What distinguishes gods from men?

The gods are great in power and knowledge; their life is not
subject to decline and fall. But all this does not touch the crucial
point, for despite their similarity to mankind they are far more
than deified and ever-living men. "Immortal" is the standing designation by which they are distinguished from men; and myth
knows of men who were raised to superhuman stature by being
endowed with immortality. But the idea of divine being is not of
such a nature that a man can become a god by the intensification
and prolongation of his existence. Here as elsewhere the essential is not made explicit.

Man is a contradictory being who participates in many conditions of existence. Day and night, heat and cold, serenity and
storm, all have claims upon him. This multiplicity, which is his
delight and his torment, makes of him a limited and transitory
being. He is everything, and nothing wholly—"wholly" in the
positive sense, not in the negative of mere exclusiveness—with the

self-sufficient wholeness and abundance of the image of life. For man, singularity means distress and a forfeiture of life. Only in change can he breathe freedom and strength. It is preposterous to think of such a nature raised to the divine, the temporal to the timeless, the contradictory to the uncontradictory. Only for moments can man be wholly swept into the enchantment of singular being, and then he touches upon the perfect and the divine. Whether it be love or cognition, the higher world has begun, and as proof of its presence ego and personality are extinguished, for these belong to the transitory. But earthly nature cannot abide in this majestic singularity and wholeness; that only the god can do. Indeed, the god is this majesty and fullness. But man, who must never forget that he is only man, may ever and again leave the petty constraints and enticements of transitory existence to be submerged in the great elemental image of divinity.

If we reflect upon this profound distinction between men and gods we shall not be surprised to find that in large areas of life the gods follow a different law from that followed by man. That is why puritanical judgments have found the morality of the Greek gods questionable. It cannot be denied that many legends concerning them are at odds with obligations of conjugal fidelity and extra-conjugal chastity. Many erotic myths received their character from the fact that the diverse forms and names which originally figured in the legends were fused in the course of time: a god whose consort was invoked in various places under different names could only appear as a very inconstant lover in the combined tradition. But we need not invoke this circumstance to exculpate the gods' conduct. The Homeric Greeks took no offense at the uninhibited love-life of their gods. The truth is that the idea of Olympian divinity is hard to reconcile with notions of conjugal ties; it is therefore very noteworthy that ancient cult sites united the god with his goddess and that the celebration of the Sacred Marriage was highly revered in the ancient cult. Hera was the divine consecration of the marriage bond and of womanly dignity; it was impossible to think of her as unmarried. But it can be plainly seen that she is much more the wife than Zeus is the husband. This is no whim of the poet and no moral frivolity but a necessary consequence of genuine Homeric belief, which could imagine gods involved in the most passionate amours but not as married after a human fashion. It was only when this belief began to waver and when legends of the gods turned to a pastime that these lovers' adventures assumed the character of light-hearted pursuit of pleasure. We cannot wonder that criticism raised its voice in Greece itself at a relatively early date. Abstract speculation and rationalism, which took special exception to the human form and character given the divine, resented such transgressions most strongly. Xenophanes levels serious charges against the gods of Homer and Hesiod for their "adulteries."

But in the earlier and more pious age only the uncommon was expected of the eternal beings who set forth pure humanity. Indeed, even the coarsest naturalism cannot equal middle-class propriety and respectability in stripping the divine of its magic. The ancient nobility who derived their lineage from the union of their ancestress with a deity did not imagine that the benefactor was bound by a personal relationship and that he could have jeopardized his honor by a love affair. The great hour when the majesty of heaven descended to an earthly woman in love they regarded with pious awe. That the deity's night of love might also serve some marvellous design is beautifully shown in Hesiod's *Shield of Heracles*. Here it is told how the father of men and gods took counsel with himself how he might raise up a deliverer for gods and man. "So he arose from Olympus by night pondering guile in the deep of his heart, and yearned for the love of the well-girded woman."[11] The fruit of this love was Heracles, the deliverer, the pattern of all heroism.

5

It is objected that the Homeric age itself had lost reverence for its life-loving gods and made sport of representing them in questionable and discreditable situations. The most explicit and traditional support for this view is the Love of Ares and Aphrodite, which Demodocus sang to the Phaeacians and Odysseus for their delectation—how cuckolded Hephaestus bound the goddess and her paramour with invisible fetters and thus made their em-

braces a laughing-stock for the gods.[12] Even in antiquity many
readers, Plato among them, found this story offensive, and in
modern times it is generally regarded as a frivolous burlesque.
But even if the subject may appear bold it is hard to see how it
can be considered salacious and how it can yield the impression
that the society which heard it regarded their gods lightly.

Ares, whose embarrassment is the object of laughter, is not a
distinguished god, and indeed can hardly be considered a god
at all. None of the other gods could for a moment be imagined in
his situation, not even Hermes, though Hermes says that he is
ready to change places with Ares. There can be no question of
frivolity here. If any of the mythical figures could serve as a
butt for a spirited jest it would be this passionate savage whom
the true Olympians did not regard as their equal. And Aphrodite?
If we consider the story carefully we suddenly realize that she
receives no attention whatever. All interest centers upon the discreditable rôle played by Ares. The poet had no intention to
lessen respect for Aphrodite. In the epic tradition she is married
to Hephaestus, but at many cult sites she was regarded as the
wife of Ares. Actually, being an Olympian deity, what was said
above about marriages of the gods in general applies to her to a
special degree. She is really not to be thought of as married. She
is the power of charm and longing, the magic that sets the
heart afire and suffers all prudence to perish in the rapture of an
embrace. To her realm also belong all the trials that beset love,
including gossip and ridicule. If a man is snared in her trap it is
he that is mocked, not she, for hers is the triumph. Though on con-
ventional grounds the poet has been condemned as impudent and
godless, we must realize how vividly he senses the true meaning
of the elemental goddess. Even in so novella-like and high-spirited
a tale he does not forget who she is; he cannot imagine that she
would compromise her true nature; and while virtually eliminat-
ing her person, he demonstrates the effect of her eternal power.
The enamored warrior, on the other hand, he makes a butt for
ridicule. But the thing which rouses the hearty laughter of the
gods is not the indecency but the successful trick of the deceived
cripple whose ingenuity overtakes speed of foot and who gives
validity to the saying that ill deeds never prosper.[13] The more

insidious the story appears, the more noteworthy it is that the
narrator passed over its piquant phases and found pleasure only
in the spirited and witty aspects. The only indication that the
spectacle to which the irate husband invites the gods violates
decency is the fact that the goddesses stay away from it.[14] Not a
word is said of the performance which the amorous pair must
have provided for the spectators nor of their own feelings the
while. The story is naturally not a moralizing sermon, but that
does not make it frivolous. Its tone of lofty humor removes it
from both moralizing and frivolity.

The humor reaches its most brilliant effect in the conclusion,
which reveals the feelings of the three great gods who are spectators: Apollo, Hermes, and Poseidon. Of the appearance of the
helpless lovers we learn nothing; instead the three gods speak of
the unpleasantness of such a contretemps, and the few words
they utter present a characterization in masterly strokes. Poseidon, who speaks last, feels only sympathy; he is so touched by
Ares' situation that, unable to laugh, he prevails on Hephaestus
to release his hapless victim and is so kindly as to provide a guar-
antee for him. But before this there had been a dialogue between
Apollo and Hermes. The noble god of insight is witty enough to
ask his brother whether he would not like to be in Ares' place,
and to introduce this question with a ceremonial address to the
divinity of his interlocutor; he knows perfectly well what the
feelings of this rogue among the gods must be. And the god of
thievery and lucky chance responds, reciprocating the highly
ceremonial form of address, that thrice so many fetters and the
laughter of all the gods in heaven would not deter him from the
voluptuous embraces of golden Aphrodite. The bard who attributes such language to Hermes is not offending the honor of
the god; rather is he characterizing him precisely as the Greek
spirit conceived him, that free and spacious spirit capable of
honoring the divine even in luck and roguery because these too
are eternal images of life. It is therefore altogether mistaken to
conclude from the tone of this intrinsically true and witty tale
that an age which could tolerate it must have thought lightly of
the gods who appear in it or even of the gods in general. What
could be made of the story by a poet who really loved high season-

ing and to whom the life of the gods was only a game of fancy is demonstrated by Ovid, who includes it as an instructive example in his *Art of Love*.[15] Here our interest is wholly occupied by the spectacle of the chained lovers: Venus can hardly restrain her tears; she and her lover are eager to hide their faces and cover their nakedness with their hands, if their bonds only permitted. Here attention is no longer directed to the overreaching of strength and agility by a cripple, but only to the erotic and seductive, and Ovid's lesson is that in future detected sinners will be only the more unconcerned.

6

Are such divinities capable of giving moral support? If so, what sort of moral support would it be?

Early Christians naturally answered in the negative. Students of religion have seldom posed the question in express and serious terms. This is regrettable, for the question has always occupied the background of their researches, and since it was not itself made an object of study it merely blurred their vision. They were disappointed to find that the assurances and incentives which other religions, and mainly Christianity, gave their votaries were missing in ancient Greek religion; but they were unaware of the possibility of other forces which might deserve our attention and perhaps even our admiration.

To be sure, Greek deity reveals no law to stand as an absolute body above nature. It is no holy will before which nature trembles. In it there speaks no heart to which the soul of man can render perfect devotion and trust. Its large gaze demands worship and prayer, but it maintains its own dignified distance. Ready as it may be to help, there is not inscribed upon its visage an infinite love which will be vouchsafed to man and redeem him from all his woes.

Here is a more biting wind: everything great is dangerous and may confound the man who is not on his guard. In the realm of the gods there abides danger; as the eternal forms of this realm, they are themselves the danger. Often they crash into the well-ordered life of man like a storm. Aphrodite can set life into such confusion that the holiest bonds are shattered, faith is dishonored, and deeds are perpetrated that the doer himself later finds incredible. Artemis caused the downfall of the innocent Hippolytus. While he was wholly beguiled by the enchantment of her pure and virginal world and had only contempt for the realm of love, that realm advanced upon him in its most formidable aspect and destroyed him. Here only vigilance and strength avail.

But the vigilant finds powerful assistance. The character of the deity itself becomes his illumination. The large world, whose form the deity is, embraces the whole realm of being, from brute primal force to the serene ethereal heights of freedom; and at this highest point it reveals its perfect image. The hand of the artist has caught the image, and at sight of it our eyes can still experience the miracle of the wedding of pure nature with sublimest spirit. Divinity is and remains nature, but as nature's form it is spiritual and as its perfection it is majesty and dignity, whose rays illumine the life of man. For the Greeks this is the prime meaning of insight and intelligence. Without these the truly divine is inconceivable.

It is to be expected that among the manifold forms of Homeric religion savagery, fanaticism, and ecstasy would find a place. But the ideal of intelligence stands opposed to all blind surging and to every form of excess. Other peoples have frequently thought of their gods, especially when they were war-like, as quick to anger and destructive in their wrath. Their celebrated heroes too distinguish themselves in battle by mad rage, as if they were possessed. Not so the Homeric Greeks. That their society found delight in battle and heroism is shown by the *Iliad;* its glorification of warriors has remained the most powerful poetry of Hellenism. But out of it there breathes a spirit which looks down with noble contempt upon blind unchaining of gigantic strength. Indeed we notice with astonishment that these men who rejoice in battle and are accustomed to perceive the basic forms of existence as a reflection of divine forms ignore the existence of a war god in the proper sense of the term.

Every reader of Homer, of course, knows Ares and remembers that the Achaeans are often called his "servants." But this bloodthirsty[16] spirit of carnage, who enters men like a demon,[17] whose

power makes the spent spear quiver,[18] never attained the full
dignity of a god, though belief in his frightful presence is undoubtedly ancient. Only rarely does he appear in myth as a complete personality. If we compare his image with that of the warrior
Athena, it crumbles into the horrid gloom of the demonic. Though
the heroes, and in particular Menelaus, are called "favorites of
Ares," they never pray to him. And though the divine family of
Olympus count him as one of themselves, they do so reluctantly
and treat him with less respect than any other. Only Ares is overthrown in a duel with an Olympian deity, and there is satisfaction in knowing that the crude monster has for once been humbled
by the superior strength of a nobler power. It is Athena, goddess
of genuine, intelligent Hellenism, who makes him feel her superiority with the single cast of a stone—Athena, friend of con-
quering Heracles, bright spirit of noble manhood. This triumph
makes a magnificent introduction to the battle of the gods which
precedes the decisive encounter between Achilles and Hector.[19]
Once before Ares had yielded to Athena: standing upon a chariot
at the side of her protégé Diomedes, she had made his spear-cast
ineffective with a light hand, and had so hurt him, through the
spear of the hero, that he was forced to leave the field howling.[20]
Then we hear what the father of the gods, to whom he complained, thinks of him. He calls him "the most hateful of all the
gods that dwell on Olympus" because he "always loves strife and
war and battle."[21] This implies that the others do not; they do not
"always" wish battle. The figure of Ares derives from the antiquated earth-religion, where his savagery had its proper place
among other pitiless forces. He is the spirit of imprecation, vengeance, blood-guilt.[22] As the daimon of bloody slaughter he still
possesses fearful stature for Homer—the more fearful, indeed, the
less his personality is delineated. His element is manslaughter;
he is called "the destroyer," "the slayer of men," and his companion Eris "the bane of strife," "she who moves mightily through
the throngs of men, augmenting the groans of heroes."[23] He rages
among the Trojans no less than among the Greeks.[24] His name
frequently denotes little more than "bloody battle"; hence Zeus
reproaches him as having no character, consorting with all or
rather against all.[25] In the battle scene depicted on the shield of

Achilles, Ares and Pallas Athena are shown striding forth from a warrior throng.[26] This conception corresponds to the actual belief concerning Ares better than his decided partiality for the Trojans in many individual episodes in the *Iliad*. He cannot sustain the rôle of a partisan because he is basically only a daimon whose character is blind savagery. He is far removed from Athena, who is also mighty in battle but who, as goddess of intelligence and dignified bearing, reveals true heroism in heavenly brilliance. But Ares is consumed in the ecstasy of bloodshed, and so is wholly lacking in the breadth and depth which distinguish the character of all the genuine figures of this religion.

Excess may also be a true revelation of the divine. Aphrodite is a lofty goddess for Homer, and yet her nature and effect is unchaining elemental passion. Women like Helen, Phaedra, Pasiphaë, testify to her fearful power, which mocks all law and order, all shame and restraint. But in contrast to a figure like Ares, she represents a profound aspect of life. As spirit of seductive grace, as inciter to the ecstatic madness of lover and beloved she possesses no little share of the blindness and savagery of the demonic. But however mad her doings may be in an individual case, they still belong to the venerable elemental forms of life, and the enchanted world which is reflected in her divine figure extends eternally from the lust of the worm to the sublime smile of understanding. And therefore despite the demonic force of her nature she stands before our eyes in illuminating serenity. In the large sense of life excess finds its counterpoise. That form to which other peoples attributed characteristics of bestial lust and sensuality the Greek looked upon not as licentious but as a noble goddess, because to him she explains not the surface but the wonderful depths of the world. Here too, then, the spirituality of his religion is sustained.

In the statues of Aphrodite and the other gods, created by plastic art in thoroughly Homeric spirit, we perceive the thought of the Greeks: the spiritual is not alien to nature; in nature itself is born that sense which is expressed as nobility and majesty in the human figures of the gods. The natural may retain its abundance and vitality entire and yet be one with the spiritual, which desires to be nothing more than its consummation. Immediacy and bodily presence and at the same time eternal validity—that is the marvel of the Greek formulation. In this unity of nature and spirit the earthy, without forfeiting aught of its freshness and warmth, combines with the freedom of proportion and perceptivity to produce nature perfected. Measure, delicacy, taste, determine attitudes and gestures and testify to the intelligent being of the divine personage. It is impossible to associate any trace of vulgarity, offensiveness, or barbarism with the aspect of a genuine Greek likeness of a god.

This nobility makes itself felt in the first colloquy of gods in the *Iliad*. Thetis ascends Olympus to petition for honor for her great son for whom so early a death is decreed. She had appeared at the seashore at his call, and had wept with him at the affront he had endured. Now she is to remind the king of the gods that it was she who had delivered him from serious trouble and to ask him, for her son's sake, to suffer the Greeks to be routed by the Trojans at their ships so that Agamemnon might realize what folly he had committed in denying honor to the best of the Greeks.[27] She sinks at the feet of the son of Cronus, who is throned in solitary grandeur, embraces his knees with her left arm and with her right touches his chin in supplication. In this posture she utters her request. Yet she says nothing of the saving deed she had once performed at a horrifying moment, the details of which she had recalled to her son, but only: "Father Zeus, if ever I have given you aid amid the immortal gods, fulfill my petition." And the petition contains none of her son's imagined vengeance but only satisfaction and honor: "Give honor to my son, short-lived beyond all other mortals. . . . So long put strength into the Trojans until the Achaeans do honor to my son and exalt him with recompense." She holds his knees in her embrace, and when he keeps a long silence she begins again: "Bow your head and promise me to accomplish this thing, or else, you have nothing to fear, refuse it, that I may know by how much I am the most dishonored of all gods." Then Zeus speaks and nods his divine head.

Threats are frequently uttered on Olympus, or an earlier deed of violence is recalled,[28] but nothing crude or unseemly ever takes place. Indeed it is almost as if the expressions which might seem crude show all the more clearly how seemly and dignified the

conduct of the gods, really is. When Zeus realizes that Hera's
tender affection was only a trick to distract him from events on the
battlefield, he grimly reminds her how severely she had been chas-
tised on a previous occasion, and with her all the gods who wished
to succor her. But when she swears that it was not she who had
instigated Poseidon to his deed, the father of the gods smiles and
his wish shows his belief that his wife is at one with him.[29] At
his bidding Iris then goes to Poseidon to enjoin him to leave the
battlefield.[30] In this scene also the initial violence of the words
makes the actual motives for the gods' conduct all the clearer.
Peremptorily Iris threatens Poseidon with Zeus's superior power
if he should act contrary to his will. This argument the ruler of
the sea proudly rejects: he had as great a share in the world as his
brother, who could save his threats for his daughters and sons;
he himself was strong enough to be in no fear of them. But Iris
refuses to receive this unfriendly answer. "The hearts of the great
can be changed. You know the Furies, how they always side with
the elder." This is an admonition to remember the ancient order,
and Poseidon is won over in a moment: "It is a fine thing when a
messenger is conscious of justice."

So the quarrels of the gods end in a dignified manner. Indeed,
they conclude with jollity and cordiality, as the fine and significant example at the end of the first book of the *Iliad* shows. It is
unthinkable that the conduct of the gods to one another could be
unrestrained and insolent. Their attitude and behavior are determined by propriety. Athena shows ruthless force in dealing
with Ares, but here force itself is meaningful, as we have seen
above. The poet of the twenty-first book of the *Iliad* has shaped
the so-called battle of the gods with such fine perception that,
apart from the set-to between Athena and Ares, there is actually
no battle at all, and Apollo can say to Poseidon, with noble dignity, that it is folly for god to strive with god for a mortal's sake.[31]
Only Hera, the most vigorous of all Olympian divinities, after
having scolded Artemis boxes her ears with her own bow, as a
mature woman might deal with an impudent young girl.[32] But
Hera's very animosity and her frequently bitter outbursts, which
are correctly pointed out by critics of the Homeric gods, should
make us notice that she is never carried away to the point of ir-

rational or undignified behavior. To see in this only hopelessness
of resistance against the will of Zeus is superficial, for she would
still be able to perpetrate many kinds of mischief in great things
and small. The ideal of intelligent and dignified conduct is given
life in Hera also. When Athena admonishes raging Achilles to
sobriety she requires of him the dignity which is taken for granted
in a Hera. She herself provides proof of this just before the much
maligned battle of the gods begins. She had summoned the fire-
god Hephaestus to subdue Xanthus, whose waves were threatening Achilles. But the moment the river-god is ready to yield, she
holds Hephaestus back, and though her words can sometimes be
relentless and savage, here she speaks almost like Apollo himself
in the battle of the gods which follows: "Unseemly it is so to mal-
treat an immortal god for the sake of a human."[33]

But a larger ideal is revealed to mankind by the superior deities,
Apollo, Athena, and Zeus. In the figure of Apollo man honors the
nobility of serenity and freedom, the rays of the sun, which furnish
light not for mysteries of the soul but for virile realization of life
and worthy achievement. His stately bearing in the battle of the
gods, the magnificent utterance with which he sent the son of
Tydeus back to his place as a mortal, his flaming protest against
the inhumanity of Achilles and his admonition that gentlefolk
must observe measure and worth even in deep anguish—these
genuine expressions of his character are amply noticed in the
section devoted to him.[34] So Athena, who so loved Tydeus that
she wished to present him with the cup of immortality, turned
from him with distaste as he lay dying because she deemed him
degraded by a base act. Her fiery glance fell upon Achilles at the
very moment when he was in danger of being carried away by a
senseless act of rage unworthy of himself, and her word admonished him to guard his composure. We have dealt with these
significant stories in a previous section,[35] where account was taken
of modern prejudices to the effect that the original character of
Athena, as far as it can be judged from the *Iliad*, was not yet affected by ethical considerations. It is true that she holds out to
Achilles the prospect of triple satisfaction in the future if he but
control his passion in the present. But it is to seemliness of conduct that she admonishes him. Does she forfeit moral stature by

her awareness that seemly conduct promises desirable results while impetuous assault would only bring a barbarous victory? Only a narrow and hidebound concept of ethics can lead to the view that the attribution to Athena of motives other than a will to victory was the work of later writers. Does not the character of Athena as presented by the *Iliad* and the *Odyssey*—one may say, for all time—with its essential nobility contradict such a view? Is it not significant of the ideal that she is opposed to Ares, the goddess of intelligent power as against the wild spirit of carnage? Is it not indicative of a lofty ethic that she deems only the noblest masculine characters worthy of her friendship and that she makes the nearness of her spirit felt at moments of their greatest tension of energy and thought? Do not the heroic achievements of Heracles, the clever deeds of Odysseus and the trials which he so manfully withstood breathe the nobility of Athena's character? In that case we should have to understand ethics as merely the observance of certain categorical commandments and regard all else as morally indifferent. Then, at least, Athena, like the Olympian gods generally, would take interest in anything but morality. Her divinity does not oblige this immortal to watch over strictly formulated moral laws and even less to set up a canon of what must forever be called right or wrong, good or evil. How far a powerful nature may go in a given instance remains open. Nevertheless she does raise certain requirements, and through her own being she sets them up as a living ideal before the eyes of men. In a higher sense we may indeed call her moral, for she is not concerned with details but with the bearing of the whole man. From her we may recognize nature refined and capable of freedom, which neither follows impulses blindly nor is subjected to the categorical demands of a moral legislation. It is not to dutifulness or obedience that decision is allowed, but to insight and taste; and thus everywhere the intelligent is bound up with the beautiful.

It may be objected that this noble concept of Athena is stultified by the cruel deceit worked upon Hector, who was doomed to death;[36] in modern times this has been called not only immoral but even diabolical. But the true meaning of this story (from which we have previously drawn implications concerning modes of divine intervention[37]) we can understand fully only in connection with the idea of fate;[38] it will then evoke not revulsion but awe and reverence. Athena is here no other than the path and fulfillment of higher necessity; the trick by which she deceives the faith of Hector is the trick of fate. It is foolish to attempt to measure the enormity of this event by the gauge of morality and to demand that fate should requite fidelity and uprightness as if it were a man dealing with his fellow-man. We are indeed appalled to see how her powers mock human insight, but out of the fateful gloom there bursts the splendor of the divine. Athena misleads Hector on the path of fate, but as goddess she recalls him to honor. When does he play a worthier rôle, before the divine intervention, when he fled as if demented, or afterwards, when he offered manly resistance? If his fall was already determined, would it have been better for the deity to allow him to be overtaken and cut down by Achilles? The deity does not deal lightly with the great figures whom she must destroy. Her deception, gruesome as it may appear to us, restores his hero's honor to Hector. Now he knows that his doom is sealed, but he knows also that posterity will be filled with his fame. This achievement of divine sway is not accidental, but valid testimony for its spirit.

7

The greatest deities, Zeus, Athena, and Apollo exhibit the ideal of ennobled manliness in threefold form.

One of them is a woman, and indeed the one in whose image courageous and vigorous masculinity seems to be deified. This remarkable circumstance we have discussed above, in our consideration of the image of Athena.[39] Here we need add only this: Freedom of thought and art, spiritual creativity, is wholly in the realm of masculinity and hence as deity has a purely masculine character. But the energy and drive of active life requires illumination through the feminine if it is to be uplifted above brute force. All great men of action have a feminine trait which mitigates hardness and ennobles strength. That is the significance of the feminine in these high levels of Greek religion. But beyond this the feminine has lost its power. In the worship of the goddess Athena there is not the slightest trace of the love of women.

Nietzsche has said that it was the will of the Greeks to subdue the feminine in the human, and this observation is applicable even here. It is a familiar characteristic of ancient religions that they conceive their great deities as a pair or a triad. In either case the female element regularly plays a significant rôle. In eastern civilizations it frequently occupies the principal position, and the man, or in the case of a triad the two men, are subordinate to the lofty female. In the ancient Greek triad, on the other hand, the female nature is not even of equal weight with the other sex. Indeed, in a sense it is not even present, for of its characteristic traits Athena possesses only a sublime reflection. She possesses neither love nor motherliness; she is a virgin, but has none of the maidenly aloofness of an Artemis which may at a moment be transformed into motherly warmth and tenderness. Her disposition is masculine, and it is quite in keeping with the conception of her presented by the Homeric epic when Aeschylus has her declare, in the *Eumenides,* that she stands heart and mind on the side of the man and feels herself wholly the daughter of her father.[40] Whereas other religions, then, frequently endow even the male deity with unmistakably feminine traits, the Greek asserts its masculine temper even in the female member of the supreme triad.

Woman is more elemental than man and much more centered upon individual existence. Her physiological organism induces in her a concern with the bodily which man seldom comprehends. She deals with the whole sphere of the sensual and the concrete with a devotion and respect naturally alien to masculine sensibility. Her power lies in her presence and person. Whereas man strives for the general, the impersonal, the non-sensual, her energy is wholly concentrated upon the immediate, the personal, the present reality. Just as man worships her as his idol in the moment of ecstasy, she is herself formed by nature to feel her uniqueness and to make use of it with all her resources.

It is very interesting to note how many significant traits of various religions and views of the world can be subsumed under one or the other of these basic characteristics. The Greek deity with its masculine temper does not assert its personality with the zeal of other gods. It does not expect that man should live only to serve it and should perform his highest achievements to glorify its per-

son. The honor it claims is not of the exclusive sort that admits
recognition of no other beside it. It rejoices in freedom of spirit
and requires of human life intelligence and insight rather than
devotion to specific formulae, acts, and objects.

Nowhere is the difference between specifically Greek religious
feeling and others more striking than in its attitude towards the
elemental and towards concrete objectivity. The world of primal
matter and primal force is sacred to it, but its thoughts of the
divine soar far above it. Whereas in other religions and cults connection with the material in its objective reality is indissoluble,
the truly masculine faith of the Greeks is committed to freedom
and spirituality. Just as, in its Homeric form, it requires no con-
tinuance of the objective body and the objective soul in order to
comprehend past, present, and future in a single large idea, so it
is able to perceive and adore the profundity of everything concrete in an eternal image.

This religious spirituality stands clearly revealed in the supreme divinities. Of all earthly beings only man has access to their
realms. But they too are form, not absolute spirit, to which nature
would stand opposed as a thing of lesser worth. None of them
reveals himself in perceptions or premonitions that reach out beyond this world. None categorically differentiates between good
and evil in order to master nature by prescriptions set down once
and for all. Their desire is nature, which is itself consummated
through insight and magnanimity. This consummation of nature
itself became divine form in them, and stands forth as perfect
being above the shortcomings and transitoriness of human life.
Thus once more these divinities perpetuate a quite specific reality,
here a spiritual one—higher humanity.

8

The loftiness by which Zeus, Apollo, and Athena tower over the
other Olympians is everywhere plain to see. Their presence is surrounded by the highest splendor, their appearance is always decisive. Where some great wish is directed to divine power, these
three names, formally united, appear. It is so in the Homeric

poems,[41] and there is something similar later in the religious language of Athens. The incomparable quality of Zeus's children Athena and Apollo is given somewhat symbolic expression in the battle of the gods in *Iliad* 21, which has several times been mentioned. At first Athena overthrows raging Ares with magnificent composure, and then Apollo's lofty temper refuses conflict with the god Poseidon for the sake of a mortal. In addition to intelligence and beauty, the three supreme divinities possess grandeur also.

Later ages were ever more inclined to see the highest manifestations of the divine in general providence and justice. In his *Oenomaus* Euripides has one of his characters say: "When I see the wicked come to grief then do I believe that a god dwells in heaven."[42] The rustic Hesiod in his hard struggle against unfaithfulness and corruption of justice imagines that the deity esteems the values that are uppermost in his own way of life. In him we recognize the temper of a bourgeois existence reduced to dependence. The history of religion considers this a sublimation and a deepening of religiosity; but a call to justice is rather a sign of a de-deification of the world. The rightful claim to prosperity which the individual believes he possesses signifies that the awareness of divine presence has declined. In the Homeric world too, to be sure, there was a belief that the justice of Zeus would prevail. After the treacherous bowshot that broke the sacred oath, Agamemnon cried out that the destruction of Ilium and Priam and his whole folk was certain, for Zeus's wrath would surely exact requital for their heedlessness even though the punishment might be delayed.[43] Menelaus, too, the victim of the initial wrong, firmly maintains his confidence in the justice of heaven despite strenuous opposition.[44] A famous simile mentions the burst of wrath which Zeus visits upon unjust judges.[45] Indeed, the poet of *Odyssey* 24 has Laertes exclaim, when he hears that the suitors have been destroyed, "Father Zeus, ye gods still live in the heights of Olympus if it is true that the insolence of the suitors has been punished!"[46]

But such thoughts as these do not occupy the foreground of Homeric belief. That could not be in a world whose most brilliant and best-loved personage is not blessed by a long and prosperous life but must fall in the first bloom of youth, that handsomest among the sons of earth, whose brief span held only battle, and separation from a beloved friend, and tears—and who yet for the sake of glory preferred such fleeting brilliance to a long life free of trouble.[47]

For a spirit which craves glory rather than prosperity, the justice of divine sway is a different thing from what the husbandman or commoner intent on possessions and gain might wish it to be. Otto Gruppe has acutely remarked on the great thread which winds through the *Iliad*:[48] Zeus fulfills the wish of Achilles that during his wrathful absence the Greeks should fall into desperate need;[49] but for this he must pay with the deepest sorrow, for the need of the Greeks draws his dearest friend to his death, and since, in order to avenge him, he must again be reconciled to the Greeks, his own doom is sealed, for his own fall must follow directly upon Hector's.[50]—Man may choose. His choice is fulfilled—and in the end it was much sorrow and renunciation. Then he may, like Achilles, sit down amicably with the enemy and weep.[51] But it was not life's pleasure that he chose, but glory. This magnanimous humanity might say to the generations whose religion reputedly grew more mature and more serious, "Why do you complain of injustice and arraign heaven when you think you have not received your deserts? Did not your program of possessions and gain also choose, along with the justice that would strengthen you, the injustice that shatters you?"

Justice does not tower above the all too human. Glory is another matter. Beyond fortune and misfortune, justice and injustice, love and hate, it can bestow honor upon the great man, and knows that a single moment may counterbalance a whole life. It can extend a hand to an enemy, it can see the guilty and the victim of destiny in a halo, not, however, because it loves or is humble, but because its own loftiness knows regions where measures and evaluations are futile. Such glory the highest Olympian god shows to Hector in the seventeenth book of the *Iliad*.[52] Hector must fall. The overthrow of Patroclus was the highest point of Trojan triumph and now fate has turned. Dying, Patroclus prophesies to his conqueror, "Now is death near you, and unavoidable fate."[53] But Hector does not believe; in pride of victory he thinks that he himself will overcome Achilles.[54] His last great hour has come, which is at the same time the darkest for the Achaeans. The armor of Achilles, taken from slain Patroclus, is carried to Troy as a trophy;[55] but Hector, who had himself ordered this done, hurries after the bearers: he wishes to accouter himself in "the god-like armor of Peleid Achilles, the gift of the heavenly beings," and thus arrayed in the splendor of supreme triumph to storm into battle. We know what awaits him, and so for us his pride turns to a lamentable picture of human blindness. But the father of gods has larger thoughts than self-righteous man would desire of deity.[56] Fate must take its course. Hector will not return from battle; no loving hand will help him off with this armor. But in return he is now to experience his loftiest moment. "But when Zeus that gathers the clouds beheld from afar off Hector arming himself in the armor of Peleus' god-like son he shook his head and spoke thus to himself: 'Ah, hapless man, no thought is in your heart of death that is already close upon you, and yet you put on the armor of a hero before whom many another trembles. His comrade, gentle and brave, you have slain; and his armor you have unmeetly stripped from his head and shoulders. Yet now for a while I will put into your hands great might, in recompense for your never coming home from battle to put down the armor of the son of Peleus before Andromache.'" This is the Zeus whose mighty image the poet has shown us at the beginning of the *Iliad*, when he responds to Thetis's petition after a long silence and by the nodding of his head makes great Olympus quake.[57]

The unforgettable manifestation of divine glory stands at the beginning of the *Iliad*, and the *Iliad* closes with a picture of human glory. The gods desire that Hector's body should be delivered to his father Priam, and Achilles, who persecuted the slayer of his dear friend with horrible cruelty, hearkens without demur. It is altogether in the Homeric spirit that charity to an enemy springs from no act of voluntary self-denial but receives its impulse from the divine. And yet the sensitivity and the deed belong to the human, for never has a man received his enemy with more natural humaneness and magnanimity. Suddenly the obdurate man sees the graybeard at his feet, kissing the man-slaying hand

which had done so many of his sons to death.[58] And he weeps with
the old man. The king of the enemy people, the father of Paris
who had caused the war and of the hated slayer of his friend, is
still only a man, born for sorrow and tears, like himself, like all
others. And he complies with his request, he guards him carefully
from the eyes of the Greeks; he even promises a truce for the duration of the funeral rites in Troy. And with the dark glow of the
funeral obsequies which the most irreconcilable of enemies had
guaranteed would be completed without molestation, the *Iliad*
comes to a close.

VII

FATE

1

THE DARKEST SPHERE of life yet remains, and if here too the gods are encountered they would themselves seem to contradict the impression of brightness which they have communicated to us.

How is it possible that the geniuses of life, abundance, and fortune should likewise be the source of distress, doom, and destruction? Can life so turn against itself? That a power must be the doom of any who mock it we can understand. But how can we reconcile ourselves to the fact that the power of itself confounds man and flings him into the abyss, that it is not merely light and warmth but likewise the dark and chilly shadow which so uncannily falls across life? Can it be that those gods are not the luminous figuration of the living world that they seem to be, but superhuman powers which issue sovereign decrees on life as on death?

The contradiction is resolved if we understand the peculiar image by which the ancient Greek spirit comprehended the nocturnal aspect of existence and its effect upon the attitude of the gods. This nocturnal aspect is death and all that necessarily leads to death. Here, where life is forfeited, the essential power of the gods ends and they vanish. But most mysterious of all, there is a point where their living forms are converted into hostile demonic forces and thus seem to become powers of fate and death—but only seem to do so, as will become apparent in the final section of this examination.

Sometimes it is said that the gods "can do all things," but a glance at the stories of the gods shows that this is not to be taken literally. Their oneness with nature would of itself contradict their ability to do all things. In a desperate situation men do not hesitate to say that even the gods could be of no help. When Nestor expresses the wish that Telemachus may succeed, with Athena's help, in mastering the suitors, Telemachus answers: "I dare not let myself think of it. Even though the gods themselves willed it no such good fortune could befall me."[1] However we may explain the impotence of the gods in these special cases, there is a fixed limit to their power, a basic "so far and no farther." That limit is death. No god can restore life to a man once dead, no will of the gods can reach into the shadowy realm of the departed. But this applies to other religions also, even to the Old Testament. The Greek view goes much further and has an additional and profounder meaning. Here the deity not only possesses no power over the dead: it cannot shield the living from the death which is determined for him.

> Nor did his immortal mother save the hero divine
> When, falling at the Scaean gate, he fulfilled his doom.

With these words Schiller's Nänie reproduces Greek thought precisely. In the *Odyssey* Athena herself says: "Death is certain, and when a man's fate (Moira) has come, not even the gods can save him, no matter how they love him."[2] And Thetis prays Zeus to give her son, who is doomed to an early death, due honor, and Zeus nods assent;[3] that she might ask that Achilles' life be lengthened does not occur to her, nor is it in the power of the great god to grant such a prayer. When Hector puts on the armor of Achilles, Zeus deplores his failure to realize how near he is to death,[4] and wishes to give him glory while he may, for Hector will not survive the battle; but despite his sympathy, the dark doom itself Zeus cannot rescind. Apollo, who had so faithfully supported Hector, forsakes him when the scales of destiny show that he is doomed to death.[5]

These examples suffice to illustrate the limitation of the gods. There is a saying which the ambassadors of Croesus heard from the prophetess at Delphi,[6] and which is often repeated in later literature,[7] to the effect that against destiny or necessity even the gods are powerless. Indeed they themselves sometimes avow that they are subject to destiny's decree.[8] This decree is not only withdrawn from the gods' sphere of authority once and for all; it is essentially different from the functions of the gods.

It is in the nature of the divine to bestow, to assist, to illumine. Sometimes it may appear that the decree of fate allots some positive good to man; but from the totality of its functions there can be no doubt that its character is not positive but negative. It sets

a boundary to limit duration, catastrophe to limit prosperity, death
to limit life. Catastrophe, cessation, limitation, all forms of "so
far and no farther," are forms of death. And death is itself the
prime meaning of fate. Whenever the name of Moira is uttered,
one's first thought is of death, and it is in the inevitability of death
that the idea of Moira is doubtless rooted.

We must accustom ourselves to the thought that death, which is
the most important and decisive of all destinies, can be dependent
upon a power other than the gods'. Surely death is the epitome of
all pain and terror from which we should expect that the gods
would graciously preserve man, and if their power falls short in
this respect, of what use are they? Can there be room for divine
help if catastrophes, issues, death, are immovably fixed?

For a faith whose deity operates from without upon natural
existence, this question can only be answered in the negative.
But where the divine is one with the abundance of life, then
death must be separated from it by a wide chasm. For whatever
lives regards death as the thing most alien, and cannot believe
that it can be comprised in the meaning and scheme of life. Thus
we can understand that the powers of life and the law of death are
not the same. Thus we comprehend the unbridgeable difference
which keeps them apart.

One strand, to be sure, does connect the gods and Moira, and
that is the conception that the gods, unlike mortals, know what
Moira has determined. But often we see the gods taking cogni-
zance of destiny with sorrow and accommodating themselves to its
decree very unwillingly. They may not, indeed cannot, do otherwise. The more vividly this notion is expressed the plainer it is
that their essence is here in collision with another which is alien
to it.

> So the gods weep, weep the goddesses all
> For that beauty perishes, for that the perfect dies.
> SCHILLER

Experience demonstrates two things to the spirit and temper
of the Greek: burgeoning life, which the deity confronts on all
the paths of its development; and strict necessity, which cuts
through life at the points it has itself determined. The gods belong on the side of life. In order to encounter them the living must

move, go forward, be active. Then the gods encompass the living with their strength and majesty and in sudden revelation even show their heavenly countenance. Hence one who is no longer in the path of life can no longer be encountered by deity. With the dead whose whole *is* is a *was,* with the figures of the departed who are cut off from all that is present, the deity can no longer have dealings. But neither can it present itself to one whose way is to be ended. Here the two spheres intersect. What takes place at this intersection remains a mystery for rational thought. But there do arise imaginary representations which unmistakably derive from experience of life.

2

The notion of a destiny that fixes decline and death is rooted in the prehistoric belief whose earthy forms the Homeric religion, in many cases, pushed back from the foreground and made into a respectable background for itself. Moira was a daimon of doom and death. The name denotes allotment or share, which is self-explanatory. It is the feminine form of the noun *moros,* which also means death and doom and appears in Hesiod[9] as the proper name of a divine being which, like Moira herself, has Night for its mother. Figures of this sort usually occur in the plural—for example, Keres, Erinyes, and the like—and so whereas Homer has Moirai in the plural only once,[10] Hesiod[11] names three Moirai, daughters of Zeus and Themis. The domain in which these dark beings are at home is unmistakably indicated by another genealogy, also given by Hesiod:[12] they are daughters of the primal goddess Night, who also gave birth to Moros and the Erinyes, whom Aeschylus[13] too designates as sisters of the Moirai by their mother. The fifty-ninth *Orphic Hymn* also calls them daughters of Night. The fact that they are linked with Uranus and Gaia, with Cronus, and with Aphrodite points to the same circle of thought and imagery. The Orphic theogony calls them children of Uranus and Gaia.[14] In Epimenides[15] Cronus and Euonyme are parents of the Moirai, Aphrodite, and the Erinyes. Aphrodite Urania is designated "the eldest of the Moirai."[16] Their kinship with the Erinyes

appears in the cult also: in the grove of the Eumenides at Sicyon
the Moirai had an altar where they received sacrifices like those
offered to the Eumenides, namely such as were characteristic of
the earth-deities and the deities of the nether-world.[17]

All of this plainly indicates that we are dealing with denizens of
that primeval world of gods whose earthiness and whose ties to
earth distinguish them sharply from the Olympians. Like so many
of the figures of that gloomy and austere sphere, the Moirai too
administer a sacred ordinance and are inexorable avengers of any
who transgress it. According to Hesiod[18] the Moirai and the Keres
follow up transgressions against men and gods and do not rest
until they have exacted due punishment from the transgressor.
According to Arcadian legend,[19] when sorrowing Demeter destroyed Earth's vegetation, Zeus sent the Moirai to her, and their
solace assuaged the goddess's wrath. In this sense Pindar[20] can
say of them that they turn aside when blood-kin fall to feuding. In
a hymn an unknown author[21] prays to these daughters of Night
to send Order (Eunomia) and her sisters, Justice (Dike) and Peace
(Eirene). Hence myth often presents the Moirai in connection
with the ancient forces of order, with Erinyes, the Hours, and
above all with Themis. The *Iliad's* remark on Achilles' speaking
horse[22] is significant: the horse said that great Moira would master Achilles, but the Erinyes stayed his speech.

Beginning and end, birth and death, are the great seasons of the
Moirai, and along with these marriage is a third. They bring
Themis to Zeus to be his wife,[23] and they marry Olympian Hera
to him.[24] They sing at the wedding of Peleus and Thetis.[25] In
Aeschylus they pray their sisters the Eumenides, after the latter
have become reconciled, "to order marriages for lovely maidens."[26]
As goddesses of birth they are associated with Eileithyia.[27] Their
connection with the Eileithyiae may still be seen in Horace's
Carmen Saeculare. Their appearance at the birth of Meleager is
well-known. "To men, when they are born, they give good and
evil."[28] According to the familiar and surely extremely ancient
notion they "spin" his fate for the newborn child—but this means,
in the first instance, his death. In this sense the image is employed by Homer also. This day, says Hera, no harm shall befall
Achilles, "but hereafter let him suffer whatever fate (*aisa*, which

has the same meaning as *moira* and is often used in place of it) may have spun for him."[29] Hector's own mother says of him, when his corpse is in the possession of cruel Achilles, "When I gave him birth, the threads of overruling fate were spun for him."[30] The Phaeacians wished to carry Odysseus safe to his native shore, so that no misfortune should befall him on the journey; "but once he is at home he will have to take whatever fate the heavy spinning women (*Klothes*) spun for him when he was born, when his mother gave him birth."[31] "With an evil fate did I bear you," Thetis says to sorrowing Achilles, who was doomed to an early death.[32]

So the Moirai stand, in the sphere of the ancient earth-religion, as dark powers which determine death. Determination of death is the proper sense of the notion of allotment or share which the name Moira implies. Though the name was and continued to be transparent, pre-Homeric religion thought of its bearers as personalities. Consideration of the testimony cited above can leave no doubt on this point. In the battle of the gods and giants the Moirai appear to have fought with a cudgel, which is characteristic of other deities of fate also.[33] How coarse and sensual primitive imagination could paint them is shown by the story, surely very ancient, that Apollo once made them drunk.[34] In Homer the word *moira* is frequently used in an impersonal sense; but the personal conception persists in certain formal expressions and in the remarkable word *moiregenes* ("son of Moira") which Priam applies to Agamemnon as a laudatory term.[35]

3

The primeval image of the Moira who "allots" death is still potent in the range of thought which characterizes the Homeric poems, but like everything ancient which retains validity in that range, it has been transformed in essentials.

At first blush it might appear that the Moira is as vital a personal figure for Homer as she ever was. He places her beside gods who possess personality, and like the latter represents her as intervening in human affairs. "Not ours is the blame," says the horse, suddenly endowed with human speech, when it foretells his early death to Achilles, "but the great god's and the mighty Moira's."[36] To Hector gloating over his triumph dying Patroclus says: "They that overpowered me were Moira and the son of Leto, and among mortal men Euphorbus; you are yourself only third in the killing of me." And then he adds: "You too shall live but for a little season, for already death and mighty Moira have taken their stand near you."[37] Along with Zeus, Agamemnon names Moira and the Erinyes as having caused his fatal blindness.[38] The work of Moira is described in colorful transitive verbs. Amphius possessed much wealth in his homeland, but "Moira brought him" to Troy as ally of Priam, and there he fell by the hand of Ajax.[39] Lycaon "destructive Moira put into the hands" of Achilles.[40] Strong Tlepolemus "mighty Moira drove" against Sarpedon, whose spear laid him low.[41] Peisander strode against Menelaus; "him evil Moira led to his death," for Menelaus slew him.[42] "Now Moira hurries me on," says Hector, knowing that "the gods have summoned me to death."[43] "Moira fell upon Dioreus,"[44] for the Thracian Peirous struck him with a stone and finished him with a spear. When all the other Trojans fled into the city from before Achilles, "destructive Moira constrained" Hector to remain outside, at the Scaean gate.[45] Moira seems to be the power which—like Death conceived of as a person—attacks a man and plunges him into night. So it is said of a man fatally wounded that "dark Death covered his eyes, and the mighty Moira."[46] If a man must die, "the destructive Moira of death casts him down."[47] The spinning of the Moira is also a familiar image to Homer, as the passages cited from *Iliad* and *Odyssey* prove. He has even preserved an expression, apparently unknown in later literature, which gives particular stress to Moira as a living being—*Moira krataie,* that is, the strong or mighty.[48] This recalls Krataiis, Homer's name for the mother of Scylla[49] whose connection with the nether-world is plain to see and whose descent is sometimes derived from Hecate. This is clearly a parallel to Moira's connection with Night, the Erinyes, and other beings of the murky realm.

And yet the Homeric Moira is by no means the same as that primeval figure which persisted in popular belief in post-Homeric times. First of all we must notice that a significant ancient aspect of Moira which linked her with a group of powers in primitive and popular religion is no longer present in the Homeric figure: Moira does not institute and watch over earthly ordinances. Nor is it her character to bestow gifts and blessings, as the Moirai of popular belief do. Of them Hesiod says that "they give good and evil" to men.[50] In Homer the only suggestion that Moira bestows blessings is the old word *moiregenes* ("child of Moira"), which occurs along with *olbiodaimon* ("favorite of the rich deity").[51] A characteristic which can clearly be recognized as basic in the ancient Moira now determines her whole being in all its aspects. The ordinances of the Homeric Moira are wholly negative: she ordains a man's fall and destruction. In certain cases it may appear, for reasons easy to understand, that her designs may be positive also. But this is nothing more than appearance. One need only compare the passages which speak of the gods' designs to notice the difference at once. Of the lot which the gods determine the poetic language may say that they "spin" it (*epiklotho*).[52] But then Homer can also speak of "a man for whom the son of Cronus has spun bliss in the marriage bed and in the procreation of fair children, even as now he has granted to Nestor for all his days that he should glide peacefully into old age in his comfortable halls, surrounded by sons prudent and adept with their spears."[53] Of the power over destiny it is said only in one passage (where the Moirai are thought of in the plural, in the manner of folk belief) that it *gave* man something: "An enduring soul have the Moirai given unto men."[54] That is not true of the genuine Homeric Moira, whose saying is Nay. This nay-saying fixes death —the "day of fate"[55] is death—but it also introduces great catastrophes and major errors, such as the fall of Troy or Agamemnon's unhappy quarrel with Achilles.

We do occasionally read that it was "fated" for one man or another to attain some desired goal. For Odysseus it was fated (*moira* or *aisa*) that he should return safe to his home.[56] He shall sail alone on his raft, says Zeus to Hermes when he sends him to Calypso, and shall suffer much until he reaches the Phaeacians and they bring him back to his home; "for this is how he is fated (*moira*) to return to his tall house and his native land and to see his friends once more."[57] But when Hermes speaks to Calypso he says:

"It is not his fate (*aisa*) to perish in this place, far from his friends; it is decreed (*moira*) that he shall see his friends again and re- turn to his tall house and his native land."[58] So clairvoyant Hel- enus says that Hector may safely venture to fight, for it is not now fated for him to die and fulfill his fate.[59] For Odysseus there is a special fate (*moira*) which does not imply death but which never- theless plainly reveals the negative character of Moira: he must endure great suffering, and *only if* he reaches the land of the Phaeacians will it be possible for him to recover his native land.[60] Here too the decree is restrictive and enjoins a limit. "Not until" is the characteristic note of Moira, and the qualification is so griev- ous that it can break a man's heart.[61] Menelaus, who uses this ex- pression of himself, was told that it was *not* fated (*moira*) for him to recover his country *before* he had accomplished the difficult voyage to Egypt and had there offered sacrifice to the gods.[62] So it is only in superficial appearance that Moira also promises man advantages or success; in actuality her function is always denial.

When it is said of Aeneas that it is "fated" (*morimon*) for him to escape with his life,[63] the meaning is that fate (*moira*) had *not* ordained that he fall in battle.[64] To prevent his doing so Posei- don intervenes, for, as this passage puts it, his death would be "beyond fate" (*hyper moiran*). Thus it is quite conceivable that a thing may take place which goes "beyond fate" (*hyper moron*). But, as we see, this does not mean that the fate might have re- mained unfulfilled and that its fulfillment required the timely intervention of a god. The substance of fate is always a Nay, which implies a fall or some painful strait; and anything that goes beyond fate does not abolish but only accentuates it. The language of the formula is not "contrary to fate," but "beyond fate."

If, therefore, there is ground to fear that a fall may take place which is not, or not yet, fated, then gods enter the scene to avert the excess. How thoroughly in keeping this is with their nature we shall see directly.

There are, moreover, not merely absolute but also qualified principles which may be called fate in the degree that they ordain specific consequences for specific deeds with inexorable severity, without, however, specifying whether or not the initial step would take place. For this myth supplies a series of famous examples. *If* Metis bears a son he shall be king of the gods.[65] *If* Zeus marries Thetis, he will be overthrown by his own son. *If* Laius raises a son by Jocasta, he will prove his father's murder. In this case the result of the act is absolutely determined, but it is itself free. It would be beyond fate if the act too were obligatory. From such steps the gods are preserved by their knowledge of fate. The gods wish to preserve man from fateful decisions by giving him too an insight into the inevitability of the causal nexus. If he nevertheless enters upon a path which must lead to destruction, then he has fashioned his own misfortune "beyond fate" (*hyper moron*). This is the perceptive thought which the poet applies to the fate of Aegisthus at the opening of the *Odyssey*. Men, says Zeus, blame us gods for their misfortunes, whereas they bring trouble upon themselves through their own perversity "beyond fate" (*hyper moron*): "Look at Aegisthus; he married Agamemnon's wife beyond fate (*hyper moron*) and killed her husband when he came home, though he knew the ruin this would entail, for I had sent Hermes the keen-eyed slayer of Argus to warn him neither to kill the man nor make love to his wife, inasmuch as Orestes was sure to take his revenge when he grew up and wanted to return home. Yet with all Hermes' friendly counsel Aegisthus would not listen, and now he has paid for everything in full."[66]

This is a direct hit on an important problem of life. Human existence is struck not only by bolts of fate which are unavoidable; there are also catastrophes which, by the judgment of ordinary experience, the victim might have avoided. They are no less necessary and fated than the others, once man has committed an act pregnant with consequences. He can be restrained from committing this act by knowledge, and this knowledge is itself, according to the Homeric view, the work of the gods: the moment a good thought enters a man's consciousness a god encounters him, and the good thought is the word the god speaks to him. So Hermes appears to Aegisthus and informs him of the consequences which must be involved in this act. When he perpetrates the act notwithstanding, his fall is caused by himself. In the post-Homeric age when mythic thought had lost much of its force, a man enlightened by insight was no longer thought to be visited

by a god, but the total conception remained the same. The great
Solon thought precisely as the poet of the Aegisthus passage. In a
famous elegy he says to his fellow-citizens: "Our city will never
be destroyed by the 'fate' (*aisa*) of Zeus . . . but the citizens
themselves shall destroy it by their folly."[67] Elsewhere he says:
"If you experience evil because of your perversity do not place the
blame upon the gods; for it is *you yourselves* who have made our
oppressors great."[68] For Solon too fate becomes self-imposed by
the fact that men have foreknowledge.[69] But now it is no longer a
god who appears to arouse knowledge; it is Solon himself who
instructs his fellow-citizens through his own insight,[70] and so
causes them to have knowledge. So the mysterious concatenation
of free will and necessity is explained to the thoughtful mind. The
Homeric idea is no theodicy, and least of all in the sense that divine providence is to be theoretically justified as against natural
experience. For it is in fact life's experience that forces man to
draw a distinction between the inevitable doom of fate whose
symbol is death, and the lot which he himself fashions, with at
least the appearance of free will, but which knocks at his door as
inexorably as the other, once he has himself stirred his fate.

4

It is very significant that the gods, who must step aside when
Moira enters into action, regularly intervene whenever there is
reason to fear some catastrophe not decreed by Moira, that is,
some event "beyond Moira" (*hyper moron*).

In the *Iliad* there is several times danger that Troy, which fate
has doomed to destruction, may be conquered "beyond fate,"
that is, prematurely, and upon each occasion some deity intervenes to prevent such an outcome.[71] Odysseus was on the point of
perishing "beyond fate" if Athena had not taken his part.[72] Just
as it is the character of Moira to set limits to life, so it is the nature
of the gods to protect life as long as possible. But one day the
end comes, and the gods must needs give way once Moira is determined to take over.

The gods have knowledge of fate in advance of man. "Zeus

surely knows, and the other immortals, for which of the two the doom of death is fated," says Priam, before the duel between Paris and Menelaus begins.[73] Zeus knows that Hector is near death and the only thing he can do for him is to allow his glory to blaze once more before his final extinction.[74] But at the moment of decision the great god is filled with sorrow because the irreproachable hero who was always meticulous in discharging his obligations to his godhead, must now be delivered to death.[75] He asks the other gods whether he might not even now save Hector, and Athena replies: "What mean you? Would you pluck this mortal whose doom has long been decreed out of the jaws of death? Do as you will, but we others shall not be of a mind with you." Then Zeus reassures his daughter: "I did not speak in full earnest." Now fate takes its course. But in the moment of decision it must be made to speak unequivocally. "Then the father balanced his golden scales and placed in each of them a death-bringing doom (*ker*), one for Achilles and one for horse-taming Hector. As he held the scales in the middle Hector's fated day (*aisimon emar*) sank deep into Hades."[76] That is the sign. At that moment Apollo forsook Hector, to whom he had previously given strength. The scene enacted on Olympus before Zeus took up his scales shows that the gods know the will of fate and do not require the process of weighing, in order to be informed of it. The primeval image of the scales is therefore not employed by Homer with its original meaning; it serves merely as a visible expression of the necessity whose moment has now arrived. So we are to understand that the "scales of Zeus" upon which fate is again weighed in another passage[77] is elsewhere merely a manner of speaking to designate the will or resolve of Zeus.[78] Upon the tragic stage at Athens, at the presentation of Aeschylus' *Psychostasia*, the grandiose picture of Zeus with his scales was to be seen on high while Achilles and Memnon were fighting; in one pan was the "life" of Achilles, in the other Memnon's, and at the sides were the two mothers, Thetis and Eos, weeping for their sons. On another occasion also Zeus strives against fate. When Patroclus and Sarpedon came to blows "Zeus looked down upon them in pity and said to Hera, his wife and sister, 'Alas, that it should be the fate (*moira*) of Sarpedon whom I love so dearly to perish by the hand of Patroclus. I am in two minds whether to catch him up out of the fight and set him down safe and sound in the fertile land of Lycia or to let him now fall by the hand of the son of Menoetius.'"[79] Hera protests in the same terms Athena had used in the scene cited above, "and the father of gods and men assented, but he shed a rain of blood upon the earth in honor of his son whom Patroclus was about to kill."[80]

The grief of the gods when the moment of Moira comes, and even more their resistance, which must nevertheless at once yield to resigned assent, are clear proof that two disparate realms are here opposed to one another. Their rôle as consummators, which is a function of the gods at decisive moments, cannot alter this situation; as we shall see, the meaning of that rôle is quite different from the meaning usually assumed. The sum of the matter is that gods and fate are separated from and opposed to one another because of a distinction in essence. But what is this Moira against whom the resistance of even the mightiest god is futile and at whose intervention divine helpers can only withdraw?

For Homer, Moira is not a person. To be sure he speaks of its functioning, as we have noticed, in terms of a personal and acting agent. But all of these terms, in particular such images as "mighty," "compelling," "overwhelming," and even "spinning," are merely formulary and point to a conception shaped in the early period rather than to Homer's own. Aside from the area of these formulae Moira is never thought of as a personal figure in any living context, as even such faded deities as Ocean, Tethys, Night, and others occasionally are. Latterly the remarkable conjecture has been advanced that in the Homeric age Moira gradually developed into a personality out of an antecedent impersonal "force"; but it is quite obvious that in Homer's mind Moira has lost her primeval plastic existence, though she may have retained it in popular thought. Related to this is the fact that Homer knows of no plurality of Moirai (with the single exception noted above), whereas in the case of similar figures, insofar as they are imagined as persons, mythic and popular thought has a predilection for plurality. In addition to Ker, which is very like Moira, Homer has a plurality of Keres; he can even speak of "spinning women" (*Klothes*) in the old-fashioned way.[81] But Moira is one. There is only one "fate." Even though each individual has his own "fated day" (*morsimon emar*), we cannot say that he has his own Moira. Moira is the law which stands over all of life, and for each fixes and allots his doom, namely, collapse and death.

Not only does Moira possess no personality but—and this is of the highest significance—she cannot even be designated a "power" in the proper sense of the word. We have seen how conscientiously the gods respect her, even though their hearts are anguished. But there is never any suggestion that the gods yield to a higher power perforce or need fear any consequences if they should refuse. Even when fate is consummated through their actions, there is no suggestion that they are acting at the behest of a higher power. There is only one statement concerning their relationship to Moira: They have knowledge of it, and guide themselves according to this knowledge.

Thus the primeval and popular belief in personal powers of fate was supplanted by the idea of an irrefragable order and destiny which is a factual datum for the living and personal gods and exists independently of them. Hence the only consequence that may be expected of a possible disregard of the fact is a disruption of order. That is what Athena and Hera say to Zeus in the scenes discussed above. His willfulness would evoke the disapproval of the gods, and the bad example would be imitated; confusion would be introduced into the great order.

But this "destiny" certainly implies no fatalistic determination of all happenings. Nowhere do we find any trace of a belief that all happenings are predetermined. Destiny means death and the great catastrophes allied to death. Death is determined for all living things, and on this principle even the power of the gods is frustrated. It is quite conceivable that a man may depart this life even before the day determined. This "excess" (*hyper moron*) he may have incurred by his own guilt, specifically by affronting a deity, and in such a case it is the gods themselves who bring it about. Otherwise, however, they endeavor to hinder it with all their strength. The gods are life, and therefore they combat death so long as its peremptory hour has not come. But then the ordinance takes its course, and with it they have nothing more to do. Limitation, cessation, is a law which is alien to life and to the gods, but life must be subject to it and the deity must yield. Beyond this limit begins the realm of the has-been, which is remote from life; its peculiar being we have examined in an earlier chapter.

Such is the idea of fate as it took shape in the Homeric spirit. It denotes the negative in the world of life, whereas deity denotes the positive. Thus the contrasting idea of fate puts the idea of deity into clearer focus.

5

Now it may fairly be asked how the law of Moira is executed, seeing that Moira herself possesses no power. Naturally Homer has no theory on the subject; his thoughts are presented to us in figures and images. But if we follow up the meaning of these images we glimpse a view whose truth and profundity can only evoke astonishment.

It has been said that it is the gods who "execute" the will of Moira. This would imply a unity of the two which is in flat contradiction to our understanding of their natures. But the Homeric statements which are used to prove the gods' rôle as consummators only imply prevention of such happenings as might go "beyond fate" (*hyper moron*), which is not consummation of what is fated. The actual sequence in these matters may be perceived most plainly in the circumstances that attend the death of Hector.[82]

Zeus has lamented the doom of death by which Hector must fall. He has even invited the gods to consult whether Hector might yet be saved. The alternative was: "Or shall we let him fall, valiant though he be, before Achilles son of Peleus?" At the earnest admonition of Athena he decides at once, and we might expect that he himself would proceed to arrange the catastrophe. But his attitude is purely negative. "I will let you have your way," he says to his daughter, "do without let or hindrance as you are minded." At once she darts down from Olympus to the battlefield. Now the scene of which we have spoken above is enacted. As soon as Zeus has shown the will of fate with his golden scales, Apollo forsakes Hector and Athena approaches Achilles.[83] She aids him in a manner which to modern critics seems repulsive, but only because they have not comprehended the meaning of the event. In the deceptive guise of a brother-in-arms the goddess encourages Hector to stand fast and fight with Achilles. Grateful and pleased, Hector proceeds to fight, believing that he has a loyal second at his side. But when he is needed, the second has vanished without a trace. Athena has therefore delivered him to his overpowering adversary and Hector at once realizes that he is doomed; his only desire is to fall honorably. The magnanimity of conception which makes the goddess, who here represents fate, actually help the unfortunate man achieve an honorable and glorious death should have been noticed long ago. Instead, critics have balked at Athena's telling an untruth and deceiving Hector's confidence. But on the main point she speaks the simple truth: "Verily, swift-footed Achilles will overtake you."[84] Of that there could be no doubt after he was deserted by Apollo, who, as the poet emphasizes, "had sustained his strength and nerved his running."[85] For us, however, that is not as important as the observation that Athena here represents fate. In all of her action the sway of fate is reflected with frightening accuracy. After Hector, beguiled by the phantom, had entered upon his unhappy course, his initial success made him bold, but only paved the way for the great failure which leads to his destruction. His success is nugatory because Achilles recovers his spent spear through Athena whereas his own is lost, and eventually his attack thrusts him upon the spear of his enemy, which he had at first, apparently luckily, evaded. So Athena is the personal figure of the misfortune ordained for him. But she is his misfortune by the very fact that she is Achilles' fortune. Just as everything goes wrong for Hector in demonic fashion and even his gain leads to his loss, so Achilles has luck in everything and even his failure leads to success.

The poet has thus expressed himself plainly enough on the effects of the gods on the path of fate. If Hector's life were not doomed, this conflict with the far superior Achilles would have involved the danger of "going beyond fate" (*hyper moron*) and would have been obviated by a god. Actually, until the very moment that Hector's fate is revealed by the scales of Zeus,

Apollo is at his side infusing him with strength and preventing his opponent from overtaking him, as the poet expressly says. But then he must withdraw and leave the field to Athena, that is, to the fortune of Achilles. And in protecting and exalting the life of Achilles, Athena becomes fatal to the life of Hector. To us the demonic element in the events leading to Hector's fall communicates a feeling of horror; for the man summoned by fate the divine becomes demonic.

If it were literally true that the gods consummate fate, then some god or the gods as a group would have to take the life of the man doomed. But that is not the case. A life which is finished is always destroyed by the tutelary deity of another life which is opposed to it. When the hour of fate has arrived, something takes place that is worth our pondering. We hear that the god who had hitherto loyally attended the hero vanishes from his side. Deity and fullness of life are one. If the divine has taken its departure, life has, to be sure, not yet perished, but it has lost its genius. The negation of existence has already thrown its chill shadow over it. The immediate effects are false thoughts and blind resolves. Divine presence illumines man and preserves him from such errors. For the man whom the divine has forsaken everything turns to deception; for him the divine itself is transformed into the demonic—and he stumbles into a region where there is no footing. Blindness drives him defenseless into the arms of the opposing life, which is guarded by a deity.

The story of the death of Patroclus brings this process home to us in vivid and terrifying detail.[86] Patroclus was doomed. He was seized with the blind folly of venturing against the city of Troy, which was still spared by fate, and thus against Apollo, the protector of the city. We know Hector's cry when he notices with horror that he has fallen victim to a deception: "Alas, the gods have summoned me to my death!"[87] The same significant sentence is uttered by the poet in the passage where he tells of Patroclus's blindness. He had forgot the earnest admonition of his friend and had stormed against the city whose tutelary deity was to destroy him. "Foolish man! Had he but obeyed the bidding of the son of Peleus he would have escaped the evil Ker of black death. But the counsels of Zeus pass man's understanding; it was Zeus who then kindled the spirit in his breast."[88] His fate had been set in motion. At his going forth Achilles had prayed Zeus to inspirit his friend with valor: "Zeus grant that when he has succeeded in turning the battle from the ships he may return unscathed."[89] But Zeus granted only the first part of the petition; Patroclus's safe return he denied.[90] With his dying breath Patroclus says to Hector: "Destroying Moira and the son of Leto have overpowered me, and among mortal men Euphorbus; you are yourself only third in the killing of me."[91] Here fate and Apollo coincide. The doom is consummated by Apollo (and Zeus). "Vaunt as you will," this final speech of Patroclus begins, "for Zeus the son of Cronus and Apollo have vouchsafed you victory; it is they who have vanquished me so easily, and they who have stripped the armor from my shoulders."[92] His speech concludes with a prophecy for Hector: "You too shall live but a little season; death and mighty Moira are close upon you."[93] Just as Hector, summoned by fate and forsaken by the divine, falls into the hands of Achilles and his goddess Athena, so Patroclus is hurled against Apollo, who must protect Troy. And this comes about by his becoming blinded. Achilles had warned him not to advance against Troy "lest one of the ever-living gods from Olympus attack you, for Phoebus Apollo loves the Trojans."[94] But in the excitement of victory Patroclus forgot this friendly counsel. Hence arises the situation whose character we have now come to know. "The sons of the Achaeans would now have taken Troy by the hands of Patroclus . . . had not Phoebus Apollo taken his stand upon the wall, contriving destruction for him and aiding the Trojans."[95] Thrice Patroclus charged at the wall, and thrice did Apollo beat him back, but when he charged for the fourth time Apollo shouted to him with an awful voice: "Draw back, noble Patroclus, it is not your lot to sack the city of the Trojan chieftains, nor yet will it be that of Achilles, who is a far better man than you are." And now he goes to meet his end. He is allowed, indeed, to triumph once more: a stone he throws crushes Hector's charioteer to earth, and in the ensuing battle over the corpse the Greeks at last gain the upper hand. But this very success induces that same constellation for the second time, and this time it leads to destruction. "When the sun went down the Achaeans were 'beyond fate' (*hyper aisan*)

stronger."[96] They won possession of the fallen man and his armor. "Patroclus sprang like Ares with fierce intent and a terrific
shout upon the Trojans, and thrice did he kill nine men; but as
he was coming on like a god for a fourth time, then, O Patroclus,
was the hour of your end approaching, for Phoebus fought you
in fell earnest."[97] And now there followed the harrowing collapse
we have discussed above. What else is Phoebus here than the
protected and triumphant life of the Trojans upon which the
doomed and forsaken life of Patroclus is shattered?

That same path great Achilles himself was to take. The epic
account of his fall has unfortunately not been preserved, but re-
ports of it and indications in Homer himself make its principal
features clear. He was doomed to an early death,[98] and was to
fall shortly after Hector.[99] His conqueror was Apollo, whether
he slew him himself or by the hand of Paris.[100] He was to fulfill
his fate beneath the walls of Troy as he was about to conquer
the city.[101] It was "the great god and mighty Moira" who brought
about his fall.[102] It has been alleged that Apollo appears here as
a god of death. But the intention of the poet was different. Like
Patroclus, Achilles succumbs to the fortune of the city which was
not yet doomed to fall; like Patroclus he was overthrown by
Troy's protector. And this happened when an issue "beyond fate"
was to be feared for Troy. Already Achilles was storming through
the gate of the city—but it was not fated that the city should fall
by his hand.[103] Thereupon the fatal arrow struck him. And so
ended the brilliant career of the most glorious hero, whom only
a god could lay low:

> There like a pine by biting axe-stroke shorn,
> Or cypress brought to ground by eastern gust,
> Stretched all abroad he laid his neck forlorn
>   In Trojan dust.
>   HORACE[104]

6

Without theory, then, and without dogmatism a consistent view
of the world, clear and meaningful, takes shape. Because it is not

theoretical, because it makes no postulates, because its point of departure always follows experience and always grows out of existence itself, its apparent contradictions also prove consistent. There are indeed mysteries—and they are as great as existence itself—but there are no mystifications, no artful transvaluations, and no compromises.

Because there was no dogma to fix the belief that fate—which means, in the first instance, the doom of death—and the gods were independent of one another, that belief was intersected by another, which held that all things flow from the hand of the godhead, including also the tragic aspects of human life. It is not merely the conception that the gods are unfathomable that suggested this thought: there is a strong impulse towards it even in the relationship, as we have come to know it, between the gods and fate. If "doom" is not a person or an independent power, if only the gods know it and exercise their providence accordingly, may it then not be their own decree? Actually this conception not infrequently takes shape in Homer's language. In a sense it is the counterpole to the conception that the gods accommodate themselves to the demands of fate unwillingly and with sorrow. But we must not overlook the fact that this divine with whose thoughts and purposes fate can merge is only that great and infinitely enhanced being which is called "Zeus" or "the gods." Plastic art placed the Moirai directly in the hands of Zeus, and Zeus himself bears the name—though not in Homer—of Moiragetes, "leader of the Moirai." As the giver of all things he appears in the image of the two urns from which he distributes good gifts and evil to mankind,[105] and in the *Odyssey* it is said of him that "to this one or to that one he giveth of good or of evil; to him all things are possible."[106] So at the opening of the *Iliad*, when the poet speaks of the many deaths caused by Achilles' wrath, he makes no mention of Moira but attributes the disaster to the counsel of Zeus.[107] In the account of the fall of Patroclus, Moira is indeed specifically mentioned, but it may easily appear that the sequence of events was willed and ordained by Zeus. His name is cited along with Moira, as if there were no distinction between the two. Lycaon, who had once escaped Achilles but eventually fallen into his power, cries out: "Now again cursed Moira has put me into your

hands; I think I must be hated by Zeus the father who has given
me once more to you."[108] So says Hector also when he sees death
before him: "Here at last the gods have summoned me to death.
. . . So it must long since have been pleasing to Zeus and his son
who strikes from afar. Before this they defended me gladly, but
now Moira attacks me."[109] When dying Hector warns Achilles
that he too will shortly die, Achilles says: "Death will come upon
me whenever Zeus and the rest of the immortals choose to accomplish it."[110] When Telemachus despairs of recovering his father
he says: "For him the immortals have decreed death and dark
doom."[111] Sorrowing over the mischief she has caused, Helen
says of herself and Paris that to them "Zeus gave an evil destiny."[112] And Odysseus himself says to the angry shade of Ajax in
the underworld: "None other was to blame, but Zeus was angry
with the Greek host and upon you laid the fate (*moira*) of
death."[113] The gods' determination of fate is not infrequently
designated by the image of spinning.[114] So we can easily understand that a "decree of Zeus" or "of the gods" is occasionally
spoken of in the ancient terms of *moira* or *aisa*, which in any case
retained their literal meaning of share or allotment. Though it is
"going beyond fate" (*moira, moros*) that the gods are called upon
to prevent, in one passage we read that "the Argives even beyond
Zeus's destiny (*aisa*) might have won glory by their own force and
strength had not Apollo intervened."[115] "Hapless men that we
were," says Odysseus,[116] "an evil destiny of Zeus overtook us."
"Grievous fate (*moira*) trapped Melampus," one passage begins, and closes with the words "and the counsel of Zeus was accomplished."[117] When Clytemnestra yielded to Aegisthus, it was
the "fate (*moira*) of the gods" that compelled her to submit.[118]
What caused the destruction of the suitors was the "fate (*moira*)
of the gods and their own wicked conduct."[119]

But this brings us to another level of thought. In view of the
mystery which envelops "doom" and its consummation—that is,
where the circles of the gods and of fate intersect—it is conceivable that the greater the deity is the more easily it can be
placed on a par with dark necessity or even supplant it. When
Agamemnon speaks of his fateful blindness he names Zeus ahead
of Moira.[120] But with thoughts of a "decree of Zeus" or of "the

gods" the imagination turns from murky destiny to intelligent plan and counsel. It was through their wickedness that the suitors fell, and this fall was brought about by the "decree" of the gods. Thus what is apportioned to men in this manner is no longer merely negative. Achilles knows that "honor is granted by Zeus's decree" (*aisa*).[121] In post-Homeric language advantages and blessings come through the "decree" of deity or of Zeus,[122] and in a famous passage Solon says, equating "decree" and "deity": "Decree (*moira*) bringeth to mankind both good and evil, and the gifts of the immortal gods are inescapable."[123] Even in the *Odyssey, moira* in the sense of allotment is linked with the gods in a completely neutral sense: "For everything the immortals have fixed a proper time (*moira*)."[124]

7

These ambiguities in applying the notion of decree are easy to explain and do not obscure the proper sense of the idea. This idea posits two realms, which are alien to one another: a realm of life, of development, of affirmation, and a realm of death, severance, and denial. Only the former is configured, active, personal; the realm of negation has neither figure nor personality; it only sets limits and with its cry of Halt! sharply curtails development and life. On this the gods have no more to say. They serve the consummation of fate, but only in the degree that the full and protected life must serve the fall of a life that is lost and without protection. If it is possible to say that the gods too formulate decrees, theirs (in the specific sense of "doom") belong to the other, negative, side of existence. It cannot be denied that on occasion another conception comes to the fore, and that this conception was destined to attain great power—but it is nevertheless perfectly plain that genuine Homeric thought makes not life and blossoming subject to fate but rather denial and death. This thought is so weighty and profound that no one who thinks upon it can regard it as the brilliant notion of an individual. It belongs to the primeval thoughts of humanity, which are timeless, whatever the time and place of their first formulation might be.

Life is movement, and in movement it encounters deity as
energy, revelation, and bliss; indeed the god is himself this life.
From his gifts, his benison, his illumination, fate and necessity are
as different as Yea from Nay, as death from life. That he attain
or create or enjoy this thing or that is not a matter of man's fate.
All this belongs to life's animation, to its mysterious flower, which
is at every instant of its development and enrichment natural and
at the same time wonderful, orderly growth and at the same
time manifestation and presence of divinity. But it is a matter of
fate that life does not attain this goal or that; here or there it
suffers a fall and eventually perishes—that is, must pass over to
the other side of being, which no longer knows life, flowering,
gods, but only necessity and limitation, to that twilit realm where
instead of the present there is only the past, but where, though
growth and gods are wanting, all configurations are preserved
timelessly and are sent up into life as great memories.

In the face of such a thought all fatalism must seem petty and
petulant. It diminishes the Nay of none of its rigor, and yet
leaves life its wonder. It is neither dogma nor consistent theory
but—like all truly Greek thought about the world—living actuality which bears its own proof.

8

If we direct our glance from the Greek idea to the religions of
other peoples, we observe how easily this counter-play of light
and dark can turn into a definite dualism. This only enhances
our appreciation of the Greek idea. In the deep and limpid
Homeric spirit the positive aspects of being and the negative
are alike reflected: the former with all the abundance and
plasticity of form, the latter with its limitation and its shadows
and hence no longer as form and personality. The negative falls
upon life as a shadow, and under it life's paths are darkened
and its geniuses the gods are transformed into the demonic. No
dark ruler makes a violent attack: existence itself becomes dismal
and dangerous. The good powers who previously guarded life
are changed. They no longer illumine but deceive and mislead;

that is the path to ruin. So it happens when a man mocks them. Their desire has been to advance life, but now they become his curse; his spirit is confounded, he falls into the abyss. In Sophocles' *Ajax*, Athena, with horrible mockery, displays the mighty hero in his benighted hour to his rival, Odysseus. Ajax had mocked her, and now has himself become an object of mockery. Only the grandeur of his death restores his nobility. But a similar darkness falls when fate has spoken.

However cold and bitter necessity may be, the grandeur of death remains as the last province of the brilliance of life and its gods. The goddess who has turned into danger and calamity now intervenes, and the fallen man may take her with him into the mute night which knows no more pulsing of the heart, no more immediacy.

CONCLUSION

We have reached the end, and glance backward once more.

Much that is important has doubtless been passed over and must await some future interpreter to place it in its proper light. But very soon we come to a barrier at which we must acknowledge that there is a great deal which cannot be spoken. The Greek conception of the divine is as broad as the world and therefore, like the world itself, in the last analysis ineffable. It presents itself to us candidly, without obfuscation and without pathos. In it mystery does not occupy the foreground, and hence it requires no creed or confession of faith: it abides serene in the depths and allows all thoughts upon it to issue in the inexpressible. Out of it we recognize a cosmic feeling of unexampled strength and abundance which, as unerringly as nature, always finds the right images. What possesses substance must be consistent, and so it comes about that despite the absence of creed we find agreement and unity; indeed we can discover a system of ideas which has never been conceptually apprehended. But behind the clarity of view stands the enigma of being, and here all is inexplicable.

Despite its admirable transparency the enigma is greater and weightier than in any other religion. Greek thought overwhelms us by its uniqueness. Other religions cannot help us here, because the Greek cannot be compared with any of them. Hence it has seldom been appreciated and almost always it has been misunderstood; indeed it has not even been noticed, for we have learned to seek the holy in other religions, from which the Greek stands isolated in solitary grandeur.

Thus the belief of the most perceptive of all peoples has remained unheeded and unpraised—this wonderful and admirable belief which arose out of the riches and depths of life, not out of its anxieties and yearnings—this meteor of a religion which could not only see the brilliance of life with an eye more luminous than the rest of mankind but is also unique in that its lucid gaze confronted the insoluble conflict of life with candor and out of its most terrifying darkness conceived the majestic achievement of tragedy.

287

NOTES

CHAPTER I

1. *Homeric Hymn to Apollo* 189 ff.
2. Cf. H. Oldenberg, *Die Lehre der Upanishaden und die Anfänge des Buddhismus*, Göttingen, 1915
3. Goethe, *Faust*, tr. MacNeice, p. 281

CHAPTER II

1. Aeschylus, *Prometheus* 88 ff.
2. Aeschylus, *Eumenides* 321, 416
3. Ib. 960
4. Ib. 904 ff.
5. Ib. 835, and scholia ad loc.
6. Cf. Pausanias 1.28.6
7. Sophocles, *Oedipus at Colonus* 40
8. Frg. 19, Diels
9. Aeschylus, *Eumenides* 184
10. Ib. 264 ff.
11. Ib. 186 ff.
12. Ib. 605 ff.
13. Ib. 625 ff.
14. Ib. 471
15. Ib. 735 ff.
16. *Iliad* 19.418
17. Frg. 94, Diels
18. Aeschylus, *Eumenides* 417
19. *Odyssey* 17.475
20. Cf. ib. 21.28
21. *Iliad* 13.625
22. *Iliad* 9.565 ff.
23. *Odyssey* 11.272 ff.
24. Ib. 2.135
25. *Iliad* 9.454
26. Ib. 15.204
27. Ib. 22.356 ff.
28. Ib. 24.54
29. Sophocles, *Antigone* 337
30. Cf. Aeschylus, *Prometheus* 209
31. Aeschylus, *Eumenides* 267 ff.
32. *Iliad* 3.278
33. Cicero, *De legibus* 2.36
34. Plutarch, *De facie in orbe lunae* 28
35. *Iliad* 20.65
36. Cf. Euripides, *Alcestis* 22, *Hippolytus* 1437
37. Cf. Kretschmer, *Glotta* 1
38. *Iliad* 15.195
39. Cf. ib. 21.435 ff.; *Odyssey* 8.344 ff.
40. *Iliad* 15.204
41. Hesiod, *Theogony* 453 ff.
42. Antimachus in Pausanias 8. 25.9
43. Hesiod, *Theogony* 278
44. *Iliad* 20.56 ff.
45. E.g. ib. 7.411, 16.88
46. Hesiod, *Theogony* 546, *Works and Days* 48
47. Hesiod, *Theogony* 18, 137, 168, 473, 495
48. Ib. 566, *Works and Days* 50
49. Hesiod, *Theogony* 535 ff.
50. Ib. 459 ff.
51. Ib. 494
52. Ib. 137
53. Ib. 468
54. Evidence for this and for what follows is cited in Kaibel, "Daktyloi Idaioi," *Nachrichten der Göttinger Ges. der Wissensch.* 1901
55. *Glotta* 14 (1925), 301 ff.

56. Loc. cit.
57. Aeschylus, frg. 44
58. Hesiod, *Theogony* 176
59. Ib. 154 ff.
60. Cf. Sir George Grey, *Polynesian Mythology*, 2nd ed. (1885), 1 ff. Traces of a similar myth are to be found among civilized peoples also: cf. Andrew Lang, *Custom and Myth*, 45 ff.
61. Bastian, *Die heilige Sage der Polynesier* (1881), 62
62. Hesiod, *Theogony* 453 ff.
63. Ib. 886 ff.
64. Cf. ib. 463 with 891
65. Ib. 924
66. Cf. W. W. Gill, *Myths and Songs from the South Pacific* (1876), 10

CHAPTER III

ATHENA

1. Cf. Rodenwaldt, *Athenische Mitteilungen* 37 (1912); Nilsson, *Anfänge der Göttin Athene* (Copenhagen, 1921); Wilamowitz, *Berliner Sitzungsberichte* (1921), 950 ff.
2. Cf. Frickenhaus, *Athenische Mitteilungen* (1908), 19 ff., and Buschor, ibid. (1922), 96 ff.
3. Hesiod, *Theogony* 924 ff.
4. Pindar, *Olympians* 7.34 ff.; tr. Lattimore
5. *Homeric Hymns* 28; translation based on Evelyn-White, in Loeb Classical Library
6. *Iliad* 2. 446 ff.
7. Ib. 4. 515
8. Aristophanes, *Wasps* 1086 f., version of B. B. Rogers. The flight of an owl is said to have announced the victory at Salamis: Hesychius, and scholia on Aristophanes ad loc.
9. *Iliad* 17.547 ff.
10. *Odyssey* 22.239 ff.
11. Ib. 22.205 ff.
12. *Iliad* 18.516
13. Ib. 6.305; Cf. *Homeric Hymns* 11
14. *Iliad* 10.274 ff.
15. Ib. 21.390 ff.
16. Ib. 5.761, 831
17. Ib. 5.761
18. Ib. 5.831, 889
19. Ib. 5.890
20. Cf. Pausanias 3.18.11 et al.
21. *Iliad* 1.194 ff.
22. Cf. Bacchylides frg. 41; Apollodorus 3.6.8.3
23. Cf. e.g. *Iliad* 4.390, 10.285 ff.
24. Ib. 1.193
25. Ib. 2.279
26. *Odyssey* 23.124
27. *Dii metin atalanton: Iliad* 2. 169, 407, 636; 10.137
28. *Iliad* 2.167 ff.
29. *Homeric Hymn to Athena* 2. Cf. also *Iliad* 5.260, *Odyssey* 16.282 (where the word is *polyboulos*), Simias 65 fr. (*hagna polyboule Pallas*)
30. *Odyssey* 13.297
31. Hesiod, *Theogony* 896
32. *Odyssey* 6.14
33. *enth' aut' all' enoese thea glaukopis Athene: Odyssey* 6. 112 and frequently
34. Cf. Apollodorus 1.9.16, 2.1.4
35. *Odyssey* 8.493 et al.
36. Pindar, *Olympians* 13.65 ff.
37. Pausanias 2.4.1
38. *Iliad* 21.355
39. *Odyssey* 4.227
40. Aeschylus, *Eumenides* 376

41. Hesiod, *Theogony* 886 ff.
42. Wilamowitz, *Sitzungsber. der Berliner Akad.* 54 (1921), 950 ff.
43. See p. 35.
44. Plato, *Cratylus* 407b and later writers
45. *Iliad* 23.311 ff.
46. Cf. Wilamowitz, loc. cit. 953
47. *Odyssey* 13.287 ff.
48. Aeschylus, *Eumenides* 736
49. This is the view of Nilsson
50. This is the view of Wilamowitz
51. *Iliad* 5.61
52. Ib. 15.412
53. *Odyssey* 6.223
54. Hesiod, *Works and Days* 430
55. *Homeric Epigrams* 14.2; cf. the vase paintings in *Monumenti Antichi* 28 (1922), 101 ff.
56. *Odyssey* 13.288, 16.157
57. *Iliad* 9.389
58. *Odyssey* 20.72; *Homeric Hymn to Aphrodite* 14 f.; Hesiod, *Works and Days* 63 f.
59. *Odyssey* 2.116 f.
60. *Iliad* 5.735
61. Ib. 14.178 f.
62. Hesiod, *Theogony* 573, *Works and Days* 72
63. Cf. Diels, *Fragmente der Vorsokratiker* 1².326
64. Cf. *Iliad* 16.34; Hesiod, *Theogony* 440
65. Cf. Empedocles, frg. 42 Diels; Euripides, frg. 1009
66. Cf. Sophocles, *Oedipus at Colonus* 701 et al.
67. Cf. *Iliad* 20.172
68. Cf. Pindar, *Pythians* 4.249, *Olympians* 6.45, 8.37
69. Cf. Sophocles, *Ajax* 450, frg. 760

70. Cf. Callimachus, *Hymns* 5. 17; Theocritus 20.25; Propertius 2.28.12
71. Cf. Dio Chrysostom 12.1 ff.
72. Pausanias 2.24.2
73. Plutarch, *Lycurgus* 11; Pausanias 3.18.2
74. Sophocles, *Oedipus at Colonus* 706
75. *Iliad* 1.200
76. Bacchylides 10
77. Hesiod, *Shield of Heracles* 339
78. Cf. Sophocles, *Ajax* 758 ff.

APOLLO

1. *Iliad* 5.440
2. Ib. 19.413
3. Ib.
4. Euripides, *Hippolytus* 75 ff.
5. Servius on *Aeneid* 4.143
6. Pindar, *Pythians* 10.29
7. Ib. 10.31 ff.
8. Ib. 10.45
9. Herodotus 4.36. According to a view documented only in later authors but surely original, Abaris did not carry the bolt but flew on it through the countries: cf. H. Fränkel, *De Simia Rhodio,* 35
10. Cf. Herodotus 4.13
11. Ib. 4.33 ff.
12. Ib. 4.32
13. Sophocles, frg. 870
14. Himerius 14.10
15. Cf. Wilamowitz, *Hermes* 38, and *Greek Historical Writing and Apollo;* this is refuted by Bethe in *Antidoron für Wackernagel,* but accepted by Nilsson in his *History of Greek Religion* (1925), 132
16. *Iliad* 21.461 ff.

17. Pindar, *Pythians* 8.95, tr. Lattimore
18. *Iliad* 21.461
19. Cf. Plato, *Charmides* 164d
20. *Iliad* 5.440
21. Ib. 24.40 ff.
22. See p. 18 f.
23. Cf. Plato, *Charmides* 164d
24. Cf. Plato, *Protagoras* 343b
25. Herodotus 1.30 ff.
26. Cf. R. Herzog, in E. Horneffer, *Der junge Platon* 1.149 (1922)
27. Pliny, *Natural History* 7.151
28. Valerius Maximus 7.1.2 et al.
29. Porphyry, *De abstinentia* 1.15 ff.
30. Plato, *Apology* 21 ff., 28 ff.
31. Pindar, *Pythians* 1.40
32. *Odyssey* 19.86
33. Hesiod, *Theogony* 347
34. *Odyssey* 8.79
35. *Iliad* 9.404
36. *Homeric Hymn to Apollo* 130 ff.
37. *Iliad* 1.72, 86
38. Ib. 1.603 f.
39. Ib. 24.63
40. Cf. *Odyssey* 8.488
41. Hesiod, *Theogony* 94
42. *Homeric Hymn to Pythian Apollo* 189 ff., tr. Evelyn-White
43. Ib. 182
44. Callimachus, *Hymn to Apollo*, 1 ff.
45. Claudianus, *On the Sixth Consulship of Honorius* 32
46. Pindar, *Pythians* 1.1 ff., tr. Lattimore
47. Euripides, *Alcestis* 579 ff.
48. Apollonius Rhodius 1.740
49. Cf. Callimachus, *Hymn to Apollo* 2, 47 ff.

50. Euripides, *Alcestis* 569 ff.· *Iliad* 2.766
51. *Iliad* 21.448
52. Plato, *Laws* 653, tr. Jowett
53. Plutarch, *Coriolanus* 1.1
54. Horace, *Odes* 3.4
55. *Homeric Hymn to Delian Apollo* 131
56. Cf. *Iliad* 2.827, 4.101, 119, 15.441, 23.872; *Odyssey* 21. 267, 338
57. Cf. *Odyssey* 21.338, 22.7
58. Ib. 8.226
59. *Homeric Hymn to Pythian Apollo*
60. Cf. *Iliad* 24.757 ff.
61. *Odyssey* 15.409 ff.
62. *Iliad* 1.47
63. Cf. *Odyssey* 11. 318
64. *Iliad* 12.463
65. *Odyssey* 11.606
66. Heraclitus, frg. 51, Diels
67. *Iliad* 4.125
68. Pindar, *Isthmians* 6.34 f.
69. *Odyssey* 21.410 f.
70. Pindar, *Olympians* 9.11
71. Ib. 2.89 ff., tr. Lattimore
72. Ib. 9.5
73. Hölderlin, *Poems,* tr. Hamburger, p. 149
74. Pindar, *Nemeans* 6.1 ff.
75. Id. *Pythians* 8.95 ff.
76. Id. *Isthmians* 5.14 ff., *Nemeans* 11.15 f.
77. Aeschylus, *Prometheus* 22
78. Cf. *Orphic Hymns* 34.16 ff.
79. Cf. Skythinnus, frg. 14; Neustadt, *Hermes* (1931), 389

ARTEMIS

1. Cf. Wilamowitz, *Hellenistische Dichtung,* 2.50
2. Cf. Pindar, *Olympians* 3, and the Delian tradition

3. *Homeric Hymn to Delian Apollo* 16

4. Cf. O. Kern, *Die Religion der Griechen* (1926), 1.103

5. Euripides, *Hippolytus* 1301

6. *Homeric Hymn to Aphrodite* 17

7. Cf. *Odyssey* 5.123, 18.202, 20.71

8. *Homeric Hymn to Aphrodite* 18 f.

9. *Odyssey* 6.102 ff.

10. Aeschylus, frg. 342; cf. Aristophanes, *Thesmophoriazusae* 114 ff.

11. Euripides, *Hippolytus* 75 ff. and cf. p. 63. Upon a red-figured vase she herself is named Aidos: cf. Kretschmer, *Griechische Vaseninschriften*, 197

12. Cf. *Iliad* 16.182; *Homeric Hymn to Aphrodite* 118; Callimachus, *Hymn* 3

13. Plutarch, *Theseus* 31

14. *Homeric Hymn to Pythian Apollo* 20

15. *Odyssey* 6.151

16. Ib. 20.71

17. Cf. Pamphus in Pausanias 8.35.8; Sappho in Pausanias 1.29.2; Aeschylus, *Agamemnon* 140; Euripides, *Hippolytus* 66 ff.

18. *Iliad* 21.470; Anacreon 1

19. Aeschylus, *Agamemnon* 133 ff.

20. Pausanias 5.19.5

21. Ib. 9.17.2

22. Theocritus 2.67

23. *Homeric Hymns* 27.2

24. Strabo 14.643

25. *Iliad* 6.205

26. Strabo 5.215

27. Cf. Pausanias 7.18.11

28. *Iliad* 21.483

29. *iokheaira: Iliad* 5.53 and frequently

30. *keladeine: Iliad* 16.183, 20.70 et al.

31. *Homeric Hymn to Aphrodite* 18

32. *Homeric Hymns* 9.6

33. *Iliad* 5.51

34. Cf. Diodorus 4.22

35. Sophocles, *Oedipus at Colonus* 206

36. Antoninus Liberalis 15

37. Sophocles, *Trachinian Women* 214

38. Pausanias 8.19.6

39. Ib. 8.37.4

40. Aeschylus, frg. 170

41. Pausanias 3.22.12

42. Cf. e.g. idem 7.19.4

43. Cf. Euripides, *Iphigenia among the Taurians* 21

44. Plutarch, *Themistocles* 22

45. Porphyry, *De abstinentia* 2.54; cf. Usener, *Götternamen* 51

46. Pausanias 1.19.6

47. Cf. ib. 4.13.1 et al.

48. *Odyssey* 5.124, 11.172 ff., 199, 15.411, 18.202

49. Cf. ib. 18.202, 20.61 ff.

50. Cf., in addition to passages already cited, *Iliad* 6.428, 19.59, *Odyssey* 11.324, 15.478

51. *Iliad* 21.483

52. *Orphic Hymns* 36.4

53. Callimachus, *Hymns* 36.4

54. *Iliad* 11.269; cf. Theocritus 27.28

55. Euripides, *Hippolytus* 166

56. *Palatine Anthology* 6.271

57. Aeschylus, *Suppliants* 676

58. Callimachus, *Hymns* 3.127

59. Cf. Euripides, *Iphigenia among the Taurians* 1462 ff.

60. *Palatine Anthology* 6.269
61. *Skolion* 4
62. Sophocles, *Electra* 626; cf. Aristophanes, *Lysistrata* 435, 922, *Ecclesiazusae* 84
63. *Palatine Anthology* 6.271
64. Cf. Diodorus 5.73
65. *Odyssey* 20.71
66. *philomeirax:* Pausanias 6.23.8
67. *Palatine Anthology* 6.242
68. Callimachus, *Hymns* 3.122
69. *Homeric Hymn to Aphrodite* 20
70. *Homeric Hymns* 1.14
71. *Iliad* 5.447
72. E.g. Aeschylus, frg. 200
73. *Homeric Hymns* 2.21, 27.15
74. *Odyssey* 15.410

APHRODITE

1. Jeremiah 7.18, 44.18
2. Herodotus 1.105; cf. also Pausanias 1.14.7
3. *Iliad* 5.330
4. *Odyssey* 8.362
5. Ib. 8.288
6. Hesiod, *Theogony* 192 f.
7. Pausanias 1.19.2
8. Epimenides, frg. 19, Diels
9. Hesiod, *Theogony* 934
10. *Iliad* 5.312, 370
11. Hesiod, *Theogony* 188-206
12. *Paul.-Fest.* 52
13. Pausanias 5.11.8
14. Ib. 2.1.8
15. Lucretius 1.4, tr. Bailey
16. *galenaie:* Philodemus, *Palatine Anthology* 10.21
17. *Palatine Anthology* 9.143 f., 10.21
18. Polycharmus, *Frag. Hist. Graec.* 4.480
19. Tacitus, *Histories* 2.4; Suetonius, *Tiberius* 5

20. Pindar, *Olympians* 7.25 with scholia
21. Athenaeus 6.253e
22. Pausanias 9.16.3
23. *Odyssey* 18.194
24. Ib. 8.364
25. *Iliad* 5.338
26. Cf. Strabo 14.683
27. Pausanias 1.19.2
28. Euripides, *Medea* 835 ff.
29. Hesychius s.v. *Antheia*
30. *Pervigilium Veneris* 13 ff.; cf. Ausonius, *De rosis nascentibus* 409, Peiper
31. 4th century A.D.: *Poetae Latinae Minores* 3.264, 1.10
32. Ibycus, frg. 6, Diels; cf. Wilamowitz, *Sappho und Simonides* 122 f.
33. Aelian, *Historia animalium* 10.50
34. Hesychius s.v. *myrikai*
35. Athenaeus 3.84c
36. Cornutus 24
37. Pausanias 2.10.5
38. Ovid, *Metamorphoses* 10.644
39. *Odyssey* 22.444
40. Hesiod, *Works and Days* 521
41. *philotes chrysees Aphrodites:* Hesiod, frg. 143, Rzach; *aphrodisiazein* and *ta aphrodisia:* Democritus frgs. 137 and 235, Diels
42. *Homeric Hymns* 4.1 ff.
43. Sophocles, frg. 855
44. Euripides, *Hippolytus* 447 ff.
45. Lucretius 1.10 ff.
46. *Homeric Hymn to Aphrodite* 69 ff.
47. *Odyssey* 20.73 ff.·
48. Pausanias 2.34.12
49. Ib. 10.38.12
50. Ib. 3.13.9
51. *tan parthenois gamelion Aph-*

roditan; Euripides, frgs. 781, 16

52. *Iliad* 3.54 ff.
53. Ib. 3.391 ff.
54. *Homeric Hymn to Aphrodite* 76 ff.
55. Cf. also Plutarch, *Quaestiones conv.* 3.6.4
56. *Iliad* 24.30
57. *marmaironta:* ib. 3.397
58. Ib. 1.200
59. Hesiod, *Works and Days* 65
60. *kallos:* *Odyssey* 18.192
61. Ib.
62. *Iliad* 14.214
63. Antiphanes, *Palatine Anthology* 6.88
64. Aeschylus, *Suppliants* 1040
65. Pindar, *Pythians* 4.214 ff., tr. Lattimore
66. Sophocles, *Antigone* 796 ff.
67. *Iliad* 3.413 ff.
68. Euripides, *Medea* 632 ff.
69. See especially Euripides, *Hippolytus*
70. Ib. 443 ff.
71. Ib. 474 ff.
72. Pausanias 9.16.3
73. Cf. Ovid, *Fasti* 4.133 ff. et al.; Valerius Maximus 8.15.12; Pliny, *Natural History* 7.120
74. Pindar, frg. 122, tr. Sandys
75. Cf. Xenophon, *Hellenica* 5.4.4; Plutarch, *Comparison of Cimon and Lucullus* 1; id., *Non posse suaviter vivi sec. Epic.* 12
76. Plutarch, *Greek Questions* 44
77. Cf. idem, *Non posse* etc. 16, *An seni gerenda resp.* 4
78. *Odyssey* 18.192
79. *Iliad* 23.185
80. Athenaeus 13.571c
81. Socrates in Xenophon, *Symposium* 8.15

82. Euripides, *Medea* 844 ff.
83. Pindar, *Pythians* 6.1, cf. *Paean* 6
84. Lucretius 1.28
85. Cf. Plato, *Symposium* 204c
86. Plutarch, *Amatorius* 5
87. Hesiod, *Theogony* 937
88. Plutarch, *Amatorius* 23
89. Aeschylus, *Suppliants* 1042, and cf. Wilamowitz' notes ad loc.
90. Sappho, frg. 135
91. Cf. Wilamowitz, *Sappho und Simonides*, 42 ff.
92. Aeschylus, frg. 44
93. Euripides, frg. 898
94. *Pervigilium Veneris* 59 ff.
95. Lucretius 1.31 ff.

HERMES

1. *Iliad* 24.24
2. Ib. 10.267, *Odyssey* 19.395
3. *Iliad* 21.498 ff.
4. *Odyssey* 8.339 ff.
5. *doteres eaon:* e.g. *Odyssey* 8.325; cf. Lucian, *Prometheus sive Cauc.* 18
6. Cf. *Odyssey* 8.335; *Homeric Hymns* 29.8
7. Aristophanes, *Peace* 394
8. *Homeric Hymns* 29.8
9. Aeschylus, *Eumenides* 945
10. Horace 1.10.11, after Alcaeus
11. *Iliad* 24.24
12. Cf. ib. 5.390
13. Hesiod, frg. 112, Rzach
14. *Homeric Hymn to Hermes* 282 ff.
15. Euripides, *Rhesus* 216 f.
16. Hipponax, frg.1
17. *Homeric Hymn to Hermes* 66
18. Ib. 274
19. *Iliad* 10.267, *Odyssey* 19.395
20. Plutarch, *Greek Questions* 55

21. Hesiod, *Works and Days* 77 f.
22. Pausanias 2.3.4
23. *Homeric Hymn to Hermes* 497, 567
24. *Odyssey* 14.435; the scholia ad loc. refer to verses of the iambic poet Simonides which say that shepherd folk are all subject to Hermes and the Nymphs
25. Hesiod, *Theogony* 444 ff.
26. *Iliad* 16.490 f.
27. Ib. 16.179 ff.
28. *Homeric Hymn to Hermes* 511
29. Cf. Pausanias 9.22.1
30. Wilamowitz, *Aischylos Interpretationen* 179, on vv. 89 ff.
31. *Homeric Hymn to Hermes* 286
32. Hesiod, *Theogony* 444 ff.
33. *Odyssey* 8.339 ff.
34. Cf. *furtum* in the Latin poets, and the instructive conclusions of W. Jaeger, *Hermes* (1915)
35. On Tychon cf. Herter, *De dis Atticis Priapi similibus*, diss. Bonn, 1926
36. *Homeric Hymn to Aphrodite* 262
37. *Iliad* 16.179 ff.
38. Pausanias 8.14.11
39. Ib. 6.26.5
40. Cf. *Homeric Hymn to Aphrodite* 117 ff.
41. Cf. Buschor, *Griech. Vasenmalerei*, fig. 124
42. Cf. *Odyssey* 11.626; Apollodorus 2.5.12
43. *Odyssey* 24.1 ff.
44. Aeschylus, *Choephorae* 622
45. Sophocles, *Ajax* 832
46. Id., *Oedipus at Colonus* 1547
47. Valerius Maximus 2.6.8
48. Cicero, *De legibus* 2.65

49. Aeschylus, *Persians* 629
50. Cf. Apollodorus, *Epit.* 3.30; Hyginus, *Fabulae* 103, 104
51. Cf. Cornutus 16.24; *Planudean Anthology* 4.254
52. *Odyssey* 16.471
53. Cf. Babrius 48
54. *Iliad* 24.340
55. Cf. Apollodorus 3.28; Apollonius of Rhodes 4.1135
56. Pausanias 3.18.11
57. Published in *Jahrb. des Archäologischen Inst.* 1892 (Anzeiger 166)
58. Cf. Wilamowitz, *Aischylos Interp.* 179
59. *Homeric Hymn to Hermes* 146
60. Plutarch, *De garrulitate* 2
61. *Homeric Hymn to Hermes* 282 ff.
62. *nyktos opopeter: Homeric Hymn to Hermes* 15
63. *euskopos: Iliad* 24.24, *Odyssey* 1.38
64. *Iliad* 10.40
65. *Battou skopiai:* Antonius Liberalis 23
66. *Index:* Ovid, *Metamorphoses* 2.687 ff.
67. *Odyssey* 7.138
68. *Iliad* 24.343
69. Ib. 24.445
70. *Homeric Hymn to Hermes* 448 f.
71. Ib. 14
72. Cf. Apollonius of Rhodes 4.1731 with scholia
73. *Iliad* 24.334 ff.
74. Ib. 24.374
75. Ib. 24.460
76. Hesiod, *Works and Days* 729 f.
77. *epikouros: Homeric Hymn to Hermes* 97
78. Hesiod, *Theogony* 224

79. *Odyssey* 10.277 ff.
80. H. Oldenberg, *Religion des Veda,* 1st ed., 230 ff.
81. Cf. scholia on *Odyssey* 16.471
82. *Homeric Hymn to Hermes* 577
83. *Iliad* 10
84. Euripides, *Rhesus* 216; cf. Sophocles, *Electra* 1395, *Philoctetes* 133
85. *Odyssey* 15.319 ff.
86. *Homeric Hymn to Hermes* 108 ff.
87. Cf. *Homeric Hymns* 29.7 ff.; Pausanias 5.11.8. See also Callimachus, *Hymn to Artemis* 68 ff.
88. Cf. Aeschylus, *Prometheus* 941 et al.; Aristophanes, *Peace* 180 ff., *Plutus* 1102 ff.; Lucian, *Dialogues of the Gods* 24
89. Cf. Athenaeus 10.425d
90. *Iliad* 24.333
91. *Odyssey* 5.29
92. Cf. scholia on *Iliad* 5.785
93. Hesiod, *Works and Days* 79
94. Cf. *Odyssey* 15.319
95. Cf. *Iliad* 24.347, *Odyssey* 10. 278. In Lucian, *Dialogues of the Gods* 22 he boasts of his appearance
96. Pausanias 9.22.1
97. Aristophanes, *Peace* 456
98. Pausanias 9.30.1
99. Ib. 8.32.2
100. Ib. 9.5.8
101. *Homeric Hymn to Hermes* 448

CHAPTER IV

1. *Homeric Hymn to Aphrodite* 244 f.
2. Hesiod, *Theogony* 949

3. *Odyssey* 5.215 ff.
4. Ib. 6.107
5. *Homeric Hymn to Demeter* 275 ff.
6. *Odyssey* 6.42 ff.
7. *Iliad* 1.573 ff.
8. Ib. 21.462 ff.
9. Ib. 21.464
10. *Homeric Hymn to Apollo* 190 ff.
11. *Iliad* 2.412
12. *Odyssey* 15.523
13. *Iliad* 11.182 ff.
14. Ib. 17.544 ff. and 19.350 ff.
15. Ib. 5.383 ff.
16. Ib. 8.402 ff.
17. Ib. 15.17 ff.
18. Pindar, *Nemeans* 6.1, tr. Lattimore
19. *Iliad* 5.339
20. Hesiod, *Theogony* 129
21. *Iliad* 14.203, 278, 8.479, and in detail in Hesiod's *Theogony*
22. Cf. Pindar, *Olympians* 2.77 ff.
23. Cf. Hesiod, *Works and Days* 111
24. *Iliad* 14.201
25. Ib. 20.65
26. Euripides, *Alcestis* 22
27. Id., *Hippolytus* 1437
28. *Iliad* 9.457
29. Ib. 8.368; Hesiod, *Theogony* 310 ff.
30. *Homeric Hymn to Demeter* 17 ff.
31. *Iliad* 9.568, 456
32. Ib. 5.395 ff.
33. Ib. 20.61 ff.
34. Ib. 23.71
35. H. Schreuer, *Zeitschrift für vergl. Rechtswissenschaft* 33 (1915), 396 ff.
36. Cf. Otto, *Die Manen* (1923)
37. Cf. *Odyssey* 11.218 ff.
38. Vergil, *Aeneid* 4.653

39. Goethe, *Faust*, tr. MacNeice, p. 178
40. Ib. p. 185
41. *Odyssey* 11
42. Ib. 11.467 ff.
43. Pindar, *Isthmians* 5.101 et al.
44. *Iliad* 24.591 ff.
45. *Odyssey* 10.492 ff., 11.91 ff.
46. Ib. 11.385 ff.
47. Bacchylides 5.67 ff.
48. Cf. Wilamowitz, *Die Rückkehr des Odysseus*, 194
49. *Odyssey* 24.15 ff.
50. Cf. ib. 10.493
51. Ib. 11.204 ff.
52. Ib. 11.487
53. *Iliad* 16.667 ff., 23.18 ff.
54. Ib. 1.47
55. Ib. 12.463
56. *Odyssey* 11.606
57. *Iliad* 14.259
58. Aeschylus, *Eumenides* 322, 416
59. *Iliad* 19.418
60. Heraclitus, frg. 94, Diels
61. Hesiod, *Works and Days* 803
62. *Iliad* 19.260
63. Aeschylus, *Eumenides* 417
64. *Iliad* 9.454
65. Ib. 9.571
66. *Odyssey* 11.280
67. Ib. 2.135
68. *Iliad* 15.204
69. Hesiod, *Theogony* 185
70. Ib. 472
71. Cf. Aeschylus, *Prometheus* 209
72. Hesiod, *Theogony* 901 ff.
73. Ib.
74. *Iliad* 20.4
75. Ib. 15.95
76. *Odyssey* 2.68
77. Aeschylus, *Eumenides* 1
78. Sophocles, *Antigone* 337
79. Aeschylus, *Persians* 629

80. Pausanias 1.28.6
81. *Iliad* 15.36
82. Ib. 3.104, 277
83. *Odyssey* 5.125; cf. Hesiod, *Theogony* 969
84. *Iliad* 14.326
85. Ib. 2.696
86. Ib. 5.500
87. Ib. 13.322, 21.76
88. Ib. 22.460; cf. *Homeric Hymn to Demeter* 386
89. *Iliad* 6.130 ff., *Odyssey* 11.325
90. Hesiod, *Works and Days* 614
91. *Iliad* 21.442. ff.
92. Ib. 24.26
93. *Odyssey* 11.100 ff.
94. *Iliad* 20.57 ff.
95. Ib. 21.435 ff.
96. *Odyssey* 8.344
97. Aeschylus, *Eumenides* 808 f.
98. Hölderlin, *Poems*, tr. Hamburger, p. 101
99. Cf. Wilamowitz, *Pindaros*, 201 ff.
100. *Iliad* 14.272
101. Ib. 21.407

CHAPTER V

1. *Iliad* 9.49
2. *Odyssey* 5.531, 2.372
3. *Iliad* 17.99
4. Ib. 7.101
5. Ib. 20.435; cf. 17.514, *Odyssey* 1.267 et al.
6. *Iliad* 22.379
7. Ib. 22.297; cf. 16.692
8. Ib. 3.164
9. Ib. 9.136
10. Ib. 1.18
11. *Odyssey* 20.344; cf. 17.399
12. Ib. 14.65
13. Ib. 14.444
14. Ib. 18.167

15. Ib. 17.218
16. Ib. 13.317
17. Ib. 19.485 ff.; cf. 21.279, 22.288
18. Ib. 7.214, 14.198, 12.190, 17. 119
19. Ib. 4.12
20. Ib. 16.211
21. Ib. 1.17
22. Ib. 8.579
23. Ib. 11.138
24. Ib. 19.592
25. Euripides, *Trojan Women* 988
26. Cf. e.g. *Iliad* 11.603
27. *Odyssey* 20.17; cf. Wilamowitz, *Die Rückkehr des Odysseus*, 189 ff.
28. Cf. von Arnim, "Das Ethische in Aristoteles Topika," *Sitzungsberichte der Akademie der Wissensch. in Wien* (1927), 30
29. *Iliad* 2.169 ff.
30. Ib. 2.169: *Dii metin atalanton*
31. *Odyssey* 13.298
32. *Iliad* 10.507 ff.
33. Ib. 1.193 ff.
34. *Odyssey* 15.1 ff.
35. Ib. 15.45
36. *Iliad* 10.158
37. Euripides, *Trojan Women* 988
38. *Odyssey* 4.712
39. Cf. also ib. 7.263, 9.339
40. Ib. 22.347; cf. also 1.384
41. *Iliad* 9.702
42. Ib. 9.600
43. Ib. 9.254
44. Ib. 15.603
45. Ib. 9.629, 636
46. Ib. 14.214
47. Sophocles, *Antigone* 620
48. *Iliad* 19.85 ff.
49. Ib. 19.270
50. *Odyssey* 4.260 ff.

51. *Iliad* 3.162
52. Ib. 6.344 f.
53. *Odyssey* 3.264 ff.
54. *Iliad* 9.448 ff.
55. *Odyssey*, 16.282
56. *Iliad* 8.218
57. *Odyssey* 5.427, 437
58. *Iliad* 16.685 ff.
59. Ib. 18.310
60. Sophocles, *Ajax* 758 ff.
61. *Iliad* 22.270
62. Ib. 21.570
63. Ib. 6.156
64. Ib. 13.726 ff.
65. *Odyssey* 2.116
66. Ib. 14.227
67. *Iliad* 5.51
68. Ib. 5.61
69. *Odyssey* 6.139
70. *Iliad* 9.254
71. Ib. 10.5, 125
72. Ib. 10.364
73. Ib. 10.482
74. Ib. 17.210
75. Ib. 16.656
76. Ib. 17.173
77. *Odyssey* 13.372 ff.
78. So ib. 13.190 according to Aristophanes' reading; cf. Wilamowitz, *Die Rückkehr des Odysseus*
79. *Odyssey* 13.331
80. *Iliad* 2.446
81. *Odyssey* 15.158 ff.
82. Ib. 7.286
83. Ib. 5.491
84. *Iliad* 11.544 ff.
85. Ib. 16.787 ff.
86. Ib. 16.791 and 806; cf. also 816
87. Ib. 16.845
88. Ib. 20.320 ff.
89. Ib. 20.438 ff.
90. Ib. 5.432 ff.
91. Ib. 5.345

92. Ib. 22.213
93. Ib. 21.595
94. Ib. 22.8
95. Ib. 5.461 ff.
96. Ib. 5.604
97. Ib. 5.785
98. Ib. 5.793 ff.
99. Ib. 16.698 ff.
100. Ib. 16.993
101. Ib. 16.715 ff.
102. Ib. 17.1 ff.
103. Ib. 17.543 ff.
104. Ib. 17.582 ff.
105. Ib. 17.534
106. Ib. 20.79 ff.
107. *Odyssey* 6.321 ff.
108. Ib. 7.32
109. Ib. 6.321
110. Ib. 6.327
111. Ib. 8.1 ff.
112. Ib. 8.293
113. Ib. 13.221 ff.
114. *Iliad* 13.43 ff.
115. Ib. 13.62
116. *Odyssey* 5.491
117. Ib. 7.286
118. *Iliad* 13.216
119. *Odyssey* 3.329 ff.
120. Ib. 3.329, 335
121. Ib. 3.372
122. Ib. 1.103 ff.
123. Ib. 1.323
124. Ib. 1.115
125. Ib. 1.135
126. Ib. 1.180
127. Ib. 1.255 ff.
128. Ib. 1.296 ff.
129. Ib. 1.320
130. Ib. 1.155, 325
131. Ib. 1.405 ff.
132. Ib. 1.324
133. Ib. 1.420
134. Ib. 2.262
135. Ib. 2.225 ff.
136. Ib. 2.261

137. Ib. 22.205
138. Ib. 22.210
139. Ib. 22.233
140. Ib. 22.233
141. Ib. 22.237
142. Ib. 22.249
143. Ib. 22.239
144. Ib. 1.320
145. *Iliad* 15.318; cf. 308
146. *Odyssey* 22.297
147. Ib. 24.182
148. *Iliad* 1.193 ff.
149. See p. 48.
150. *Iliad* 1.198
151. Ib. 14.409 ff.
152. Ib. 15.269 ff.
153. Ib. 15.290 ff.
154. Ib. 15.242
155. Ib. 15.262
156. Ib. 15.308
157. Ib. 20.375
158. Ib. 20.380
159. *Odyssey* 20.30 ff.
160. Ib. 20.54 ff.
161. Ib. 16.155 ff.
162. Ib. 16.161
163. Ib. 16.197
164. Ib. 16.211
165. Ib. 16.454 ff.
166. Euripides, *Helen* 560
167. *Odyssey* 10.277 ff.
168. Ib. 10.254 ff.
169. *Iliad* 24.463 f.
170. Ib. 21.284 f.
171. Ib. 22.214 ff.
172. Ib. 22.213
173. Ib. 22.203
174. Ib. 22.270, cf. 279 ff.
175. Ib. 22.276
176. Ib. 22.291 f.
177. Ib. 22.295
178. Ib. 22.297
179. Ib. 22.304
180. Ib. 5.2
181. Ib. 5.4 ff.

182. Ib. 5.85 ff.
183. Ib. 5.95 ff.
184. Ib. 5.103 ff.
185. Ib. 5.115 ff.
186. Ib. 5.122
187. Ib. 5.124 ff.
188. Ib. 5.135 f.
189. Ib. 5.174
190. Ib. 5.240
191. Ib. 5.256
192. Ib. 5.260
193. Ib. 5.290 ff.
194. Ib. 5.298
195. Ib. 5.312 ff.
196. Ib. 5.343
197. Ib. 5.434
198. Ib. 5.440 ff.
199. Ib. 5.449
200. Ib. 5.456
201. Ib. 5.462
202. Ib. 5.469
203. Ib. 5.512 ff.
204. Ib. 5.592
205. Ib. 5.604
206. Ib. 5.704
207. Ib. 5.765
208. Ib. 5.785
209. Ib. 5.826, 828
210. Ib. 5.835
211. Ib. 5.835-867
212. Ib. 5.177
213. Ib. 5.290
214. Ib. 5.856
215. Ib. 5.123
216. Ib. 18.239
217. *Odyssey* 23.242
218. *Iliad* 15.307
219. Ib. 15.320 ff.
220. Ib. 15.355 ff.
221. Ib. 15.308

CHAPTER VI

1. Ovid, *Metamorphoses* 1.82 ff.
2. Propertius 1.3.1 ff.
3. Goethe, *Myrons Kuh* (1812)
4. Cf. E. Norden, *Agnostos Theos*
5. Plato, *Apology* 21 ff.
6. *Odyssey* 13.287 ff.
7. *Iliad* 24.602 ff.
8. Cf. ib. 24.30
9. Euripides, *Hippolytus* 99 ff.
10. Cf. Wilamowitz, *Euripides Hippolytus*, introduction
11. Hesiod, *Shield of Heracles* 27 ff.
12. *Odyssey* 8.267 ff.
13. Ib. 8.329 ff.
14. Ib. 8.324
15. Ovid, *Art of Love* 2.561-592
16. *Iliad* 20.78
17. Ib. 17.210
18. Ib. 17.529
19. Ib. 21.385 ff.
20. Ib. 5.851 ff.
21. Ib. 5.890
22. Cf. Kretschmer, *Glotta* 11. 195 ff.
23. *Iliad* 4.439 ff.
24. E.g. ib. 24.260
25. Ib. 5.889
26. Ib. 18.516
27. Ib. 1.393 ff.
28. Ib. 1.39 ff., 587 ff., 8.10 ff., 15.16 ff.
29. Ib. 15.13 ff.
30. Ib. 15.173 ff.
31. Ib. 21.461 ff.
32. Ib. 21.479 ff.
33. Ib. 21.379
34. See p. 66 f.
35. See p. 45 f.
36. *Iliad* 22.214 ff.
37. See p. 238 f.
38. See p. 274
39. See p. 54
40. Aeschylus, *Eumenides* 735 ff.
41. E.g. *Iliad* 2.371
42. Euripides, *Oenomaus* frg. 577

43. *Iliad* 4.160 ff.
44. Ib. 13.622 ff.
45. Ib. 16.384 ff.
46. *Odyssey* 24.351
47. Iliad 9.410 ff.; cf. Plato, *Symposium* 179e
48. Otto Gruppe, *Griechische Mythologie und Religionsgeschichte*, 1013
49. *Iliad* 1.409
50. Ib. 18.96
51. Ib. 24.509 ff.
52. Ib. 17.198 ff.
53. Ib. 16.852 ff.
54. Ib. 16.860
55. Ib. 17.130
56. Ib. 17.198 ff.
57. Ib. 1.528
58. Ib. 24.478

CHAPTER VII

1. *Odyssey* 3.228
2. Ib. 3.236 ff.
3. *Iliad* 1.505 ff.
4. Ib. 17.198 ff.
5. Ib. 22.213
6. Herodotus 1.91
7. Cf. Plato, *Laws* 5.741a
8. Cf. Aeschylus, *Prometheus* 515 ff. and several famous myths; also *Iliad* 15.117 and Hesiod, *Theogony* 220
9. Hesiod, *Theogony* 211
10. *Iliad* 24.49
11. Hesiod, *Theogony* 904 ff. In Delphi there were two: Pausanias 10.24.4; Plutarch, *On the E at Delphi* 2
12. Hesiod, *Theogony* 211 ff.
13. Aeschylus, *Eumenides* 960
14. *Orphica*, frg. 57, Kern
15. Epimenides, frg. 19, Diels
16. Pausanias 1.19.2
17. Ib. 2.11.4

18. Hesiod, *Theogony* 220
19. Pausanias 8.42.3
20. Pindar, *Pythians* 4.145
21. Diehl, *Anthologia Lyrica Graeca*, 2.159
22. *Iliad* 19.408 ff.
23. Pindar, frg. 30
24. Aristophanes, *Birds* 1731
25. Catullus 64; cf. illustration on François vase
26. Aeschylus, *Eumenides* 957 ff.
27. Cf. Pindar, *Olympians* 6.42, *Nemeans* 9.1; Antonius Liberalis 29
28. Hesiod, *Theogony* 218 f.
29. *Iliad* 20.127
30. Ib. 24.209
31. *Odyssey* 7.195
32. *Iliad* 1.418
33. Cf. Apollodorus 1.6.2
34. Aeschylus, *Eumenides* 728
35. *Iliad* 3.182
36. Ib. 19.409 ff.
37. Ib. 16.849
38. Ib. 19.87
39. Ib. 5.613
40. Ib. 21.82 f.
41. Ib. 5.629
42. Ib. 13.602
43. Ib. 22.303
44. Ib. 4.517
45. Ib. 22.5
46. Ib. 5.82 f., 16.333 f., 20.476 f.; cf. also 12.116
47. *Odyssey* 2.100, 3.238; cf. 17.326
48. Cf. *Iliad* 5.83, 629, 16.853, 19.410, 20.477
49. *Odyssey* 12.124
50. Hesiod, *Theogony* 904 ff.
51. *Iliad* 3.182
52. Ib. 24.525; *Odyssey* 1.7, 3.208, 4.207, 8.579, 11.139, 16.64, 20.196
53. *Odyssey* 4.207; cf. also 3.208

54. *Iliad* 24.49
55. *aisimon   emar,   morsimon
    emar:* Ib. 21.100, 15.613
56. *Odyssey* 5.41, 288, 345, 9.
    532
57. Ib. 5.41
58. Ib. 5.153
59. *Iliad* 7.52
60. Cf. also *Odyssey* 5.206
61. Ib. 4.481
62. Ib. 4.475
63. *Iliad* 20.302
64. Ib. 20.336
65. Hesiod, *Theogony* 897
66. *Odyssey* 1.32 ff.
67. Solon 3.1 ff., Diels
68. Ib. 8.1 ff.
69. Cf. W. Jaeger, *Sitz. Ber. Berl.
    Akad.* (1926), 69 ff.
70. Solon 3.30
71. Cf. *Iliad* 16.698, 20.30, 21.
    517
72. *Odyssey* 5.436 f.
73. *Iliad* 3.308
74. Ib. 17.201 ff., 15.610 ff.
75. Ib. 22.168 ff.
76. Ib. 22.209 ff.
77. Ib. 8.69 ff.
78. Ib. 16.658
79. Ib. 16.431 ff.
80. Ib. 16.459 ff.
81. *Odyssey* 7.197
82. *Iliad* 22.182 ff.
83. Ib. 22.213 ff.
84. Ib. 22.229
85. Ib. 22.202 ff.
86. Ib. 16
87. Ib. 22.297
88. Ib. 16.693
89. Ib. 16.241
90. Ib. 16.252
91. Ib. 16.849 f.
92. Ib. 16.844 f.

93. Ib. 16.853
94. Ib. 16.93 f.
95. Ib. 16.698 ff.
96. Ib. 16.780
97. Ib. 16.788
98. Ib. 1.352, 416
99. Ib. 18.96, 19.409
100. Ib. 21.277 f., 22.359
101. Ib. 21.277, 22.360, 23.80 f.;
     cf. Proclus's summary of the
     contents of the *Aethiopis*
     and Apollodorus, Epit. 5.3
102. *Iliad* 19.410
103. Ib. 16.709
104. Horace, *Odes* 4.6.9-12, tr.
     Marshall
105. *Iliad* 24.527
106. *Odyssey* 4.236
107. *Iliad* 1.5; cf. *Cypria* frg. 1.7
108. *Iliad* 21.82 f.
109. Ib. 22.297
110. Ib. 22.365
111. *Odyssey* 3.241
112. *Iliad* 6.356
113. *Odyssey* 11.560
114. *Iliad* 24.525; *Odyssey* 8.579,
     11.139, 16.64, 20.196
115. *Iliad* 17.321
116. *Odyssey* 9.52
117. Ib. 11.292
118. Ib. 3.269
119. Ib. 22.413
120. *Iliad* 19.86; cf. Aeschylus,
     Eumenides 1045: *Zeus ho
     panoptas houto Moira te
     xugkateba*
121. *Iliad* 9.608
122. *Homeric Hymn to Apollo*
     433, *To Demeter* 300, *To
     Aphrodite* 106; Pindar,
     Olympians 2.23
123. Solon 1.63
124. *Odyssey* 19.592

INDEX